P9-AGF-154

DATE DUE

DE 19'01			

DEMCO 38-296

SUPERINTENDING THE POOR

Superintending the Poor

*Charitable Ladies
and Paternal Landlords
in British Fiction,
1770–1860*

BETH FOWKES TOBIN

Yale University Press   New Haven and London

Riverside Community College
Library
4800 Magnolia Avenue
Riverside, California 92506

PR 868 .P66 T63 1993

Tobin. Beth Fowkes.

Superintending the poor

Copyright © 1993 by Yale University.
All rights reserved.
This book may not be reproduced, in whole or in part, including illustrations,
in any form (beyond that copying permitted by Sections 107 and 108 of the U.S.
Copyright Law and except by reviewers for the public press), without written
permission from the publishers.

Designed by James J. Johnson.
Set in Monticello type by The Composing Room of Michigan, Inc.,
Grand Rapids, Michigan.
Printed in the United States of America by BookCrafters, Chelsea, Michigan.

Library of Congress Cataloging-in-Publication Data

Tobin, Beth Fowkes.
Superintending the poor : charitable ladies and paternal landlords in British fiction,
1770–1860 / Beth Fowkes Tobin.
p.   cm.
Includes bibliographical references and index.
ISBN 0–300–05559–5 (alk. paper)

1. English fiction—19th century—History and criticism.   2. Poor in
literature.   3. English fiction—18th century—History and
criticism.   4. Literature and society–Great Britain—History.   5. Moral
conditions in literature.   6. Social conflict in literature.   7. Economics in
literature.   8. Poverty in literature.   I. Title.
PR868.P66T63   1993
823.009′355—DC20   93–8312

A catalogue record for this book is available from the British Library.
The paper in this book meets the guidelines for permanence and durability of
the Committee on Production Guidelines for Book Longevity of the Council on
Library Resources.

10 9 8 7 6 5 4 3 2 1

IN MEMORY OF

my father,

Frederick M. Fowkes (1915–1990),

AND

my mother-in-law,

Eunice M. Tobin (1929–1991)

Contents

Acknowledgments

The research for this book was funded in part by the Newberry Library, the National Endowment for the Humanities, and the Research Council of the University of Hawai'i at Manoa. I wish to thank the staffs of the British Library, the Boston Public Library, the Houghton Library, the Newberry Library, the Portsmouth Athenaeum, and the Interlibrary Loan offices at the University of Hawai'i and the University of New Hampshire. I am grateful to Joseph Kau, who, as Chair of the English Department, supported this project from its inception, and to Richard Seymour, Dean of Languages and Literature at the University of Hawai'i, for granting me a leave of absence to complete work on this book. A version of chapter 3 appeared in *Eighteenth-Century Fiction,* and I would like to thank David Blewett and Alistair Duckworth for their helpful suggestions. Special thanks goes to Beth Kowaleski-Wallace and Mitzi Myers for sharing their knowledge of Hannah More, and to Craig Howes, Jay Kastely, Ruth Perry, and Joe Tobin for reading various versions of the manuscript. To the friends and colleagues who have supported my work and whose ideas have helped shape this project I owe a debt of gratitude: Jonathan Brent, Jill Campbell, Lawrence Kenney, Kathryn Kirkpatrick, Lisa Salem Manganaro, Marc Manganaro, John Rieder, Susan Staves, Jeff Tobin, Laurel Ulrich, and Deborah Winslow. Thanks goes, without saying, to Joe, Sam, and Isaac for being more than willing to live in an unregulated household.

SUPERINTENDING THE POOR

Introduction

THIS book focuses on discursive strategies used by middle-class men and women to undermine the landed upper classes' control over the rural economy of early industrial Britain. The middle-class struggle to find positions of power and authority in the regulation of land and labor dominated discussions of poverty and charity and surfaced in a variety of texts, including Evangelical tracts, dissertations on population and poverty, and treatises on scientific agriculture and land management. I locate novels written by Henry Mackenzie, William Godwin, Jane Austen, Charlotte Brontë, and Charles Dickens in this political context and analyze how middle-class strategies of self-regulation and surveillance operate in these novels to discredit the landed upper classes as managers of the rural economy and to promote the talent, intelligence, and expertise of the middle classes in the regulation of the countryside and its people.

A vast and varied literature on poverty and charity was produced in the late eighteenth century in response to the social and economic upheavals resulting from the transition from paternal to capitalist relations in the rural economy. The increase in the number of vagrants and impoverished laborers dependent on the parish for relief can be traced to the technologies of capitalist agriculture, primarily the enclosure of common lands and wasteland and the engrossment, or consolidation, of small farms, both of which contributed to the displacement of the agrarian laborer and his family.[1]

Pamphlets, treatises, and tracts on the Poor Laws argued that the parochial system had failed to deal with the distresses of the poor and with the increasing cost of caring for them. Some, like Joseph Townsend's *A Dissertation on the Poor Laws* (1786), argued that the Poor Laws should be abolished, forcing the able-bodied poor to starve or work for their livelihood and leaving the plight of the imbecilic, aged, and infant poor to the care of voluntary charity. Others, like Patrick Colquhoun's *A Treatise on Indigence* (1806) and Jeremy Bentham's *Pauper Management Improved* (1798), sought to do away with the parochial system run by the local gentry and wealthy farmers and to replace local and paternal control with a centralized authority and professionally run organization of poorhouses designed (like the Panopticon) to discourage indigence. Most of these tracts expressed dissatisfaction with the current local and paternal system of charity and sought to supplant this idiosyncratic, sometimes haphazard and ill-administered, but personal and face-to-face dispensing of charity with more systematic and efficient procedures.

Embedded in these pamphlets and treatises that describe the poor are discussions of who is best qualified to aid the poor and to superintend their welfare. These documents, written primarily by middle-class men and women, attacked the gentry and aristocracy, the traditional dispensers of alms in the old society's paternal system of welfare, for their failure to superintend the poor properly. Tracts, essays, and stories written by those who championed the emergent middle classes' right to superintend the poor delineated the special talents and supervisory abilities of middle-class men and women. For instance, in an issue of the *Lady's Magazine* from 1790, "J.H.," in "Essay on Riches and Poverty," portrays the upper classes as living lives of "luxury and debauchery" that, in turn, interfere with their ability to feel and act charitably: "These courses and habits have rendered them insensible to the wants of their fellow-creatures; corrupted their minds, hardened their hearts, and destroyed the sympathising tenderness of humanity. And those . . . engrossed by the prevalent customary modes of dissipation among the great, as to have but little leisure for reflection, and less disposition to attend to the distresses of those below them." Further, J.H.

argues that "those of a middle state" are best situated to aid the poor: "This rank has not only the best chance for virtue and contentment," but the middle classes are "not placed too high to see and observe the calamities of their neighbours," so "they actually bestow more" aid than the wealthier but unfeeling upper classes.[2]

This book examines how class and gender operate in texts that have charity and social responsibility as central concerns. Middle-class women writers like Hannah More and Elizabeth Hamilton frequently positioned themselves in opposition to male paternalists, placing descriptions of women's charitable activities alongside critiques of these absent or negligent "fathers." They believed that the upper classes were too preoccupied with the pursuit of pleasure to show any real concern for the misery and destitution of the growing number of acutely impoverished agricultural workers, and that the gentry and aristocracy had abdicated their paternal responsibilities, their duty as landowners to maintain the physical, moral, and spiritual well-being of the rural poor.

Middle-class charitable ladies were not the only ones who criticized the landed gentry's negligence and irresponsibility as managers of the rural economy. Men of the rural middling classes[3] who occupied such anomalous positions as steward, estate agent, agricultural expert, surveyor, engineer, and auctioneer also sought to locate in the rural landscape a space for themselves that conferred on them a position of power and authority. Like the middle-class charitable women, these middle-class men justified their activities as quantifiers, valuators, and managers of land and labor by portraying the upper classes as careless, self-indulgent, and incompetent managers of their property and the people who occupied it.

To trace in the pages of novels the battle between the landed classes and middle classes for the right to superintend the poor and, by analogy, the nation, I have made use of a broad range of such nonliterary materials as religious tracts, women's magazines, conduct books, dissertations on poverty, treatises on political economy, and the travel journals and scientific treatises of agriculturalists. Contextualizing the novels by surrounding them with contemporary economic, political, and social texts highlights ideological implications in fiction that otherwise might remain obscure to modern readers. Recovering ideological and cultural contexts defamiliarizes the familiar classics by Austen, Brontë, and Dickens, forcing readers to rethink assumptions about these canonical texts. Although I privilege literary texts by making novels the center of each chapter, my analysis of each novel demonstrates that literature is political, that novels as quiet and domestic as *Mansfield Park* participate in the conflict between classes for political and economic power.

My focus on strategies of regulation is indebted to Foucault, particularly his *Discipline and Punish,* and his demonstration of how "the eighteenth century invented the techniques of discipline." According to Foucault, the "formation of a disciplinary society" depends on "tiny, everyday, physical mechanisms" which assure "an infinitesimal distribution of power relations." This "refinement of power relations" and the "multiplication of the effects of power through the formation and accumulation of new forms of knowledge" are achieved through new "technological systems" such as "clinical medicine, psychiatry, child psychology, educational psychology, the rationalization of labor." Foucault finds in Bentham's *Panopticon* a blueprint for "a very real technology, that of individuals";[4] I have found in the works of Arthur Young and Hannah More prescriptions that detail similar disciplining strategies. Young and More both promoted new forms of knowledge that had as their goal the regulation of the self and resources. Young's scientific agriculture and cost accounting techniques were new disciplinary technologies aimed at regulating the land and its productivity while More's Evangelical doctrines of self-denial promised a new form of self-management.

Young and More were central in shaping the values and conduct of the emerging nineteenth-century British middle class. In his books detailing his tours throughout the English countryside and in his capacity as secretary to the Board of Agriculture, Young championed the new scientific agriculture and new techniques of valuation and quantification borrowed from mercantilist exchange. Along with his fellow agriculturalists, Young promoted a new way of looking at land and labor. With his tables, charts, and double-entry columns, he transformed land into a purely economic and legal relation, stressing its capital-producing potential while shearing it of its affective and social ties. Through the exercise of arithmetic and accounting, Young gave to landowners and those who managed their lands new ways of organizing their resources that enabled them to exercise a new kind of discipline and control over land and labor.

While Young encouraged the enclosure and cultivation of wastelands and wild sheepwalks, More encouraged the domestication of women's sexual impulses and avaricious desires through the exercise of self-discipline and self-denial. More's *Coelebs in Search of a Wife,* her *Cheap Repository Tracts,* her *Strictures on the Modern System of Female Education,* and her religious tracts like *Practical Piety* promote an evangelically inspired redefinition of virtue. Along with other advocates of the new domestic femininity, More relocates virtue within the domestic realm, making the middle-class woman with her capacity for self-discipline and ability to regulate time and space the locus of moral authority. In her innumerable tracts promoting middle-class feminine domesticity she portrays the upper classes as careless, selfish, and extravagant. Unschooled in self-control and lacking any notion of economy, the upper classes were incompetent in More's eyes and incapable of performing their duties as the superintendents of the poor, and they thereby forfeited to the middle classes the right to occupy supervisory roles.

In the following chapters I explore in novels the middle-class attack on the landed classes as well as the middle classes' effort to construct themselves as authorities and experts in the moral and economic regulation of land and labor. In the first part of the book, I examine the middle-class male critique of the upper classes. Chapter 1 looks at *The Man of Feeling* and Mackenzie's portrayal of the paternal relation of duty and dependence as hopelessly romantic, somewhat effete, and economically inoperable. Next comes a chapter discussing William Godwin's *Caleb Williams,* a work that seeks to discredit the paternal authority of the gentry, and Robert Bage's *Mount Henneth,* a novel that offers a blending of scientific agriculture and rational political economy as a solution to the ills of the countryside. Concluding this section is a discussion of Austen's

Emma as a defense of paternal practice, but one modified and informed by the new discourse in political economy.

The second half of the book shifts its focus to middle-class women's critique of the gentry and clergy as failed paternalists and the promotion of themselves as the proper inheritors of this endangered paternal tradition. Two chapters focus on Hannah More. Chapter 4 compares her depiction of a self-indulgent, narcissistic gentry in *Coelebs in Search of a Wife* with Austen's portrait of the Bertrams and Crawfords in *Mansfield Park*. Chapter 5 focuses on More's role in the Blagdon controversy and her critique of a negligent clergy, along with similar critiques by Anne Brontë in *Agnes Grey*, Charlotte Brontë in *Shirley*, and Elizabeth Gaskell in *My Lady Ludlow*. Each of these authors represents middle-class women as capable, competent, and talented superintendents of the poor who use their expertise in self-regulation to justify their entry into the regulation of the public sphere. The final chapter deals with Dickens's portrait of a declining gentry and his condemnation of the misguided efforts of charitable women like Mrs. Pardiggle who seek to fill the void left by the gentry's inadequacies. Here I explore the self-regulated woman and the surveillance of the police as Dickens's solutions to the problems of poverty.

The battle over the superintendency of the poor that was fought in the pages of such disparate texts as Austen's *Persuasion* and Bentham's *Pauper Management Improved* is a battle between the middle and upper classes, who strangely (or not so strangely) ignore the voices of the poor themselves. In reproducing this conflict, my book, I am afraid, reproduces this absence, and the under classes are represented only as the object of contention. This book does not deal with the working classes' resistance to middle-class and upper-class acts of coercion. But I believe that my attempt to historicize postpaternal discourses of regulation calls attention to a time and place when managed lives were not the norm. Balancing a checkbook, putting socks in a sock drawer, and going on a diet are historically constructed behaviors. It is not natural to keep accounts, to have compartments for species of things, or to look at a watch to know when to eat or work. How liberating can this realization be? Resistance to the regulating discourses that inform our lives could take the shape of refusal—not filing papers alphabetically, not balancing a checkbook, not folding the laundry—but these anarchic gestures lack the sustained effort and method of a revolutionary program. "Anti-institutional anarchism," as Bruce Robbins says, is "on this level indistinguishable from liberalism."5 Perhaps resistance to regulation requires a self-conscious and self-reflective use of regulation. Marx, for instance, uses in *Capital* the discourse of political economy to critique the assumptions and methods of political economy; he works within the discourse, using it against itself. Understanding how discourses of regulation work to manage lives is crucial therefore not only to any critique of regulation but also to any program of sustained subversive activity.

CHAPTER ONE

The Man of Feeling, Arthur Young, and the Dissolution of the Paternal Order

A ngered by the "devastation" of "rural virtues," Oliver Goldsmith in "The Deserted Village" points the finger of blame at Luxury.[1] He argues that the city, with its dazzling commodities and garish entertainments, has seduced the gentry from their rural responsibilities, making room for a new class of owners associated with trade to take their place. The word *luxury*, as John Sekora points out, was associated with money generated by speculation and with the consumption of expensive and useless commodities produced by overseas trade, colonial ventures, and the slave trade—commodities like tea, china, silk, coffee, chocolate, mahogany, ivory, and sugar.[2] Condemning London for its corruption, materialism, and avariciousness, Goldsmith is particularly upset by the city's production of new men who invade the countryside and pollute its rustic beauty by building ornate palaces and artificial gardens, destroying the economic and social fabric of the old agrarian society.

Attacking luxury and the corroding effect of money on the morals of the nation was a favorite theme of eighteenth-century writers.[3] This discourse on luxury provided a useful, persuasive critique and explanation of the social and economic changes that were occurring in the countryside—the enclosure of common property, the disenfranchisement of the small farmer, the pauperization of the laborer, and the depopulation of rural communities. Goldsmith's is one of many voices lamenting the passing of the old society's paternal social and economic relations. Beginning in the last third of the eighteenth century and lasting well into the nineteenth, a whole range of literature including poetry, fiction, tracts on poverty, and treatises on population valorized England's rural past. Coleridge in his "Lay Sermons" and Wordsworth in "Simon Lee" and "The Old Cumberland Beggar" lament the loss of community held together by reciprocal relations of obligation and gratitude. Robert Southey in his *Colloquies* and William Cobbett in his *Rural Rides* attack the new commercial spirit for promoting the dissolution of the paternal "bond of attachment."[4] Perhaps most outraged is Thomas Carlyle, who in "Chartism" deplores the substitution of the "cash nexus" for hierarchical relations of obligation and deference.[5]

It is tempting to argue that Henry Mackenzie wrote *The Man of Feeling* from within this tradition of blaming new money derived from trade and manufacturing for the dissolution of rural England's moral codes and social ties. But I will argue in this chapter that Mackenzie's narrative subtly supports the new capitalist order by depicting the old society's social and economic relations as impractical and essentially obsolete. By portraying his protagonist, Harley, as extremely sensitive and overly emotional, Mackenzie discredits Harley's benevolent actions and manners by relegating them to the margins of normal masculine behavior. By portraying Harley's benevolence as eccentric and extravagant, Mackenzie undermines the value of his charitable gestures by indicating that they exist outside the pale of normal economic relations. In *The Man of Feeling* Mackenzie depicts the dissolution of the old paternal order and the ascendence of a new economic order as if these changes, though to be lamented, are inevitable and natural processes.[6]

Harley as Paternalist

Harley embodies the best of the old paternal order, and his benevolent gestures originate in the old society's hierarchical relations of duty and dependence. Mackenzie represents Harley's generosity and compassion as anachronistic, as remnants of a rapidly disappearing social order. Harley lives in a world that no longer values benevolent actions because they cannot be calculated in terms of profit and loss.

The episodes in the novel that best illustrate the nature of Harley's paternal benevolence are those involving Edwards, a pauperized tenant farmer turned soldier. Harley barely recognizes old Edwards when he meets him on the road from London, for Edwards is dressed in the tattered garb of an old soldier. As a boy attending school near Edwards's small but prosperous farm, Harley had visited Edwards and remembered him for his kindness to him. He exclaims, "Let me clasp those knees on which I have sat so often: Edwards!—I shall never forget that fire-side, round which I have been so happy!"[7] Shocked by Edwards's beggarly appearance, Harley asks Edwards for his story.

Edwards tells how all his troubles began the day his landlord hired a London attorney as his steward. The new steward instituted a policy of engrossment and would not lease any farm for less than three hundred pounds a year, which by the practice of the time would have meant a farm of approximately three hundred acres, far more than a poor farmer like Edwards could successfully manage.[8] He insisted that if Edwards wanted to continue to rent his farm, South-hill, which had been farmed by his "father, grandfather, and great-grandfather" (87), he had to assume the responsibilities of managing a larger farm, a small portion of which was his beloved South-hill. "What could I do, Mr. Harley? I feared the undertaking was too great for me; yet to leave, at my age, the house I had lived in from my cradle!" (88). Edwards struggled to make a financial success of the engrossed farm but was unsuccessful. When he fell behind in his rent, he and his family were evicted by the new steward. Edwards's luck went from bad to worse: his son, having offended the local justice of the peace, was set upon by a press gang at the justice's instigation. Edwards bribed the press gang officer so that he could take his son's place. Returning home after years of military service in India, Edwards meets Harley, who shows him the first kindness he has experienced in many years. "Edwards, let me hold thee to my bosom," Harley exclaims upon hearing his tale. "Come, my honoured veteran! let me endeavour to soften the last days of a life, worn out in the service of humanity: call me son, and let me cherish thee as a father" (95). Edwards's response to Harley's generous spirit is tears: he "blubbered like a boy; he could not speak his gratitude, but by some short exclamations of blessing upon Harley" (95).

Though a gentleman and clearly of a higher rank than the impoverished, displaced old farmer, Harley embraces Edwards and sheds tears of sympathy over his sufferings. He accompanies the old soldier back to his village, where they learn that in Edwards's absence his son and daughter-in-law have "died of broken hearts" (97). Though Edwards's son was "a sober, industrious man," he could not overcome misfortune. "What with bad crops, and bad debts, . . . his affairs went to wreck" (97–98), a neighbor woman reports. Harley encourages Edwards, who is shattered by this news, to come with him to his home, where he offers to take care of him and his two orphaned grandchildren. Returning home with this "train" of followers, Harley felt a pleasure that was "as great as if he had arrived from the tour of Europe, with a Swiss valet for his companion, and half a dozen snuff-boxes, with invisible hinges in his pocket" (100). Harley does what he can to make Edwards and his grandchildren comfortable, and when he hears that a small farm on his estate is vacant, he bestows it on Edwards, saying, "If you will occupy it, I shall gain a good neighbour, and be able in some measure to repay the notice you took of me when a boy" (101). Edwards's response to Harley's generosity is again tears of gratitude, which "gushed afresh" (101). Later, when Edwards is settled on his new farm, Harley makes frequent visits and helps Edwards with his garden, making a miniature mill for the grandson's amusement. Watching Harley's efforts at pleasing his grandson, Edwards "with a look half-turned to Harley, and half to Heaven, breathed an ejaculation of gratitude and piety" (101–02).

Harley's treatment of Edwards is strikingly kind. Like his treatment of the prostitute and the madwoman in earlier episodes, his ready sympathy and spontaneous generosity toward Edwards are clearly out of the ordinary. Harley, Mackenzie tells us, "did things frequently in a way different from what other people call natural" (84). His giving Edwards the farm is not a prudent business move; it is an action that the world would deem foolish or sentimental. As Harley says, "The world is in general selfish, interested, and unthinking, and throws the imputation of romance or melancholy on every temper more susceptible than its own" (128). Harley ignores usual business procedures to follow the dictates of his heart. Harley was not guided by "the useful and the expedient" (84), principles that would have urged most landlords to chose a strong and healthy tenant with enough capital to stock and equip a farm, to hire agricultural labor, and to invest in its improvements. Harley, instead, chooses Edwards as his tenant, a poor, broken-down old man who needs a place to live and a means of supporting himself and his grandchildren. Harley's motives—his gratitude to Edwards for his kind attention to him as a child, his appreciation of Edwards's bravery and virtue as a soldier overseas, and his desire to prevent Edwards from further suffering and "to soften the last days of a life, worn out in the service of humanity"—are, in the eyes of the world, "rather eccentric" (84), for the world, as Harley says, is driven by desire for "power, wealth, and grandeur" and is not capable of understanding Harley's "pleasure of doing a charitable thing" (100).

Harley's economic and social relations with Edwards have all the marks of paternalism.[9] According to the historian Harold Perkin, the paternal relationship was hierarchical, bound together by "vertical links" of patronage and friendship. Perkin argues that the "social nexus peculiar to the old society" was "vertical friendship," which was "a durable two-way relationship between patrons and clients." It was "less formal and inescapable than feudal homage, more personal and comprehensive than the contractual, employment relationships of capitalist 'Cash Payment.'" These "personal bonds of the old society" formed a chain of reciprocal relations that ran up and down the ranks of society and formed a "mesh of continuing loyalties."[10] A patron was obliged to aid and to protect those dependent on him, and his dependents in turn were obliged to repay their debts with gratitude, deference, and loyalty. In almost every interaction in the old society, a person would assume at various times, depending on the situation, the role of either patron or dependent and participate in what J. G. A. Pocock calls the dynamic of "ruling-and-being-ruled."[11] Harley, for example, plays both roles of dependent and patron: he is a dependent when he seeks the aid of the Great Man in London in his effort to petition for the lease of the Crown lands contiguous with his paternal estate; and he is a patron when he bestows on Edwards a farm within his own small estate.

The hierarchical yet reciprocal relations of paternalism bound society in a chain of "connection."[12] Describing a relationship much like Harley and Edwards's in *Hints to Gentlemen of Landed Property* (1775), Nathaniel Kent explains how the paternal relation works: "The landlord, tenant, and labourer are intimately connected together, and have their reciprocal interests, though in different proportions; and when the just equilibrium between them is interrupted, the one or the other must receive injury." Kent argues that it is the landlords' duty and interest as "guardians of the poor" to "attend their accommodation, and happiness" and to "act as their friend and protector," for the landlord has "a lasting interest in the prosperity of the parish." The rich's generosity to the poor and the landlord's generosity to his tenants and laborers were key to the functioning of the paternal system, for as Robert Southey argues, without the "generous bounty" of the landlord, there is no "grateful and honest dependence," and the "bond of attachment is broken." William Marshall, expert on estate management, advises the landowner "to set a good example to the tenants under his care. He should endeavour to liberalize their minds, by good offices, and acts of kindness. There are numberless small favours which he can bestow upon them, without loss; and many with eventual advantage, to the estate."[13]

The Legal Reconceptualization of Land

Harley's kindness to Edwards contrasts sharply with the treatment the old man had received from the steward. This new steward, an attorney from London, ignores the personal understanding and verbal agreement that Edwards and his forefathers had had with the landlord and his forefathers and institutes a policy of engrossment based on the new scientific agriculture and cost-effective estate management. The new steward refuses to renew Edwards's lease of his old farm because it is under the ideal acreage to produce the maximum profit per acre. The steward is within his legal rights when he denies Edwards the leasehold of a farm the old man regards as his ancestral home. But Edwards experiences this act as a violation of trust, especially since Edwards's great-grandfather "was a younger brother of that very man's ancestor who is now lord of the manor" (87). Edwards is a victim of a new commercial ideology that perceives land as a commodity and labor as an investment and ignores customary rights of the tenantry and the laboring poor to the land they occupy. Land to someone like Edwards is not a mere commodity to be bought and sold like any other object. Edwards had loved the land he had worked: "There was not a tree about it that I did not look on as my father, my brother, or my child" (88). For him, land is enmeshed in a web of affective and social ties, and to see it only in terms of a capital investment is to strip it of its meaning.

For those like Edwards and Harley not yet engaged in the new commodifying discourse, land could not be "separated from a network of social and economic relationships that surrounded it: land was, indeed, these relationships as much as the physical commodity itself."[14] But the strictly legal definition of land as an object of private ownership freed land from social and economic obligations and dislodged it from its communal function.[15] Landowners gained "exclusive rights to the access of the land." Those who did not own but lived and worked on the land were forbidden access to it to perform traditional activities like "gleaning, grazing, the gathering of fuel or the killing of game." This transformation of land from a complex web of customary practice "embedded in the social fabric of the local community" to a "form of economic capital" represents, as Newby observes, "a fundamental, qualitative and decisive break" with the past, with the old manorial system and its protection of "traditionally defined customs, rights, and obligations."[16]

In his book *On the Management of Landed Estates* (1806) William Marshall discusses the moral authority and social significance of customary practice as opposed to purely legal rights. In a section titled "The Proper Treatment of Existing Tenantry" Marshall cautions estate superintendents that "established customs and usages" though not formed by "legal contracts . . . ought to be strictly observed by its superintendent; until better can be placed in their stead."[17] This is advice that the new steward should have heeded, for by refusing Edwards's request to renew the lease of his beloved farm, he creates a situation that results in Edwards's economic failure and loss of profit for the landlord, the very profit that the steward had been so intent upon wringing from the land.

Edwards's loss of his farm and subsequent pauperization are the direct result of the new commercial and legal reconceptualization of land and labor, a process that caused great confusion, frustration, resentment, and suffering for thousands of tenant farmers in the late eighteenth century. In *The Rural Economy of Yorkshire* Marshall traces the dissolution of customary practice and the institution of legal definitions and contracts to regulate landlord-tenant relations. Marshall describes how in Yorkshire in the past "tenants were in full possession of the farms they occupy; which, until of late years, they have been led, by indulgent treatment, to consider as hereditary possessions, descending father to son, through successive generations; the insertion of their names in the rent-roll having been considered as a tenure, almost as permanent and safe as that given by a more formal admission in a copyhold court." This "species of tenancy," Marshall says, is called being a "tenant at will," meaning that the "only tie between the owner and the occupier [is] the custom of the estate,—or of the country in which it lies;—and the common law of the land." Most of these tenants did not have formal leases, preferring the unwritten agreements that had been honored by both sides for generations. They were to maintain the property, fixing gates and repairing hedges, harvesting timber to make repairs and to fashion farm implements, and gathering brushwood for fuel. Marshall notes that "while the necessary confidence on the part of the tenants remained, these principles of management were abundantly sufficient," and the tenants "took care of the estate as their own."[18]

But when the landlords, no longer bound by custom and obligation, began charging rack rents, that is, the highest rent that could be earned on a property, tenants were unwilling or unable to maintain the condition of the property. According to Marshall, "New regulations respecting timber and the management of lands" had to be introduced. When Marshall states that the "woodlands have been enclosed, and woodwards appointed," he is referring to a complete breakdown in landlord-tenant relations. When the tenants enjoyed free access to timber, they rarely abused this privilege. With the institution of high rents and the consequent loss of the tenants' loyalty and identification with the landlord's interest, the tenants cut and sold the timber for cash. Accusing their tenants of abusing their free access to the woodlands, landlords and their stewards forbade access and hired woodwards to protect the forests from the tenants' so-called illegal use of the timber. Marshall concludes that the only remedy to this messy situation is to institute "legal agreements specifying covenants, and binding a responsible tenant." "Legal contract or written agreement" is, he writes, the only "rational method of tenanting an estate."[19]

In his youth Edwards had enjoyed the kind of tenancy Marshall describes as having once been the norm in Yorkshire. This "species of tenancy" is, as Marshall notes, "now fast going into disuse." The reason Marshall gives for the disappearance of tenants at will and copyhold leases is that long-term leases are not advantageous for the proprietors. "The depreciation of the circulating value of money, and the consequent nominal rise, in the rental value of the land" has rendered such leases impractical because unprofitable.[20]

In his discussion of the change in tenancy practices in Yorkshire, Marshall chronicles the transformation of land from an entity that is constituted by a complex system of social and economic relations based on obligation and trust into a commodity that has a strictly legal definition as an object of private ownership. While Marshall insists that legal contract is the only "rational method of tenanting an estate," he registers a note of sadness for the passing of the old manorial system based on trust and personal negotiation between landlord and tenant. Despite the tone of regret that occasionally surfaces in Marshall's description of the disappearance of the tenant at will and the institution of signed contracts granting ten-year leases, his narrative naturalizes this shift from a customary to a legal definition of land; he assumes that this change is a natural process involving the decay of old, obsolete forms and the growth of new and improved methods of conducting relations between classes.

Poor Edwards is doubly victimized: by the new commercial character ascribed to land and by the impersonal forces of the marketplace. Edwards's ruin is compounded by his having invested his savings in an enterprise run by a corn factor (a grain dealer and middleman) who has gone bankrupt. By making the grain dealer one of the agents of Edwards's failure, Mackenzie is emphasizing the penetration of commercial forces into the agrarian scene. The corn factor, as E. P. Thompson argues, represented the impersonal forces of a national market economy that by the late eighteenth century had gained control over the price of grain, which had previously been governed by local market conditions of supply and demand. Corn factors were perceived by local laborers as the ones responsible for breaking down local market customs and driving up the price of bread. According to Thompson, corn factors circumvented local, customary pricing practices by buying grain secretly and privately for a higher price than that available locally. Farmworkers then were forced to buy grain they had helped cultivate and harvest at higher prices than they could afford, prices that reflected the inflated national economy.[21] As Nathaniel Kent, one of the few eighteenth-century agricultural writers not in favor of large farms, writes, "If it were the custom for the great farmer, as formerly, to bring his corn to the public market, as is still the case in some places, the home districts would never be short of corn," and the laborers would not be deprived of bread.[22]

Enclosure and Engrossment

Edwards's distresses are caused by an emerging market-driven agrarian economy, an economy that ignores moral obligation and social custom and rationalizes estate management in order to maximize profit. In the latter third of the eighteenth century a new literature of estate management and agriculture emerged, introducing farmers and landlords to accounting techniques and agricultural practices that promoted cost-effective management of land and labor.[23] Arthur Young, the most prolific and enthusiastic supporter of the new regime of high-yield agriculture, encouraged the enclosure of wastelands and open fields, the engrossment of small farms, and the consolidation of scattered holdings.[24] Young's enthusiasm for enclosure permeates his description of agricultural improvements: "All the country from Holkam to Houghton was a wild sheep-walk before the spirit of improvement seized the inhabitants; and this glorious spirit has wrought amazing effects; for instead of boundless wilds, and uncultivated wastes, inhabited by scarce any thing but sheep; the country is all cut into inclosures, cultivated in a most husband-like manner, richly manured, well peopled, and yielding an hundred times the produce that it did in its former state."[25] One farm consisting of twenty-five hundred acres "all gained from sheep-walks" and "now . . . regularly inclosed" captures his attention because it "yields immense crops of corn" and is a very profitable enterprise. The practice of replacing many small farms with a few large ones repeatedly receives Young's praise and recommendation: "Great farms have been the soul of the Norfolk [agri]culture: split them into tenures of an hundred pounds a year, you will find nothing but beggars and weeds in the whole country. A rich man keeps his land rich and clean."[26]

Edwards, on the other hand, experiences engrossment not as improvement but as the beginning of personal economic troubles that end in his pauperization. Edwards reluctantly participates in the steward's new policy of not having "any farm under 300 £ a year value on his estate" (87–88). Lacking the capital to run such a large enterprise, Edwards finds "his affairs entangling on my hands," and after "some unfavourable seasons" fails to pay his rent punctually as he "was wont to do" (88). The steward takes Edwards's stock to compensate for loss of rent and evicts him: "Had you seen us, Mr. Harley, when we were turned out of South-hill, I am sure you would have wept at the sight" (88).

To ensure that readers weep while reading this eviction scene, Mackenzie concludes it by detailing the death of Edwards's faithful dog:

You remember old Trusty, my shag house-dog; I shall never forget it while I live; the poor creature was blind with age, and could scarce crawl after us to the door; he went however as far as the gooseberry-bush; that you may remember stood on the left side of the yard; he was wont to bask in the sun there: when he had reached that spot, he stopped; we went on: I called to him; he wagged his tail, but did not stir: I called again; he lay down: I whistled, and cried "Trusty"; he gave a short howl, and died! I could have lain down and died too; but God gave me strength to live for my children. (88–89)

The dog's name, Trusty, reminds us of Edwards's trust in his landlord's benevolence. In fact, the master-dog relation is characterized by ties not unlike the paternal relations of duty and dependence. Like Trusty, Edwards deserves to live out the remainder of his days in security and comfort after having worked hard. The dog's attachment to place, to his spot in the sun by the gooseberry bush, is like Edwards's love for South-hill, his home and the home of his family. The gooseberry bush is associated with wholesomeness, reminding one of homemade (and very English) treats like the gooseberry wine, gooseberry fool, and gooseberry tarts made and served with pride by housewives like Mrs. Primrose in the *Vicar of Wakefield* and Mrs. Wilson in *Joseph Andrews*. The dog's death signals the violation that Edwards feels with this removal and the profound rupture he experiences between himself and the surroundings to which he has deep ties of affection.

Edwards's story was a common one. Even Young, the champion of scientific agriculture, admits that engrossment can ruin those many farmers who lack the capital to employ a greater number of labors and to buy the seed and stock necessary to cultivate the land. "The bad success of great numbers" of farmers, Young observes, "is owing to their not having a sufficient sum of money to begin with, which inevitably involves them in difficulties, and reduces their profit in every article of their produce." Lacking sufficient capital, farmers like Edwards "grow poor, in spite of all possible industry, judgment, and application."[27] Nathaniel Kent was concerned that small farmers would go bankrupt trying to compete with large farmers, who could invest in capital improvements.

Kent argues that when agriculture is "monopolized and grasped into a few hands," "it must dishearten the bulk of mankind, who are reduced to labour for others instead of themselves; must lessen the produce, and greatly tend to general poverty."[28] Small farms, he believes, will make England a strong agricultural producer that is safe from the disaffection and discontent of displaced, pauperized farmers. Small farms "reward merit, encourage industry, fill the markets with plenty, increase population, and furnish the best class of men in all subordinate stations of life," and those "who persist in the ruinous practice of throwing too much land into one man's hands, are blind to their own interest, and deaf to the cries of humanity."[29]

The Commodification of Land

Nathaniel Kent's attack on engrossment stands out as a dissenting voice in the annals of late eighteenth-century agriculture, which are dominated by Arthur Young and his insistence that enclosure and engrossment were positive improvements in land management. An essential feature of the new scientific and cost-effective agriculture that Young and his colleagues promoted was the reconstitution of land and labor as commodities to be "bought and sold under conditions of market competition and according to a calculation of profitable return."[30] Young's descriptions of his tours through the agricultural districts of England exemplify the new discourse on the commodification of land and labor. When Young examines an estate, he counts the number of acres capable of producing crops and stock that can be sold for cash. He takes into account the expenditures associated with maintaining horses, oxen, and laborers, which reduce profit. Unlike Edwards, Young does not sentimentalize land or endow it with human meaning. Young sought to rid land of the system of social customs and moral obligations that prevented its rational use.

Young teaches his readers—mostly farmers, stewards, and gentlemen who took an active part in administering their estates—how to calculate profitability by quantifying and commodifying all aspects of production. Young encouraged his readers to think in terms not only of enumerating and recording every step in the productive process but of assigning a monetary figure to each step. Sprinkled throughout his books are tables and charts demonstrating the profit-cost principle. For instance, in *A Six Weeks Tour, through the Southern Counties of England and Wales* Young begins his description of the "general economy and management" of a middle-sized farm of 250 acres with a list:

> 80 of them [acres] grass.
> 10 horses.
> 2 men.
> 2 boys.
> 5 labourers.
> 25 cows.
> 60 sheep.

By indiscriminately including land, people, and animals on this list, Young reduces each to the same interchangeable category of expense. To Young's way of thinking, they are all commodities to buy and sell.[31]

Young's ability to commodify agricultural processes is most acute in his analyses of labor. In enumerating the cost of growing potatoes, he calculates the cost of ploughing, planting, harrowing, manuring, and reaping; he assigns a numerical value to each act performed by a laborer, thereby allowing work to be quantified in a profit-loss ledger.[32] Young insists that farming is like any other business in that it requires constant, careful attention to detail and the keeping of "regular accounts."[33]

Other agricultural writers, including William Marshall and John Mordant, participated in this new discourse that commodified land and labor, rationalized agricultural production, and maintained control over resources by employing rational capital accounting. In *The Complete Steward* (1761) John Mordant despairs over the sloppy and idiosyncratic bookkeeping of farmers, who, he says, are "the most ignorant and illiterate of all others that are in any creditable employ." Farmers are "dilatory in keeping accounts, there being but few of these sort of people that keep any accounts at all, either of their income, or their out-goings, which should be carefully done by every person in business."[34] Describing the kind of bookkeeping that drove agriculturalists like Mordant to frustration and anger, the historians Leonore Davidoff and Catherine Hall recount how one Essex farmer used an account book but did not distinguish between domestic and business transactions. He had entered "purchases of food, school fees, rates, wages, horse medicine and nails jumbled with incomings from sales of corn, rents from small property as well as of payments in kind."[35] Mordant as well as Young preached accounting to these "illiterate" farmers, Young exhorting them to keep a ledger and to "account for every article in the farm." Young writes that "the farmer should in this book directly without the intervention of a waste-book or a journal, enter all his expenses; . . . and before he balances his books at the end of the year, it is necessary for him first to cast up the sundry accounts, such as tythe-poor levy—various expenses—and divide them in the same manner as rent."[36]

Young's efforts to reduce complex sets of social and economic relations to cost accounting were part of a larger movement to redefine land and labor as commodities and to displace the old society's paternal and charismatic economic and social arrangements. By emphasizing legal and exclusive rights to land, middle-class agricultural writers sought to erase traditional definitions of land based on customary practice, common usage, and verbal agreement and worked to transform land from a historical and social relation into a "thing, a discreet physical commodity . . . freed of any social obligations that had hitherto rested upon its ownership."[37] Marshall's faith in the law and its ability to establish rational relations between landlords and tenants, and Young's zealous promotion of cost accounting participated in the construction of what Max Weber describes as the "preconditions" necessary for the existence of "rational capital accounting"—the cornerstone of capitalism. The agriculturalists' accounts of new breeds of cattle, new ideas on crop rotation, new ways to draw up leases, new plans for building canals to transport sheep to market, and new methods for draining wetlands and reclaiming common wastelands contribute to what Weber sees as the six preconditions necessary for capitalism to flourish. Weber's six preconditions are the use of "rational technology," "the appropriation of all physical means of production," the presence of "free labor," "the absence of irrational limitations on trading in the market," the existence of "calculable adjudication and administration," and "the commercialization of economic life."[38]

With the commodification of land and labor and the commercialization of agriculture came a new "apparatus of efficient estate management" and the managerial authority of the estate agent. Newby notes that "the estate agent symbolized the period of agricultural 'improvement' as much as the better known innovators," and Mingay observes that "the land stewards were a vital factor in this progress" and were "an essential ingredient of that complex process known as the agricultural revolution."[39] For Mackenzie, however, land agents in the performance of their "rational capital accounting" disrupt the old moral economy based on paternal relations, and with their cost-effective agricultural methods of enclosure and engrossment disfigure the rural landscape. It is, after all, a London attorney who, in his capacity as steward, insists on the efficient agricultural practice of engrossment and forces Edwards to rent a much larger farm than he is capable of handling. It is this London lawyer who, without consulting Edwards or offering him help or leniency, seizes his stock and evicts Edwards for nonpayment of the rent.

The Commodification of Feeling

In the story of Edwards's pauperization Mackenzie traces the shift from a paternal, face-to-face society that honored verbal agreement and customary usage to a society that reduces all relations to commodity exchange.[40] He locates this capitalist transformation in a new gentry composed of rich merchants who use their success in trade to purchase estates and in the sons of stewards who have learned cost accounting at their fathers' knees. These two groups, consisting of persons "so perfectly versed in the ceremonial of thousands, tens of thousands, and hundreds of thousands" (interest rates) (9), bring to the countryside their ability to quantify and commodify property and labor, techniques that transform social relations into economic relations.

In *The Man of Feeling* Mackenzie contrasts the affection, loyalty, and gratitude shared by Harley and Edwards with the cold, calculating relations that dominate in what he calls the world. Mackenzie stresses the qualities in Harley that distinguish him from his worldly contemporaries. His modesty, his integrity, his sensitivity and tenderness, his amiable and sympathetic nature, and his generosity mark him as unusual, while his lack of ambition and desire for wealth and power mark him as "eccentric." Not possessing a "forwardness of disposition" (14) or even "spirit and assurance" (13), Harley is ill-equipped to make his way in a world that is driven by desire for "power, wealth, or grandeur" (10). With phrases like "he did things frequently in a way different from what other people call natural" (84), Mackenzie calls attention to Harley's unfitness for worldly activities. Harley even says about himself, "This world, my dear Charles, was a scene in which I never much delighted. I was not formed for the bustle of the busy, nor the dissipation of the gay" (127–28).

By valorizing the man of feeling who acts without consulting expediency or even utility and who is motivated not by the desire for gain but by the prompting of his heart, Mackenzie seems to be criticizing worldly ambition and lust for profit. By idealizing Harley and Edwards's paternal relation, Mackenzie seems to be protesting the commodification of social relations and the introduction of the cash nexus into the countryside. And yet, *The Man of Feeling,* despite its posture of protest, participates in the very economy it condemns. *The Man of Feeling* was a tremendously popular book, going through thirty-nine editions in fifty years.[41] Readers were moved to tears by Mackenzie's depiction of displaced and disenfranchised victims of the coldhearted, calculating world: the laborer turned beggar and fortune-teller, the daughter driven mad because forbidden by her greedy father to marry the poor but good man she loved, the young woman seduced and abandoned by a profligate member of the gentry, and, of course, Edwards, the victim of his landlord's new profit-maximizing agricultural policies. If a reader of *The Man of Feeling* did not cry, he or she was accused of not having a heart. Lady Louisa Stuart recounts how when she first read the book, she was afraid that she "should not cry enough to gain the credit of proper sensibility."[42] In fact, readers must have purchased the volume with the expectation that they would get a good cry out of it. When readers bought *The Man of Feeling,* they purchased the opportunity to feel pity for other people's distress and to shed tears of sympathy. Readers of Mackenzie's book, by purchasing and consuming this commodity, were participating in an economy that replaced social relations with commodity exchange. Mackenzie and his readers were, as we still are, "caught up," as Marx says, "in the relations of commodity production," an economy that is marked by persons who have material relations with people and social relations with things.[43]

Not only does *The Man of Feeling* participate in the very economy it deplores, but it also encourages readers to consider as obsolete the paternal system it seems to valorize. Mackenzie's idealizing of Harley's selflessness and benevolence undermines Harley's actions as a viable code of conduct. By portraying Harley's paternal relations as unsuited to the goals and methods of the modern world, Mackenzie relegates paternal relations to an idealized, rapidly receding past. Readers were meant to recognize that no one could conduct themselves like Harley and survive in the real world. Harley understands this, and he voluntarily withdraws from the world, fully aware of his own obsolescence in a world devoted to the accumulation of wealth and power.

Power and Paternalism

In stressing Harley's benevolent patronage and Edwards's gratitude and deference, Mackenzie emasculates paternalism, erasing its power and its potential for despotism. Paternalism was a much more complicated and effective form of social and economic control than Mackenzie's sentimental portrait would imply. The workings of paternalism are very complex and subtle, containing, as Howard Newby observes, basic contradictions at every level: "At one and the same time paternalism may consist of autocracy and obligation, cruelty and kindness, oppression and benevolence, exploitation and protection."[44] Eighteenth-century observers of the rural scene record a wide range of behavior within the paternal model. Some landlords are depicted as exercising autocratic control over the estate and its closed village while others are shown struggling to negotiate a reciprocal relation with their tenants. William Marshall conveys the sense of how precarious a landlord's relation to his tenant was and how difficult it was to maintain good working relations between his tenants and himself. He urges the landowner to think about and to invest energy in maintaining these delicate ties of duty and dependence. Care ought to be exercised, Marshall argues, in choice of tenants, for one must "consider the intimate connexion which must subsist between owner and occupier and how the interest of the former depends on the conduct of the latter."[45] On the other hand, John Throsby in *Select Views of Leicestershire* (1791) describes the landlord of Throsby's Cotesback estate, owner of eleven hundred acres of land, as someone who maintains strict control over his property and environs: "If he should chuse to govern, [he] may give laws to all that breathe in this place," for "not only all the land owns him for its lord, but every dwelling also; the patronage of the church and the living, are all his own."[46]

Describing the abuses that paternal power was capable of, Joseph Arch, a radical activist who had grown up in an estate community, wrote in the late nineteenth century about his childhood: "We labourers had no lack of lords and masters. . . . There was the squire, with his hand of iron overshadowing us all. There was no velvet glove on that hard hand, as many a poor man found to his hurt. . . . At the sight of the squire the people trembled. He lorded it right feudally over his tenants, the farmers; the farmers in their turn tyrannised over the labourers; the labourers were no better than toads under a harrow."[47] While Arch's interpretation of paternal relations highlights the naked power of the ironfisted landlord, other nineteenth-century critics of paternalism, J. S. Mill, for example, stress the way in which paternalism could exercise social control and maintain the power of the landed interest by disguising class conflict and massaging away, as the historian

F. M. L. Thompson observes, the "potential disaffection or awkward independence" of the laborers by "vigilance and calculated manipulation on the part of the gentry."[48] The power of the rich over the poor is obscured and made palatable by paternalism, which, as Mill argues, represents itself as "amiable, moral, and sentimental."[49]

In his study of paternalism as a method of social control, Newby points out that it is in the landowners' interest to defuse farmworkers' anger and resentment at the unequal distribution of land and profit and that paternalism, with its peculiar mixture of kindness and authority, can be very effective in managing class conflict. Paternalism, he argues, disguises "fundamental conflicts of interest" and mediates "however unjustly, between one class and another." Paternalism's aim is to enlist the laborer's identification with the landlord's goals and to cultivate the laborer's attachment and loyalty to the landlord himself. To enlist the laborer's cooperation with a system that ultimately oppresses him requires, according to Newby, personal contact, face-to-face interaction with "traditional elite members." Newby reports that Lord Percy, a landowner and mill owner, said that any landowner, great or small, "could manage men with whom he could talk." Utilizing the "personal quality of the relationship," a landowner could elicit from the agricultural laborer his endorsement of "a moral order" and a social and economic system that legitimizes his dependence.[50] Paternalism succeeds in muting these contradictions when it can utilize personal contact, and for this reason it functions best when its scope is limited to a small area. The paternalism of the old society with its peculiar mix of power and patronage could exist only, Harold Perkin contends, "in a society distributed in small units, a society of villages and small towns in which everyone knew everyone else."[51]

Paternalism as an effective means of social control did not die in 1770 despite Mackenzie's eulogy for the passing of a noble but obsolete way of conducting social and economic affairs. Paternalism as practiced by the landed interest was a flexible and adaptive form of social control, constantly reinventing itself as it encountered ideological attacks from the middle classes, and it continued to exercise considerable, if not hegemonic, ideological, political, economic, and social control until the close of the nineteenth century.[52] Mackenzie's representation of paternal relations sought to invalidate paternalism as an effective form of social control and to install in its place a rational and legalistic model of political economy. Mackenzie was, after all, a highly prosperous urban lawyer, nothing like his creation, the man of feeling. Sir Walter Scott, an admirer of Mackenzie, wrote, "No man is less well known from his writings. We would suppose a retired, modest, somewhat affected man, with a white handkerchief and a sigh ready for every sentiment. No such thing. H.M. is as alert as a contracting tailor's needle in every sort of business—a politician and a sportsman—shoots and fishes in a sort even to this day—and is the life of the company in anecdote and fun."[53] While it may seem ironic that the London lawyer and the whole new discourse on cost accounting loom large as the villains in Edwards's tale, Mackenzie, the Edinburgh lawyer, represented his class's interests well by making his readers accept this new discourse on political economy as natural and inevitable. By idealizing Harley's benevolence to Edwards, he relegates it to the realm of the unreal and impractical and by depicting Harley's withdrawal from a world that he cannot cope with, Mackenzie signals to his readers the death of paternalism, allowing them to mourn the loss of a kinder, gentler but ineffectual way of conducting oneself in the world.

CHAPTER TWO

Economic Man and Civic Virtue: Godwin's
Caleb Williams and Bage's *Mount Henneth*

ACKENZIE is but one of many late eighteenth-century novelists who sought to undermine the authority of the gentry by representing the landed classes as inept in worldly matters and incapable of managing the finances of their own estates. These novelists associate the gentry's failure to regulate the rural economy with their failure to regulate themselves, particularly their emotions. Mackenzie's Harley, for instance, is rendered incompetent by his too-lively sensibility. Many novelists of the late eighteenth century represent male characters of the gentried class as overwhelmed by feelings, including not only tenderness and sensibility but also rage and pride. Depicting the gentry as impulsive and passionate was one way for middle-class male writers to claim authority for themselves and their role in the rural economy. Middle-class portraits of the gentry sought not only to delegitimate the power and authority of the landed classes, but also to valorize the talents, skills, and intelligence of the men of the middling classes.

Proud and Passionate Heirs

A recurring figure in novels as different as Samuel Richardson's *Pamela,* Oliver Goldsmith's *The Vicar of Wakefield,* Jane Austen's *Pride and Prejudice,* William Godwin's *Caleb Williams,* and Robert Bage's *Mount Henneth* is the proud, impulsive, and frequently violent young gentleman whose petulance and ill humor are the result of an upbringing that fails to teach self-discipline.[1] This arrogant heir typically is represented as having been spoiled by fawning servants, indulged by a silly mother, and neglected by his father. Without a firm hand to guide and chastise him in his youth, the heir grows up without ever having his will thwarted.[2] Richardson may well have been the first middle-class author to explain the pride and passion of a young gentleman in terms of his rearing. Pamela accounts for Mr. B's violent temper and extreme willfulness by blaming his mother for indulging him: "My good lady, his dear mother, spoiled him at first. Nobody must speak to him, or contradict him, as I have heard, when he was a child; and so he has not been used to be controuled, and cannot bear the least thing that crosses his violent will. This is one of the blessings attending men of high condition! Much good may do them with their pride of birth, and pride of fortune!"[3] A similar narrative is told by Darcy in *Pride and Prejudice* to explain to Elizabeth why his manner is so haughty: "I have been a selfish being all my life. . . . As a child I was taught what was *right,* but not to correct my temper. . . . Unfortunately an only son, (for many years an only *child*) I was spoilt by my parents, who . . . allowed, encouraged, almost taught me to be selfish and overbearing." Pamela and Elizabeth teach their would-be lovers the lesson they never had as children by saying no to them. The women's refusal to oblige their desires causes the young gentlemen to rethink their goals and methods. Chastised by Elizabeth's frank assessment of his proud and cold demeanor, Darcy says to Elizabeth, "You taught me a lesson, hard indeed at first, but most advantageous. By you, I was properly humbled."[4]

In *Mount Henneth* another haughty young gentleman is shocked when his suit is rejected. The novel's heroine, Julia Foston, a young woman of sense and feeling, rejects an offer of marriage from Mr. Stanley, the only son and heir of a baronet, saying, "I cannot reconcile myself to the impetuous temper" of this proud, young man, "who must have been humoured in his infancy, who displays in manhood, the petulance of a child, unable to obtain the toy he wants. He must know but little neither, of the softer affections, who imagines they can be generated by spleen and perverseness."[5] Laura Stanley, his sister and Julia's friend, laments that there is generally "both in parents and tutors of heirs of fortune a fatal bias towards indulgence" (1:91). Stanley can neither "conceal his pride nor govern his tumultuous passions" (2:32), and this combination of pride and passion results in a near-fatal duel. Provoked by the presence of Mr. Cheslyn, whom he thinks is his rival for Julia's affection, Mr. Stanley "grew outrageous, and made a most furious lunge" at his opponent, who says, "Thank heaven, I am not so mad as you are." Crazed by jealousy and enraged by injured pride, Stanley grows careless in his swordplay. His "frenzy now surpassed description. He made a most furious attack, but left himself so unguarded, that he gave Mr. Cheslyn an opportunity to pass his sword through his right shoulder" (2:36–37).

Even more violent and willful is Godwin's Squire Tyrrel in *Caleb Williams,* a depraved and vicious young man whose mother's infatuation with her "pretty" boy produces a monster possessing an unnatural appetite for power. Tyrrel had been left "under the tuition of his mother, a woman of narrow capacity, and who had no other child. . . . Mrs. Tyrrel appeared to think there was nothing in the world so precious as her hopeful Barnabas. Every thing must give way to his accommodation and advantage; every one must yield the most servile obedience to his commands. He must not be teased or restricted by any forms of instruction."[6] As a result of this kind of upbringing, Squire Tyrrel was "insupportably arrogant, tyrannical to his inferiors, and insolent to his equals" (19). Tyrrel's wealth and rank discourage his country neighbors from crossing his will and further contribute to the "refinement of tyranny" (20). Each of these arrogant, ill-tempered young men is represented as being the product of an upbringing that failed to teach self-denial. These young men, often violent and always willful, are victims of their emotions. Characters like Tyrrel and Stanley are unable to exercise any self-discipline and as a result are incapable of channeling their energies into useful activity.

This figure of the proud and passionate young heir was featured in novels written by middle-class authors who were actively engaged in political opposition to the gentry. Bage and Godwin are examples of writers who participated in a discourse that challenged the power and the authority of the landed classes while promoting the interests of those disenfranchised but meritorious men of the middling classes.[7] Bage's and Godwin's portraits of the proud and passionate man of property call into question the landed gentry's ability to manage their estates, conduct their financial affairs, and participate in the governing of the nation. In contrast to the gentry, middle-class men, by exercising self-control and self-denial, regulate not only themselves but also the world around them. By underscoring the gentry's lack of self-discipline, Bage and Godwin highlight the middle-class man's ability to manage land, labor, capital, and resources. Bage and Godwin portrayed middle-class characters not only as productive, useful members of society but also as virtuous citizens concerned about the welfare of their communities. By stressing the civic virtue of middle-class men, these writers sought to counter the popular belief that the aim of the mercantile activity of middle-class men was the accumulation of wealth for private use.

The nonfictional writings of Arthur Young and his fellow agriculturalists contain a subtle but well-defined attack on aristocratic masculinity and provide a useful context for Bage's and Godwin's fictional portrayals of men of the landed and middle classes. Like *Mount Henneth* and *Caleb Williams,* Young's agricultural writings function to define the talents, virtues, and utility of the rural professional classes, men who worked as estate agents, accountants, lawyers, surveyors, engineers, architects, and auctioneers.[8]

The New Economic Man

Agricultural writers sought to discredit the managerial abilities of the landed upper classes, portraying them as pleasure seeking, self-indulgent, and incapable of exercising the self-control necessary to run a commercial venture. Young argues that gentlemen are incapable of paying attention to detail and of giving a "farmer's attention to the business." "No profit," he contends, "can arise to any gentleman that does not give the business constant attention, and descend to *minutiae*; which may be too disagreeable for him to submit to." It cannot be expected, Young argues, that a gentleman will "forgo his diversions, his excursions of pleasure, the company of his friends, the joys of society" to supervise the daily running of a farm; neither will his wife "renounce opera or a ball for the pleasure of dancing attendance on her butter and cheese in the dairy." Without careful and constant supervision, a farm will not profit: "Cattle of no kind will thrive but in the master's eye: every variation of the season to be remarked; the lucky moment for ploughing, harrowing, sowing, reaping, etc. to be caught, and used with diligence and foresight; fences for ever to be attended to; and, in short, a million of other things, which require constant thought and endless application." Young does not believe that a gentleman can be expected to perform with consistency and regularity any of these tasks and still remain a gentleman pursuing gentlemanly pleasures.[9]

Agriculturalists describe the few farming gentlemen they meet on their tours as rough, crude, and boorish, as if they have been debased and brutalized by their involvement in the daily business of agriculture and their entry into the market economy. William Marshall describes how a gentleman "coming into a good paternal estate, discharged his tenants and commenced farmer." Without a steward or even a bailiff, he handles every aspect of farming. "He attends fairs and markets—sells his own corn and his own bullocks." As a result of his direct involvement in farming, "his person is gross and his appearance bacchanalian—his dress that of a slovenly gentleman . . . his conversation bespeaks a sensible, intelligent mind; borne away, however, by a wildness and ferocity which is obvious in his countenance." In Marshall's eyes, this gentleman farmer has lost his gentility.[10]

Arthur Young, John Mordant, William Marshall, Nathaniel Kent, and other agriculturalists argued that the business of agriculture was not something a gentleman could engage in without endangering the manners and life-style that marked him as a gentleman. They also insisted that the business of agriculture required organizational skills and a scientific education that gentlemen lacked. These writers championed the emergence of a new class of professionals, who, as the sociologist Howard Newby observes, ensured the "rational administration of estate practice" and instituted "a complex structure of managerial authority . . . whereby the estate itself was managed by professional administrators."[11] A steward himself, John Mordant argues that every large estate needs a resident agent who will manage land and labor effectively and who will compensate for the landlord's lack of business sense. Marshall writes that "there are men who are losing hundreds (perhaps thousands) annually, by neglect, or mistaken frugality, in the management of their estates, yet who will consider this executive establishment, and these forms and regulations of business, as unnecessary and extravagant."[12]

According to agricultural writers, Mordant and Marshall in particular, property can be effectively managed only by professional land agents skilled in the management of land, labor, and the law. They must possess knowledge of land evaluation, cost-accounting bookkeeping, agriculture, architecture, and engineering as well as the ability to perform scrivener's duties, for example, drawing up leases, receipts, bills of exchange, letters of credit, bills of debt, bonds, bills of sale, and letters of attorney.[13] Mordant argues that, unlike a farmer or a gentleman, a steward will possess "tolerable skill in mathematicks, surveying, mechanicks, architecture, hydraulicks, etc., and particularly that he understands bookkeeping."[14] Marshall lists among the "requisite acquirements of an acting manager" a knowledge of agriculture, land-surveying, mechanics (the business of an engineer), rural architecture, planting, natural history, and accounts.[15]

Young and Marshall stress the importance of organizing the estate's records, documents, maps, and legal transactions in a central office from which the estate or estates of a landowner can be rationally and efficiently managed. Young praises the orderly arrangement of the estate office of Sir Joseph Banks; it contains "156 drawers of the size of an ordinary conveyance . . . all numbered. There is a catalogue of names and subjects, and a list of every paper in every drawer; so that whether the inquiry concerned a man, or a drainage, or an inclosure, of a farm, or a wood, the request was scarcely named before a mass of information was in a moment before me."[16] Marshall argues that the "Office, or Place of Business" should be in the "proprietor's principal residence" and should contain

> 1. Maps . . . 2. Rentals, and books of accounts . . . 3. Books of valuation: . . . registers of the number, name, and measurement, and estimated value of each field, and every parcel of land, as well as of each cottage, or other building, not being part of a farmstead, on the several distinct parts of the estate . . . 4. A register of timber trees . . . 5. A receptacle of ordinary papers,—such as contracts, agreements, accounts, letters of business . . . 6. A safe repository of documents . . . 7. . . . pocket registers of the farms . . . 8. Mechanic instruments . . . earth borers, . . . a theodolite, . . . leveling instruments . . . also models and drawings.[17]

In stressing the importance of the routinization of time, space, and money in the responsible management of an estate, the agricultural writers were representing their middle-class skills of quantification and organization as crucial to economic viability of the landed estate.

Young and his colleagues constructed this new economic man, the professional estate manager and agricultural expert, in opposition to notions of aristocratic masculinity. While aristocratic males displayed their power and authority by indulging their appetites for blood (hunting, dueling, and cockfighting) and sex, males of the newly emerging middle class sought to demonstrate that "the pen and the ruler" were mightier than the "sword and the gun."[18]

Arthur Young and other agricultural experts held ambiguous positions in society: with the exception of Mordant, all had owned and managed a modest-sized estate, and all at one time or another had been stewards on great estates. From neither the gentried nor the servant class, they positioned themselves in between as professionals—highly trained, well-educated, and informed managers of property. With their treatises on crop rotation, turnips, and fertilizers, they used the new scientific discourse on agriculture to establish themselves as professional experts on land and productivity. With their manuals on estate management and their insistence on proper bookkeeping methods, they positioned themselves as men who possessed the uniquely middle-class skills of valuation.

By constructing the new "apparatus of efficient estate management,"[19] they inserted themselves into the rural economy between landowners and their tenant farmers, and they conferred upon themselves a position of power and authority.

Ingenuity and Industry

The opposition between the gentry and the men of the middling classes that Young and the agriculturalists had laid out in their tracts on the new scientific agriculture is echoed in Bage's and Godwin's novels. In *Mount Henneth* and *Caleb Williams* ill-tempered, spoiled, and willful young gentlemen are contrasted with men who have had to make their way in the world without any of the advantages of property and rank and who achieve their goals by exerting themselves, exercising their talents, and mastering a body of information. No novel delineates this conflict between middle-class men of talent and industry and gentlemen of rank and property as clearly as *Caleb Williams*. Godwin's aim was to reveal the social and political injustice of a system that gives to men of hereditary wealth the power to tyrannize over those less "blessed" by birth. Caleb's story is "an instance," one character in the novel says, "of the tyranny and perfidiousness exercised by the powerful members of the community against those who were less privileged than themselves" (228).[20]

Godwin portrays two tyrannical gentlemen who use their power and authority to destroy two decent, hardworking, and industrious men of the middling classes. The first of these two sets is Squire Tyrrel, who tries to crush the will of his tenant farmer Hawkins, a sturdy, independent-minded yeoman farmer. Hawkins's crime in Tyrrel's mind is his refusal to let his son become Tyrrel's huntsman. Hawkins explains that he is averse to his son becoming a servant and a member of the squire's household as he himself was the son of a clergyman and is the owner of a small freehold estate. He explains that he hopes that his son might rise in social rank rather than sink into the menial position of servant. Hawkins's refusal maddens Tyrrel, as it amounts to a refusal to do his bidding. "I am not to be trifled with," says Tyrrel. "I shall not be contented when I offer my favours to have them rejected by such fellows as you. I made you what you are; and if I please, can make you more helpless and miserable than you were when I found you" (73). Hawkins's refusal to satisfy his master's demands "contributed to raise into a temper little short of madness, the already inflamed and corrosive bitterness of Mr. Tyrrel" (69). Tyrrel does all he can to destroy Hawkins and his "sober and industrious" son (73). He raises the rent, and when Hawkins cannot pay it, he confiscates the farmer's stock and goods to make up the difference. Finally, Tyrrel invokes the Black Act, twisting the law to suit his purposes, and has the young man jailed for trespassing in a rabbit warren, a capital offense. The father helps the boy break out of jail, and both flee the area branded as criminals, dispossessed of their property and their respectability.

Even more egregious is Mr. Falkland's treatment of Caleb Williams, who in his capacity as secretary to Mr. Falkland learns that his master has basely murdered Mr. Tyrrel. Afraid that Caleb Williams will tell his secret, Falkland keeps him under close and constant supervision, until Caleb, who can no longer bear the confinement of living under Falkland's constant gaze, runs away. Falkland and his agents pursue and capture him, accuse him of theft, and have him jailed, and after Caleb escapes, hunt him down again. Falkland is so obsessed with maintaining the dignity of his family name and his reputation as an honorable gentleman that he will stop at nothing to prevent the truth from getting out, including letting Hawkins and his son hang for Tyrrel's murder.

In the beginning of the novel Falkland is represented as the flower of chivalry—noble, virtuous, generous, brave—everything that a modern-day knight should be. Falkland had self-consciously tried to imitate the knights depicted by "the heroic poets of Italy," imbibing "the love of chivalry and romance" and believing that an acute sensitivity to "birth and honour" would "make men delicate, gallant, and humane" (12). Falkland lives up to his romantic ideals until the day when, no longer able to "control his resentment and anger" (142), he kills Tyrrel, who has repeatedly offended him, and kills him not like a gentleman in a duel but like a common murderer, stabbing him in the back under the cover of darkness.

Shocked and surprised by his own behavior, Falkland does everything he can to cover up this ignoble deed. "So acute and exquisite were his notions of virtue and honour" (93) that Falkland is driven mad by his sense of dishonor and becomes the victim of "the excesses of his ungovernable passion" (117). Falkland had been warned earlier by a friend to beware of his intemperate nature: "You are too passionate, too acutely sensible of injury" (37). His friend had worried that if he should succumb to his "impetuosity" and his "impatience of imagined dishonour," he would become "eminently mischievous" and no longer "useful" (37) to his community.[21]

In contrast to this arrogant and volatile gentleman, Godwin gives us Caleb Williams, a talented young man of humble origins. Possessed of an "inquisitive mind," he had as a youth "neglected no means of information from conversation or books," and his "improvement was greater than [his] condition in life afforded room to expect" (5). Naturally curious, Caleb has an aptitude for mechanics (engineering and physics): "I was desirous of tracing the variety of effects which might be produced from given causes. It was this that made me a sort of natural philosopher; I could not rest till I had acquainted myself with the solutions that had been invented for the phenomena of the universe" (6). Caleb Williams's "mechanical turn" (6) serves him well when he twice manages to escape from prison, the first time using carpenter's tools ("gimlets, piercers, chisels" [201]) to unhinge the door of his cell and to remove the lock from the door to the prison. The way in which he tackles the obstacles to his escape reveals much about his self-discipline and rigorous application of mechanical principles: "Upon accurate observation, and much reflection upon the subject, I found I should be able, if once I got into the garden, with my gimlets and piercers inserted at proper distances to make a sort of ladder, by means of which I could clear the wall, and once more take possession of the sweets of liberty" (202).

Recaptured and confined in a cell far more difficult to escape from, Caleb contemplates his situation with an "active mind"; he studies his cell, finding relief "from the coolness of my investigation" (206). Employing his "mechanical ingenuity" (211) and tools ("a chisel, a file, and a saw" [210]), he manages to escape by working his way through "a kind of rude area between two dead walls" (212), loosening bricks with his chisel and filing iron bars as he makes his way through the building. His escape involves careful planning and knowledge of building materials, carpentry, and architecture and demonstrates his ability to manage time and space.

Later on in the novel he supports himself by becoming a watchmaker, a profession that draws on "a mind fruitful in mechanical invention," and by teaching "mathematics and its practical application, geography, astronomy, land-surveying, and navigation" (299). He occupies his leisure time by attempting to write "an etymological analysis of the English language" (305). He finds this task pleasurable as it gives his active mind "employment for a considerable time" and fulfills his "desire . . . [for] some additional and vigorous pursuit" (304–05). He derives much pleasure from engaging in tasks that involve organizing information and that require the exercise of self-discipline as well as the application of theoretical principles to practical situations. He says of his etymological studies, "I was unintermitted in my assiduity, and my collections promised to accumulate. Thus I was provided with sources both of industry and recreation" (305). Caleb's mechanical ingenuity, his knowledge of mathematics and its practical application, and his talent for organization are attributes of which Arthur Young would approve. Describing himself, his talents and abilities, Caleb Williams declares in a statement that reads like a manifesto for the rights of middle-class men: "I was born free: I was born healthy, vigorous, and active. . . . I was not born indeed to the possession of hereditary wealth; but I had a better inheritance, an enterprising mind, an inquisitive spirit, a liberal ambition" (264).

Regulating the Rural Economy

The opposition that we see at work in Godwin's novel between the irrationally proud and powerful landed gentleman and the ingenious and industrious man of the middling classes is also apparent in Bage's *Mount Henneth*.[22] Bage is particularly interested in demonstrating the folly of worshipping rank and social position, especially as this is often done at the expense of valuing moral attributes and acquired merit. To play out this conflict between blood and merit, Bage portrays two young men, the aforementioned Mr. Stanley, heir presumptive to a large estate, and Tom Sutton, a young man who has to make his own way in the world. The conflict that arises between these two young men is over Tom's marrying Stanley's sister, an act that transgresses, at least in Stanley's eyes, class and property boundaries. "The son and heir of Sir Richard Stanley," "a gentleman of infinite heraldry," thinks so well of "his illustrious ancestry" that he forbids his sister to even think of Sutton (1:267): "Do you think, sister, Mr. Foston's steward, the nephew of a dirty mechanic, a fit son-in-law for Sir Richard Stanley?" (2:166). Laura Stanley does not share her family's obsession with rank. Parodying her brother's pride in ancestry, Laura says, "Know, that we people of a certain rank, ought to keep ourselves to ourselves; and not puddle ourselves with the clay and dirt of manufacturers, or descend towards the lesser gentilities" (1:271).[23]

Sutton's origins are low, but he has a rich old uncle who, having made a small fortune with his hardware foundry, toys with the idea of making his nephew a gentleman. As a result of his uncle's generosity, Tom receives a gentleman's education, but when it comes time to be launched into the world as a gentleman, the old man changes his mind and withdraws his financial support. Tom, who possesses the "active energy and independent spirit of a man" (48), must work to support himself and prepares himself for a position as a clerk in the British East India Company by studying "Eastern lore" and by exercising his "active genius" and "determined industry, which conquers difficulties, that to more timid spirits seem insurmountable" (1:29). Tom, however, decides not to pursue his career in the East India Company when he is offered the position of steward for Mount Henneth, a large estate located in Wales. Tom's personal qualities—his energy, ingenuity, and determination—attract the attention of a Mr. Foston, an extremely wealthy merchant who has just purchased Mount Henneth and needs a man "to assist me in regulating my estate" (1:143). Accepting the position despite his uncle's warning that it is an "employ unworthy of a gentleman" (2:46), Tom writes to his sister, "I am going to be the active minister to carry into execution a plan of Agriculture, the most liberal, and the most adapted to make a tenantry rich and happy, that I believe has ever been conceived" (1:170). Tom does not mind descending a bit on the social ladder because what he loses in prestige he gains in personal satisfaction and in knowing that he is a productive and useful member of the Mount Henneth estate community. Once installed as steward and aided by his sister's husband, Tom attends to the business of managing the estate, overseeing its extensive grounds. Describing the estate, Tom says, "North . . . is a view of 'mountains piled on mountains to the skies.' West, the bay of Cardigan. South, Cardigan itself at a considerable distance. And East, a beautiful and fertile vale, that constitutes the greatest part of the estate" (1:158). Summing up this arrangement, Dr. Gordon, Tom's brother-in-law, writes, "The whole business relative to lands and houses . . . [is] under the care of Tom Sutton and myself, because it is suitable to our tempers and inclinations" (2:304). Dr. Gordon continues, "Our pursuit is happiness; let us first consider of our ways and means. In the first place we have four thousand acres of land to cultivate, and cause to be cultivated. We have houses to build, and the little village of Henneth to make into a town. We have two thousand fine oaks to sell, and twice as many to plant" (2:303).

The man who gives Sutton the opportunity to become a happy, useful member of society is Mr. Foston, a merchant whose enormous wealth has enabled him to buy Mount Henneth as his retirement home and retreat from the world of business. Mr. Foston is not, however, Goldsmith's usurper, a member of "trade's unfeeling train" who has invaded the countryside and displaced the old gentry and commoners alike with "unwieldy wealth and cumbrous pomp." Although he does buy an estate with merchant capital, he is not unfeeling, for in Bage's novel, it is the merchant class, not the gentry, who possess civic virtue. The merchants and the professional men are benevolent and invariably assume the paternal role, aiding all sorts of disenfranchised characters, while the gentry are cold, hard-hearted, and indifferent to the plight of the poor and homeless.

In possessing Mount Henneth, Mr. Foston assumes the role of landlord held previously by Sir Howell Henneth, a misanthropic old man who had lived as a hermit on his estate. The housekeeper and local workmen tell the new owners Sir Howell's history: of his idle and profligate youth, his years as a gamester and politician, his debts and mortgages, his policy of rack-renting the farms on his estate, and his cutting down of seven thousand oak trees to pay the interest rates on his debt, for "out of his income of eight thousand pounds per annum, seven flowed into the purses of aliens" (1:106)—"the swarthy sons of Judah" (1:105)—and his final disillusionment with the world and retreat into a hermitlike existence. Retiring to his estate "fully imbued with the surly spirit of misanthropy" (1:108), Sir Howell became eccentric, living in only two rooms of his immense, castlelike mansion, never receiving visits from anyone, and allowing only his steward and footman into his apartments. He "indulged this splenetic disposition," became miserly, and began to accumulate great sums of money which he kept scattered about his room, in the dust and ash that he never allowed to be swept away. Despite his misanthropic impulses, he did not "like to see a poor man starve" or "be idle" (1:112), and so he often relieved the distresses of the poor in his neighborhood; however, his charitable methods were bizarre. He employed those who needed work, paying them to carry heaps of stones from one place to another. A workman recalls how "you might see his honour peeping out of the window now and then, just to see if we kept in motion; and that was all he wanted" (1:112). Sir Howell also set his men to make bricks, "then to wheel 'em up the hill to this high ground here, in barrows; and then to pile them o'heaps" (1:112). Once Sir Howell had the laborers dig a trench to bury "one heap of a hundred thousand in it," and another time he ordered them to "burn a heap of about fifty thousand." When the laborers protested this last command, saying that this would spoil the bricks, Sir Howell's response was to damn them and say, "what was that to us?" (1:113).

Bage contrasts Sir Howell's useless, sterile charity with Mr. Foston's benevolence, which produces real good and substantial change in the lives of those he aids. Although Sir Howell's charity does keep the poor from starving to death, it also makes them completely dependent on his will and whim, for they get nothing more than wages from him. Mr. Foston, on the other hand, relieves people's immediate distresses with gifts of money, but then proceeds to provide them with a permanent dwelling and, more important, with employment that will sustain them and their families in the future. When Mr. Foston and his daughter happen upon a young woman recently widowed and with several children, they learn that she has been incapacitated by grief over the loss of her husband and has been unable to work and thus earn enough to pay her husband's debts. Mr. Foston pays her husband's debts, prevents her being evicted from her home, and then arranges through his steward, Tom Sutton, to make her a dairymaid on the Mount Henneth estate. Julia Foston, sent by her father as an emissary, offers the widow the following arrangement: "Within half a mile of the castle is an neat cottage, with betwixt twenty and thirty acres of very good grazing land. These will keep eight cows winter and summer; the butter and cheese to go to the castle at a market price. Thus you will be a dairy maid, but not in the common way. You will find the cows upon the spot, and no rent to pay till the second year; then you fix it yourself by your own experience" (1:284).

Foston provides immediate relief and long-term employment at Mount Henneth for a variety of displaced and impoverished people, many of them victims of conflicts arising out of the American revolutionary war. One of these is a crippled soldier, who, having lost his arm at Bunker Hill, had been discharged and was on his way back to England when he lost his leg in a naval battle. Once in England, the penniless veteran tries to make his way back to his home parish but is prevented by his arrest for theft, which in this case consists of his having eaten turnips out of a farmer's field. Brought before the justices of the peace, a group made up of local gentry, he is interrogated by less-than-sympathetic judges. "Do you know, Sir, that hunger is no justification for theft?" asks one justice, and the soldier replies, "No, please your worship, except to those that are hungry." This saucy reply infuriates the justice, who decides to have him "whipt for his insolence." The soldier replies with tears in his eyes, "I would help being angry if I could; but I own it makes me mad when I think of having been in fifteen engagements, shot through and through, and came home poor and pennyless, to be whipt for eating turnips" (2:84–86). At this point Mr. Foston intervenes and asks that the prisoner be released into his custody. He gives the veteran a half-crown to take care of his immediate needs and then asks the man to join his household at Mount Henneth. Having witnessed the justices' hard-heartedness toward a man who had served his country for over nine years and had lost much and gained nothing by way of recompense, Mr. Foston is disgusted with the justices' lack of charity, their inflated sense of self-importance, and their obsession with defending property that amounts to no more than ten turnips.

Mr. Foston's brand of charity is useful because he regards his expenditure of funds as an investment. He invests money in good people who are temporarily destitute with the expectation that they will mend their financial woes if provided with enough capital and, more important, with the means of production to sustain their industry. His charitable activity infuses capital into the Mount Henneth neighborhood, an area that has been depleted by its previous owner's years of extravagance and dissipation. The Mount Henneth estate was deforested to raise ten thousand pounds to pay the interest rates on loans that Sir Howell used to support his dissolute life in London and "half a dozen trips to Paris, two to Italy, a score or two of volant amours" (1:94). While Sir Howell takes money out of the estate, never investing a penny in improving it, and spends it on foreigners (Jewish moneylenders) and in foreign lands, Mr. Foston, who has earned his money in foreign places, India and Persia primarily, and not at the expense of any Englishman, spends his merchant capital on improving the estate and its surrounding neighborhood. Mr. Foston is, at least in Bage's eyes, a true patriot and good citizen, and it is he, the merchant, not Sir Howell, the baronet, who possesses "public virtue" (2:120). Addressing Mr. Foston, an American merchant comments on England's lack of civic virtue: "Your country . . . is ruined. To say nothing of the war [the American Revolution], or suppose it successful, you are verging to destruction by the silent operation of finance. Your public virtue is gone, or resident only in an inconsiderable part of the middle ranks; the head and tail of the fish—stink horribly" (2:120).

Merchant Virtue

Through these two portraits, one of the virtuous and truly benevolent merchant and the other of the profligate, parsimonious landed gentleman, Bage seeks to expose as fraudulent the gentry's claim to civic virtue, a claim that originates in the idea that as owners of real estate, as opposed to symbolic wealth (money) or mobile property (goods), they possess a real and long-lasting concern in the welfare of the community. Bage tries to show that the gentry do not invest in their land or in the people of their estate communities and that they do not act in concert with the roles tradition has assigned to them, the paternalist roles of caretakers of the people and stewards of the land. Bage's frequent association of the gentry with Jewish moneylenders, whom he represents as foreigners (with accents no less!), underscores his belief that in mortgaging their estates to pay for their high-living and high-rolling ways, the gentry are engaged in a financially and morally unsound as well as unsavory and unpatriotic practice.

Hard at work reconstructing the merchant into a man of benevolence, Bage deflects onto two other groups, the gentry and the Jews, traditional concerns about merchants and their means of capital accumulation. Bage's treatment of the Jewish moneylenders stresses their foreignness and their avariciousness: "We Benjamin Ben-azar, Joshua Solomons, and Moses Levi, do jointly consent and agree to pay Mr. Thomas Sutton the full and entire sum of six hundred pounds sterling, provided the said Thomas Sutton do bind himself, his executors, administrators and assigns, to pay unto the said B.B. J.S. and M.L. two thousand five hundred and twenty pounds after the 1st of January next, to be recovered in the court of common pleas" (1:31). The absurdly high interest rate is meant to be ridiculous, but Bage's treatment of the moneylenders, despite its humorous tone, underscores how corrupt *their* form of commerce is: "Vary low terms, Maishter Sutton, says honest Benjamin on delivery.—Vasht great risques.—But me and my broders do consent to do you, because it ish good vork, though it ish not von of our ten commandments. Sho you vill take times to consider and let us know your minds" (1:32–33). Bage discredits the gentry and their management of the rural economy by linking Sir Howell Henneth's exorbitant and immoral expenditures to Jews and their exorbitant and immoral usury: "Out of eight thousand pounds per annum, seven flowed into the purses of aliens" (1:106). Sir Howell's payment of interest to the Jewish moneylenders, "the sons of chance," makes him "the original grantor of life annuities to the swarthy sons of Judah. . . . A statue ought to have been erected to him in the front of the synagogue. But public virtue now-a-days, hah, Harry?" (1:105).

Bage's emphasis on the corrupt moneylending practices of the Jews functions to deflect any investigation into the moral origins of Mr. Foston's wealth, which, as it so happens, was derived in part from moneylending. Any anxiety that readers might have about the origin of Mr. Foston's wealth and his past as a factor in the East India trade is displaced onto these Jewish moneylenders whom Bage represents as obviously corrupt. In this use of the Jewish stereotype Bage merely has tapped into readily available culturally shared prejudice that serves his purpose, much as Defoe did in his representation of the Jewish merchant in *Roxana*. Defoe, who like Bage was eager to refigure the merchant as virtuous, introduces his admirable Dutch merchant in the company of a wildly avaricious Jew whose bizarre behavior attracts our attention and shields the Dutch merchant from any inquiries into his economic motives or the origin of his wealth. Roxana describes the Jew's extreme reaction when he recognizes some jewels that she is trying to sell as those belonging to a murdered jeweler:

> As soon as the *Jew* saw the Jewels, he falls a jabbering in *Dutch,* or *Portuguese,* to the Merchant . . . ; the *Jew* held up his Hands, look'd at me with some Horrour, then talk's *Dutch* again, and put himself into a thousand Shapes, twisting his Body, and wringing up his Face this Way, and that Way, in his Discourse; stamping with his Feet, and throwing abroad his Hands, as if he was not in a Rage only, but in a meer Fury; then he wou'd turn, and give a Look at me, like the Devil; I thought I never saw any thing so frightful in my Life.[24]

The Jewish merchant's wild, animal-like antics serve to obscure Roxana's own culpability in trying to sell jewels that were not rightfully hers and also serves to highlight the kindness and charity of Roxana's protector, the Dutch merchant. Roxana grows to love and admire this merchant for his honesty, industry, and merit and concludes that "a true-bred Merchant is the best Gentleman in the Nation."[25] Both Defoe and Bage participated in the reconstruction of the figure of the merchant from the greedy, selfish, and petty character of seventeenth-century drama into what Addison was to call the "Citizen of the World."[26] Addison and Steele assured their audiences that "there are not more useful Members in a Commonwealth than Merchants."[27] As Steele's character Sealand says in *The Conscious Lovers,* "We merchants are a species of gentry that have grown into the world this last century, and are as honorable, and almost as useful, as you landed folks."[28]

An even more aggressive promoter of the idea that merchants are exemplary citizens of the nation is George Lillo in his tragedy *The London Merchant.* The great merchant Thorowgood, whose generosity and hospitality rival that of the aristocracy, remarks that "honest merchants" such as himself, "contribute to the safety of their country." Echoing Addison's panegyric for the merchant who knits "mankind together in mutual Intercourse of Good Offices,"[29] Thorowgood instructs his apprentices in the science of trade. It is not "merely . . . a means of getting wealth," he says, but "it is founded on reason and the nature of things":[30] "I have observed those countries where trade is promoted and encouraged do not make discoveries to destroy, but to improve, mankind; by love and friendship to tame the fierce and polish the most savage; to teach them the advantages of honest traffic by taking from them, with their own consent, their useless superfluities, and giving back to them in return what, from their ignorance in manual arts, their situation, or some other accident, they stand in need of."[31]

Lillo, Addison, Steele, and Defoe argued for the value of merchant activity and insisted that the merchant could be as virtuous as the landowner. These writers did not seek to eclipse or supplant the gentry with their virtuous merchants. Bage, writing fifty years later, aimed to demonstrate how mercantile codes of conduct could be more beneficial to the rural economy than the gentry's noblesse oblige. Mr. Foston's abilities as a man of business are what make him a good landlord and a benevolent patron. He has vision and energy; he knows how to invest capital in the long-range improvement of the estate; and he knows how to create meaningful and gainful employment for the local people of the estate community. Mr. Foston is Adam Smith's ideal landowner, the retired merchant. In *The Wealth of Nations* Smith describes the benefits such a landowner would bring to the countryside. When merchants become country gentlemen, "they are generally the best of all improvers": "A merchant is accustomed to employ his money chiefly in profitable projects, whereas a country gentleman is accustomed to employ it chiefly in expense. The one often sees his money go from him and return to him again with a profit; the other, when once he parts with it, very seldom expects to see any more of it. . . . The habits . . . of order, economy, and attention, to which mercantile business naturally forms a merchant, renders him much fitter to execute, with profit and success, any projects of improvement."[32]

Like Smith's capitalist landowner, Mr. Foston brings merchant capital, merchant practice, and merchant virtue to Mount Henneth, rejuvenating the political and moral economy of a moribund community. "All over the globe," says one likable and benevolent young man (a merchant, of course), "merchants adhere strictly to two principal articles, which may be called their points of honour, payment of debts, and performance of contracts" (2:172). These principles, along with industry and talent, are employed in reforming the Mount Henneth neighborhood. Mr. Foston puts into play a whole new kind of political economy that will transform the estate and its environs into a happy, thriving community. He announces that "we must have manufactures, that other folk may be as happy as ourselves, and . . . we must have commerce, or the manufactures will be useless" (2:304).

In the course of the novel, Mr. Foston has gathered around him many bright young men to help him create an ideal community, men like Tom Sutton, whose merits have been ignored by society and who have not been able to find a place in the economic structure to practice their talents.[33] At the end of the novel both of these energetic men announce what they will do to make themselves useful to the community. While Tom Sutton acts as steward, concerning himself with agriculture and housing, two others propose to start a shipbuilding industry, using the remaining woods for timber and the bay fronting the castle as a site. "In two years, the business, in all its branches, may give employment to about one hundred of your people" (2:305). Another young man, a Scotsman, proposes to set up a linen manufactory, for "Welchwomen may be taught to spin, and Welch land to bear flax" (2:306), and to build a "dome to make glass bottles." He has noticed that the surrounding hills abound "with excellent flints for the purpose; and when we have made glass, man, it will be the easiest thing in the world to make spectacles" (2:306). "We shall have a thriving colony" (2:306), declares Mr. Foston and announces that "every man amongst us, should be a man of business, of science, and of pleasure" (2:304).

Bage and Godwin sought to demystify the paternalism of the landed classes by depicting the gentry as selfish, useless, and even positively destructive to their estate communities. Godwin attacks the unequal system of land distribution as a system productive of arbitrary power that corrupts even the most virtuous and benevolent members of the gentry, whereas Bage portrays the gentry as parasites who contribute nothing to their rural communities. Bage's solution to what he sees as the exploitation of England by the gentry to foot the bill for their private pleasures is to replace the corrupt and selfish gentry with hardworking, capable men like Mr. Foston. Middle-class values and middle-class skills could save this nation from ruin, according to Bage, or at least they could improve existing conditions so that agriculture, manufacturing, and commerce could flourish and enrich not just individuals but the nation.

CHAPTER THREE

The Moral and Political Economy of Property in Austen's *Emma*

O NE author who came to the defense of the embattled gentry was Jane Austen.[1] In her depiction of Mr. Knightley as an exemplary gentleman and landlord and of Emma as a less-than-exemplary member of the wealthy but landless gentry, she links Mr. Knightley's gentlemanly virtues with his ownership of landed property and Emma's moral inadequacies with her money and her lack of property. Austen's *Emma* is a defense of the "paternal system of government"[2] from attacks stimulated by the new discourse on political economy, attacks like Bage's and Godwin's that challenged the hereditary right of the gentry and aristocracy to the exclusive monopoly of the land.[3]

On Being Knightley

The words *gentleman* and *gentlemanlike* recur in *Emma* as characters attempt to define what it means to be a gentleman. Emma tries to teach Harriet Smith to appreciate the difference between Mr. Knightley's gentlemanlike air and Robert Martin's plainer ways; Mrs. Elton, assessing her husband's friend "Knightley," proclaims him "quite the gentleman, . . . a very gentleman-like man";[4] and Mr. Knightley fiercely defends Robert Martin's virtues as a "gentleman-farmer" (56), while he declares Frank Churchill not to be a gentleman for shirking his duty (132).

But of all the characters in the book, Emma is the most concerned with what it means to be a gentleman. When Emma notices that Mr. Knightley has come to a dinner party at the Coles in his carriage, she is very pleased, for she disapproves of his getting "about as he could" and his not using "his carriage so often as became the owner of Donwell Abbey" (191). Speaking her approbation "warm from her heart," she says to him, "This is coming as you should, . . . like a gentleman" (191). Too concerned with appearances, Emma misreads Mr. Knightley's motives. While she thinks he is displaying his rank as a gentleman, he is really using his carriage to perform a gentlemanly deed of consideration and courtesy: fetching Miss Bates and Jane Fairfax to the Coles. Later on at the dinner party when Emma and Mrs. Weston discuss Mr. Knightley's generous attention to these "less worthy females" (192), Mrs. Weston expresses her surprise at "so thoughtful an attention" (201) and is inclined "to think that it was for their accommodation the carriage was used at all." "I do suspect he would not have had a pair of horses for himself, and that it was only as an excuse for assisting them" (201). Agreeing without fully appreciating Mr. Knightley's action, Emma says, "He is not a gallant man, but he is a very humane one" (201).

Emma's attempt to define a gentleman in terms of his use of a carriage elicits the epithet "nonsensical girl" (192) from Mr. Knightley. She has mistaken shadow for substance, equating the accoutrements of gentility with being a gentleman. Though acknowledging his capacity for generosity and humanity, she fails to understand that these virtues make Mr. Knightley a true gentleman. Over the course of the novel, Emma learns that gentlemanlikeness is derived not from riding in carriages or from owning large houses or even from being witty and charming; rather, being a gentleman involves doing one's duty, carrying out responsibilities, and being considerate.

Emma learns to value Mr. Knightley's qualities, especially after encountering Frank Churchill's gallant deceitfulness. After Mrs. Weston tells Emma of Frank's secret engagement to Jane Fairfax, Emma says of him, "So unlike what a man should be! None of that upright integrity, that strict adherence to truth and principle, that disdain of trick and littleness, which a man should display in every transaction of his life" (360). Clearly, this is a portrait of Mr. Knightley, the man she loves although she does not yet know it. Mr. Knightley, "always so kind, so feeling, so truly considerate" (409), is the opposite of Frank Churchill, whose greatest faults are "faults of inconsideration and thoughtlessness" (406). Mr. Knightley condemns Frank Churchill for his having induced Jane Fairfax to place herself in a "situation of extreme difficulty and uneasiness." "It should have been," he argues, "his first object to prevent her from suffering unnecessarily" (405). Churchill's conduct toward Jane and the rest of the deceived community attests to Mr. Knightley's perspicuity and judgment.[5] Even before meeting him, Mr. Knightley is disgusted by Churchill's "leading a life of mere idle pleasure, and fancying himself extremely expert in finding excuses for it" (134). He condemns Frank for not doing his duty, for not acting "on principle, consistently, regularly" (133), and for his lack of "vigor and resolution" (132). Mr. Knightley argues that Mr. Weston's pampered, spoiled son has no "delicacy towards the feelings of other people" (134–35). Emma learns that Mr. Knightley is right about Frank Churchill and that being "well grown and good-looking with smooth plausible manners" (135) does not make one a gentleman, and that duty, right conduct, and consideration are the hallmarks of a man, or more precisely, an English gentleman. By the end of the book Emma can comprehend Mr. Knightley's "worth" (437), especially when she compares him with the younger man: "Pleased as she had been to see Frank Churchill, she had never been more sensible of Mr. Knightley's high superiority of character" (437).

The Landlord

For Austen, Mr. Knightley's gentlemanly virtues are inseparable from his position as an owner of an estate. Mr. Knightley's usefulness and benevolence are the requisite virtues of a responsible landowner, who because of his economic, political, and social role has duties and obligations to perform within his community. The landowner's duties were, as Thomas Gisborne in his *Duties of Men in Higher and Middle Classes of Society* (1795) asserts, incumbent upon him by virtue of "the actual power which the landlord enjoys over his estates, and the tenants who occupy them; and partly from the influence which the possession of those estates gives to him in their neighbourhood even over persons who are not his immediate dependents."[6] According to the nineteenth-century agricultural expert Sir James Caird, the landlord's duties included the management of his estate, oversight of the welfare of those who lived upon it as well as an actual concern in the business of the parish, the administration of justice in the county, and the supervision of roads, public buildings, and charitable institutions.

The landowner's economic duties included employing knowledgeable and trustworthy land agents to manage his property, choosing industrious and respectable farmers to whom to lease his farms, and maintaining a good working relation with the laborers who cultivated and usually lived on his land. His social duties ranged from providing some kind of relief for the poor, the ill, and the aged to building cottages for laborers and schools for the children of the estate and neighborhood. "His influence," Caird maintains, "where wisely exercised, is felt in the church, the school, the farm, and the cottage."[7] This influence "which he enjoys over others as a trust" makes the landlord, according to Gisborne, responsible for exerting his power "without grudging the trouble," in maintaining his tenants, laborers, and neighboring community's "rights, composing their differences, increasing their comforts, and improving their morals."[8]

Austen's Mr. Knightley is not a passive receiver of rents, an ornament on top of the hierarchy of labor, but an active and useful member of society. Mr. Knightley's productivity is underscored by the energy and the enthusiasm with which he talks about superintending his estate. "As a farmer, as keeping in hand the home-farm at Donwell" (90), he has eager discussions with his brother about "the plan of a drain, the change of a fence, the felling of a tree, and the destination of every acre for wheat, turnips, or spring corn" (90–91). Mr. Knightley's estate is much more than lime avenues framing pleasant vistas and strawberry gardens planted to provide ladies with diversions; his estate has a working farm that produces wool and crops for market. With his steward William Larkins, he has intense and private conferences (that spark Emma's jealousy) about improving his land and its productivity. "I would rather be at home," Mr Knightley declares to Emma, "looking over William Larkins's week's account" than dancing at a ball (231). A prudent as well as a generous man and a good neighbor, Mr. Knightley takes time to instruct his tenant farmer Robert Martin in modern agricultural methods and to encourage his reading of agricultural journals and newspapers, the reading of which Emma, in one of her many demonstrations of misguided sensibilities, finds sordid and low. Mr. Knightley's skill as a farmer is matched by his physical vigor, his walking out in all weather, and his constant, personal supervision of his property. The mud on his boots, his conferences with his steward, and his apples sold at market firmly establish him as a productive and useful member of his community.[9]

Mr. Knightley, however, is much more than an improver of property. He is what David Davies, the author of *The Case of Labourers in Husbandry* (1795) admires in a landlord, a man of authority who secures his community from "injustice and oppression."[10] "As a magistrate, he had generally some points of law to consult John about, or at least, some curious anecdote to give" (90). His sensitivity to the traditional rights of his community is reflected in his concern over his plan to move a path that cuts through his "home-meadows": "I should not attempt it, if it were to be the means of inconvenience to the Highbury people" (97). With "all the parish to manage" (202), Mr. Knightley is busy both as a magistrate and as a benefactor to the less fortunate of the parish. References to Mr. Knightley's involvement with parish business and to the parish's dependence on his judgment underscore his value to this community. Although Austen does not directly describe the poverty of the rural underclasses, she does represent the quiet desperation of the lives of many impoverished gentlewomen who inhabit Highbury.[11] Documented in detail are Mr. Knightley's kindnesses to Miss Bates and Mrs. Bates, his gifts of food, his frequent inquiries after their health, and his special concern for Jane Fairfax and eagerness that Emma treat her as her merit deserves. These acts of consideration are evidence of his active supervision of estate and community, duties incumbent upon him as lord of the manor.

Austen also links virtue with land stewardship in her description of Robert Martin, Mr. Knightley's tenant farmer. Although not an owner, Martin, as a renter of a farm, is responsible for managing the land and employing the latest agricultural and husbandry techniques. He is, as Mr. Knightley says, a "respectable, intelligent gentleman-farmer" (56) who "always speaks to the purpose; open, straight forward, and very well judging" (53), an "excellent young man" (53) who has "more true gentility than Harriet Smith could understand" (59). Robert Martin and Mr. Knightley share many qualities; they are both responsible, vigorous, hardworking, capable of generous feeling and romantic attachment. They even express themselves similarly. The language of Martin's proposal of marriage to Harriet is "plain," "strong," and "unaffected" (45), while Mr. Knightley's proposal to Emma is "in plain, unaffected, gentleman-like English" (407). Even Emma, far from an impartial judge, recognizes that Martin's letter of proposal "would not have disgraced a gentleman," for it "expressed good sense, warm attachment, liberality, propriety, even delicacy of feeling" (45).

In contrast to Martin and his "delicacy of feeling," Austen gives us Mr. Elton, who refuses to dance with Harriet at the ball intentionally to slight her and hurt Emma. Mr. Knightley, who rescues Harriet from her mortification, is "warm in his reprobation of Mr. Elton's conduct; it had been unpardonable rudeness" (297). It is no coincidence that both Mr. Elton and Frank Churchill, who also has gallant manners, are landless gentry. Even though he will one day inherit his uncle and aunt's estate, Frank is without any sense of landowning responsibilities; Mr. Elton, as a minister, is a passive receiver of tithes. Neither has productive economic ties to the Highbury community. They stand in sharp contrast to Mr. Knightley and Mr. Martin, both of whom are described as possessing "true gentility" (59).

Emma's "Solitary Grandeur"

Emma's ability to assess Mr. Martin's qualities coupled with her inability to value them is quite like her reaction to Mr. Knightley: she can recognize his virtues but does not fully appreciate them.

That she can so easily persuade herself to like Frank's "effusion of lively spirits" (178), however extravagant and heedless they are (184), indicates that Austen thinks Emma has much to learn about appreciating Mr. Knightley and apprehending his worth. For Emma to value and to love Mr. Knightley she must have a clearer understanding not only of what a gentleman is—kind, considerate, resolute in the performance of duty—but also of what a gentleman does.

Emma's difficulty in appreciating Mr. Knightley's worth, as well as her inability to think well of Mr. Martin, stems from her having no real economic ties with her community. Her attitude toward Mr. Martin as "a man whom I could never admit as an acquaintance of my own" (55) underscores her estrangement from the economic relations that structure her community. "The yeomanry," she says, "are precisely the order of people with whom I feel I can have nothing to do" (25). She proudly (and perversely) declares her alienation from an order of people who were considered in Austen's era to be the backbone of English society. "A degree or two lower, and a creditable appearance might interest me; I might hope to be useful to their families in some way or other. But a farmer can need none of my help, and is therefore in one sense as much above my notice as in every other he is below it" (25). She feels she has no social or economic basis for developing a relationship with the likes of Mr. Martin, and she is right. She, unlike Mr. Knightley, has no real tie to him. The only economic relation she can have with someone beneath her is as a lady bountiful, a role she assumes with cool grace when she visits a poor, sick cottager.

Emma's snobbery, not only as it manifests itself in her dealings with the Martins but also in her strained encounters with other supposed less worthy people in her community, namely, the Coles, the Perrys, and even the Bateses, is the result of her family's lack of landed property. Hartfield, a house surrounded by a lawn and shrubberies, is not an estate: "The landed property of Hartfield certainly was inconsiderable, being but a sort of notch in the Donwell Abbey estate" (123). The Woodhouses are relatively recent newcomers to the area, purchasing the land for their home from Mr. Knightley's family, who could, we are meant to assume, trace their possession of Donwell Abbey from Henry VIII's dissolution of the monasteries. In comparison to Mr. Knightley's ancient, "rambling and irregular" abbey with its extensive grounds, which include "an abundance of timber," "ample gardens," meadows, and streams (323), Emma's home is "modern and well-built" and its grounds are "small, but pretty and neat" (244). The purchaser of Hartfield, a younger branch of an ancient family as Emma tells herself, derived his fortune not through inheritance of property but "from other sources" (123), and Emma's personal fortune as an heiress of thirty thousand pounds is derived from these other sources.

Exactly what these other sources are, we cannot know for sure, but judging from Mr. Woodhouse's complete lack of involvement with any kind of business matters and his naivete about the world beyond his hearth, contemporary readers would have readily assumed that the Woodhouses must live off of the interest of a fortune accumulated either in trade or in the late seventeenth- and early eighteenth-centuries London money market. Emma says her family has lived in Highbury "several generations," which given the fact that the house is modern might not mean much more than three or four generations. That Hartfield is only sixteen miles from London, a distance that can be traversed by horseback in a few hours, would indicate to Austen's readers that the Woodhouse fortune was most likely made by someone who retired to Highbury not far from London and its money market, where he could have bought and sold stocks in corporations and colonialist ventures like the East India or South Seas companies or lent money to the government for William III and Anne's imperialist wars.

The fact that Emma's fortune is not derived from owning property, that its origin and essence is money, can explain Emma's alienation from her agrarian community. Having no real estate, she has no real ties to Highbury, and unlike Mr. Knightley, she has no clear-cut role to perform vis-à-vis those in the "gradations of rank below" her (123). Her fortune, though it has purchased rank, has not purchased the kind of useful activities she craves, duties that can come only from owning land.

Emma's economic origins are underscored by her behaving,

talking, and thinking like Mrs. Elton, who, as the daughter of a Bristol merchant, is, in Emma's words, a "vulgar being" (250). As many critics have pointed out, Emma and Mrs. Elton relate similarly to their protégés; they adopt as companions women who are economically or socially vulnerable, and they take great delight in feeling superior to these "less worthy females." Emma says of Harriet, "Shewing so proper and becoming a deference, seeming so pleasantly grateful for being admitted to Hartfield, and so artlessly impressed by the appearance of every thing in so superior a style to what she had been used to. Encouragement would be given. . . . She would notice her, . . . and introduce her to good society" (20). Mrs. Elton says of Jane Fairfax, "She is very timid and shy. One can see that she feels the want of encouragement. I like her the better for it. I am a great advocate for timidity—and I am sure one does not often meet with it.—But in those who are at all inferior, it is extremely prepossessing. . . . However, my resolution is taken as to noticing Jane Fairfax.—I shall certainly . . . introduce her wherever I can" (254–55). Mrs. Elton's sentiments and her language— "notice," "introduce," "encouragement"—echo Emma's thoughts about Harriet.

Though Emma is a much better person than Mrs. Elton, far more intelligent, creative, and talented as well as capable of real feeling and depth of attachment, she shares with Mrs. Elton a self-involvement that enables each to assume that she is the center of every social occasion. Each of them thinks that the ball at the Crown Inn has been given in her honor. "Thinking much of her own importance" (244), Mrs. Elton says, "the Westons—who I have no doubt are giving this ball chiefly to do me honor" (291), while Emma "must submit to stand second to Mrs. Elton, though she had always considered the ball as peculiarly for her" (292–93). Perhaps most significant, both of them are obsessed with status and rank, and as a consequence have in common a language of class. They both have a "horror of upstarts" (280), a phrase spoken by Mrs. Elton, which Emma applies to her, calling her "a little upstart" (250). Both are also very conscious of who is in the "first" and "second set" (17) and who "moves in the first circle" (270), and Emma's pleasure in Mr. Knightley's carriage is not very far removed from Mrs. Elton's delight in her brother-in-law's barouche-landau.

Emma's snobbery, her obsession with rank and social hierarchy, can be explained as stemming from an insecurity often felt by the nouveaux riches. But a more precise explanation can be found in her lacking an economic function in her community. All the characters but Emma and her father have economic ties to Highbury or Donwell. Of the "second and third set," even the least distinguished belong to Highbury: Mrs. Goddard runs a boarding school, Miss Nash teaches in it, the Coles have prospered from conducting trade in Highbury, and even Miss Bates, who, being "neither young, handsome, rich, nor married" (17), is the most disenfranchised of these "lesser women," belongs to Highbury, for she is the daughter of the deceased vicar, a tenuous but a real tie. Jane Fairfax, as Mrs. Bates's granddaughter, also "belonged to Highbury" (144). Mr. Weston, "a native of Highbury, and born of a respectable family," though recently returned from the world of trade, has resettled there, purchasing "a little estate adjoining Highbury" (13). Even Frank Churchill is regarded "as sufficiently belonging to the place to make his merits and prospects a kind of common concern" (14). Emma and her father stand out as the only characters who do not belong to Highbury.[12]

Unconnected to her community, Emma has difficulty negotiating social interactions with people whom she sees as her inferiors. She can be kind and considerate to family members and to those she regards as equals, and she can graciously condescend to bestow favors on someone who, like Harriet, is clearly an inferior, but when it comes to those in the gradations of rank just beneath her, she is not very generous or even kind. When the Coles invite the Westons, Frank Churchill, and Mr. Knightley to their dinner party, Emma is shocked when she discovers that her friends have accepted the invitation. She thinks the Coles should not dare to invite the "best families" (186) and need to be taught "that it was not for them to arrange the terms on which the superior families would visit them" (186). She thinks it her duty to slight them and to teach them their place; they are after all of "low origin, in trade, and only moderately genteel" (186). Clearly, Mr. Knightley and

Mr. Weston do not regard the Coles as beneath their notice. They regularly meet with Mr. Cole to discuss parish business and to enjoy a dinner together or a game of whist. Mr. Knightley says, "I was with Mr. Cole on business" when Mr. Elton's letter announcing his engagement to Miss Hawkins arrives. "He had just read Elton's letter as I was shewn in, and handed it to me directly" (155). Mr. Knightley has an open and casual relationship with Mr. Cole, so much so that Cole suggests to Knightley that he might be in love with Jane Fairfax (258). Mr. Knightley moves effortlessly up and down the social hierarchy, enjoying an intimacy with people like the Coles, the Perrys, the Coxes, and the Martins, an intimacy that Emma is unable to comprehend and unwilling to cultivate.

Emma's money places her in a state of "solitary grandeur" (187). Emma's isolation is reinforced by her father's retirement from life, his valetudinarian ways, or more accurately, his habits of gentle selfishness, which prevent him from taking a more active role in his community. Self-involved and lacking any sense of civic responsibility, he is not a man in the sense that Mr. Knightley uses the word or in the sense that Emma later adopts, for he has none of the physical vigor or moral rectitude of Mr. Knightley, nor any sense of duty to his community other than admonishing his friends for eating too much rich food. Having such a father, Emma cannot benefit from the ties that men forge as they discuss parish business or play cards. She is left entirely on her own to make connections with her community, and she does not do a very good job of it, focusing too much attention on the wrong people and slighting those who deserve her attention.

Emma adopts Harriet Smith as her companion out of boredom and the fear of spending long, lonely days with a father whose "talents could not have recommended him at any time" (5). She justifies her relationship with Harriet by saying, "Harriet would be loved as one to whom she could be useful" (56). The way in which Emma chooses to make herself useful to Harriet is to invest her time and energy in improving her, in giving her those qualities that could catch her a husband of a higher social status than Robert Martin.

Emma's interest in improving Harriet's marriage prospects as well as her neglect of the Bateses is symptomatic of her not understanding social relations in Highbury and not knowing how to be truly useful. As part of her charitable duties, a woman in Emma's position is expected to focus her attention on the special needs of women who are less fortunate than she, many of whom "may be considered in the light of long-established acquaintance."[13] As a pamphlet published by the Friendly Female Society asserts, "The knowledge which one woman hath of what is proper for the relief of another" makes women's involvement in benevolent activities vital. Of those who stand in need of female kindness, "some of them are widows, destitute of a husband's industry, a husband's counsel, a husband's sympathy. There are others who have been reduced from ease and competency, by what are called the accidents of life, to a state of dependence and want." "Poor aged women of good character," women like Miss and Mrs. Bates, are particularly "entitled to the humane notice of the female heart."[14]

Emma knows she should be kinder to the Bateses, that she should visit them more frequently, inquire into their welfare, and establish a "regular, equal, kindly intercourse" (341). She knows how much the Bateses "loved to be called on" (137) and how welcome a visit from her would be, and yet, she avoids calling on them, though she does send them a joint of meat. Her excuse for avoiding them, these "tiresome women," is fear of "falling in with the second and third rate of Highbury" (137). She knows Mr. Knightley regards her "as rather negligent in that respect, and as not contributing what she ought to the stock of their scanty comforts" (137). "She had had many a hint from Mr. Knightley and some from her own heart as to her deficiency," and "she had been remiss, her conscience told her so; remiss, perhaps more in thought than fact; scornful, ungracious" (341).

Emma neglects Jane Fairfax, who has also been "reduced from ease and competency . . . to a state of dependence"[15] despite Mr. Knightley repeatedly reminding her that it is she who must make the overtures and invite Jane to her home, offering her friendship and the opportunity to enjoy Hartfield and to escape the confines of her grandmother's home. After Mr. Knightley explains to Emma "with a reproachful smile" (257) why Jane Fairfax, a woman of taste and intelligence, accepts Mrs. Elton's friendship—"she receives attentions from Mrs. Elton, which nobody else pays her"—Emma is "more conscience-stricken about Jane Fairfax than she had often been." "I ought to have been more her friend.—She will never like me now. I have neglected her too long" (262).

Emma's dislike of the cool and reserved Jane Fairfax, while not laudable, is understandable. Her dislike of visiting the tiresome Mrs. Bates and her talkative daughter is forgivable. But her cruel remark to Miss Bates at Box Hill is inexcusable. Mr. Knightley chastises Emma for her thoughtless, inconsiderate, and irresponsible behavior: "How could you be so unfeeling to Miss Bates? How could you be so insolent in your wit to a woman of her character, age, and situation?" (339). While perhaps Emma's clever remark is not so much a product of ill will aimed at Miss Bates as it is a reaction to the tension and dis-ease created by Frank Churchill, Emma's display of wit evinces a lack of self-control. She relieves her sense of the ridiculous without considering the effect of her words. Mr. Knightley reproves her for being irresponsible, for not thinking of how Miss Bates would feel, and for humbling her "before her niece, too—and before others, many of whom (certainly some,) would be entirely guided by *your* treatment of her" (340). Once again Emma has not understood her role in her community, and Mr. Knightley has to spell it out for her: "Were she your equal in situation—but, Emma, consider how far this is from being the case. She is poor; she has sunk from the comforts she was born to; and, if she live to old age, must probably sink more. Her situation should secure your compassion" (339).

The Moral Bankruptcy of Speculation

Austen links Emma's faults—her snobbery, her inability to understand complex social interactions, and her spurious speculative powers—to her economic origins.[16] Without property and the responsibilities that come with owning land, Emma lacks two important virtues: consideration for the feelings of others and a firm sense of her duty to her community. Austen associates these virtues with owning property in much the same way that Country Tories of the eighteenth century identified civic virtue with landowner-ship. The historian H. T. Dickinson describes how Country Tories believed that "those who possessed a real and substantial stake in the country were the only true citizens and natural leaders of those who were merely inhabitants." The Country Tories' ideology was founded on "an ethic of civic virtue which maintained that society and civil government could only be preserved by the patriotic ac-tions and public spirit of men of property." Austen shares with this Country Tory ideology a distrust of money, for "property had to have a real and stable value, not a fictitious and mobile one." Those who made money in trade were suspect because merchants could leave England and continue their business elsewhere, taking their movable property with them. Even more morally and politically suspect were those who traded in money and shares. The money trade, according to Dickinson, "did not confer the rights of citizen-ship upon financiers because their wealth was based on fantasy and speculation." The Country Tory ideology feared that with their money financiers, bankers, and stockjobbers could gain control of the government by loaning money to the monarchy to conduct wars and by selling bonds to bankroll colonial expeditions. The Country Tories "mistrusted the new financial system of the na-tional debt, the Bank of England and the great chartered corpora-tions" and feared that the monied men would "devour the country gentlemen and work the most ancient families out of their inheri-tance" and corrupt the "moral, social, and political order."[17]

There is a parallel between the Tory attack on the financiers' speculation in money and shares and Austen's portrayal of Emma, who, as an "imaginist" (302), deals in fantasies rather than in production and who enjoys speculating about romantic relation-ships for others, yet declines to engage in one herself. Like the Tory portrait of the monied man who seeks only to gratify his own needs and is completely uninterested in maintaining the welfare of the polis, Emma, engaged in "fantasy and speculation," to use Dickin-son's words, and lacking the real ties of real estate, behaves irre-sponsibly toward her community.

Having no experience relating to people in the old society's paternal and nurturant manner, Emma relates to them as if they were commodities to possess or stocks to invest in. When Emma meets Harriet, she is "convinced of Harriet Smith being exactly the something which her home required" (22), and she decides to "improve her" by forming "her opinions and manners" (22) with the aim of marrying her to a gentleman and firmly establishing her "in good society" (26). In short, Emma is a speculator in the marriage market.

In linking Emma's disruptive behavior to her monied status and Mr. Knightley's virtue to his property, Austen employs this old Tory argument that equates land with virtue and money with corruption. Pope and Swift in their attacks on Walpole used this Country Tory ideology to oppose the Court's system of patronage, its standing army, and the financial revolution, and Oliver Goldsmith and William Cowper used it to attack the new money of wealthy merchants and colonists. But in *Emma,* Austen is not simply reverting to this rather worn opposition of land to money. She is not parroting old Tory doctrine derived from eighteenth-century poets and playwrights, but responding to current political and economic issues, specifically the attack on the landowners by a new breed of thinkers, the political economists.

The Attack on the Country Gentleman

Her portrait of Mr. Knightley defends property and its power to confer virtue from the attacks of writers who challenged the efficacy and utility of the old paternal and local system of government. These writers scrutinized the paternal system of economic and social relations in a series of tracts, pamphlets, and treatises on population and poverty that were prompted, in part, by the concern over the dramatic increase of the population of the rural poor and the consequent sharp rise in the poor rate.[18] In 1803 more than one million people out of a total of nine million received poor relief, at a cost of £4,267,965.[19] The plethora of tracts and treatises on the condition of the poor—for example, Joseph Townsend's *Dissertation on the Poor Laws,* David Davies's *The Case of Labourers in*

Husbandry, Sir Frederic Eden's *The State of the Poor,* and Jeremy Bentham's *Pauper Management Improved*—contributed to an examination of the relation between the rural poor and those who were traditionally viewed as their guardians, benefactors, and superintendents, namely, the landlords. Many of these political writings on population and poverty as well as such poems as George Crabbe's "The Village" and Wordsworth's "Simon Lee" and sermons like Coleridge's "Blessed are Ye that Sow beside All Waters" directly or obliquely portrayed the landed upper classes as selfish, nonproductive members of society, remiss in their customary custodial duties. Some writers, mostly political economists and proponents of laissez-faire capitalism, argued that the traditional ties of paternal responsibility and grateful dependence were insufficient or inadequate to deal with the increasing numbers and distresses of the rural poor.[20] Other writers, often Tory, accused the landholders of abdicating their role as governor and substituting for the old system of paternal obligation a new capitalistic system of power and privilege minus duty and responsibility.[21]

Tories like Coleridge, Southey, and W. Johnstone of *Blackwood's* criticized the landed gentry and aristocracy for abdicating their paternal role as custodians of the soil and superintendents of their rural communities. They felt that the landowner's lack of interest in agriculture and indifference to the welfare of those who occupied his estate constituted a breach in ties that bound the landlord to his tenants in a system of obligation and gratitude. When there is no "generous bounty" on the part of the landlord, there is no "grateful and honest dependence," Southey argues, and so "the bond of attachment is broken."[22] At the core of the Tories' critique was the belief that a combination of selfishness and negligence was responsible for the increase in the number of the poor and the degree of their distress. "The rich and the high," an article in *Blackwood's* asserts, have "indolently and slothfully" neglected "those whom nature, providence, and law have placed beneath them."[23]

Radical Tories criticized landlords for adopting, at the expense of their tenantry and dependents, two methods of modern and efficient agriculture—enclosing wasteland traditionally held in common and farm engrossing. Both methods, by sacrificing the public's good for the landlord's private gain, smacked too much of the marketplace for many advocates of the paternal system.[24] Farm engrossment, according to Nathaniel Kent, is a "destructive practice" that ignorant or negligent landlords engage in, persuaded "by the specious inducements" of greedy farmers and land agents.[25] The Tory critics argued that both enclosure and farm engrossment resulted in the expulsion of great numbers of small farmers and farm laborers from land they had farmed or used for grazing cattle. Davies states that "the land-owner, to render his income adequate to the increased expense of living, unites several small farms into one, raises the rent to the utmost, and avoids the expense of repairs. . . . Thus thousands of families, which formerly gained an independent livelihood on those separate farms, have been gradually reduced to the class of day-labourers." He concludes that "the depriving the peasantry of all landed property has beggared multitudes."[26] A *Blackwood's* article titled "Hints to the Country Gentlemen" also blames the "system of great farms" for the distresses of the poor. An "outcry should be directed against the Country Gentlemen, who have depopulated their estates. . . . The Country Gentlemen were remorselessly driving their tenantry like herds of swine into the market towns, and burning and destroying their cottages, that they might return no more." The author concludes, "They, and they only, are the class who have lessened the employment for the poor. From them, and only them, the country at this time has a right to demand relief."[27]

A second kind of criticism leveled at landowners was made by political economists, who argued in terms of utility, productivity, and economic contribution to society. Advocates of laissez-faire capitalism like N. W. Senior and David Ricardo criticized the landowners' passive role in the economy, for, as receivers of rent, landlords contributed neither capital nor labor. Unlike the High Tories, who attacked the landowners on moral grounds, these political economists attacked the landed classes and in particular the figure of the Country Gentleman from a utilitarian point of view, on the grounds that the landlord was nonproductive and therefore superfluous and parasitic. Patrick Colquhoun in *A Trea-*

tise on the Wealth, Power, and Resources of the British Empire describes "royalty, nobility, and gentry" as "unproductive labourers, whose exertions do not create any new property." Landlords, like paupers and indigents, do not produce capital:

> It is only those who pass their lives in vice and idleness, or who dissipate the surplus labour acquired by inheritance or otherwise in gaming and debauchery, and the idle class of paupers, prostitutes, rogues, vagabonds, vagrants and persons engaged in criminal pursuits, who are real nuisances to society—who live upon the land and labour of the people, without filling any useful stations in the body politic, or making the smallest return or compensation to society for what they consume.[28]

Nassau Senior says of the landlord, who epitomizes for him "the indolence and selfishness of the superior classes,"[29] "A considerable part of the produce of every country is the recompense of no sacrifice whatever; is received by those who neither labour nor put by, but merely hold out their hands to accept the offerings of the rest of the community."[30] In his *Essay on the External Corn Trade* and *Principles of Political Economy and Taxation,* David Ricardo criticizes the landed classes' promotion of the Corn Bill as a supremely selfish measure designed to protect their profits derived from the artificially high wartime price of grain. Arguing against the Corn Bill, he insists that "all classes . . . except the landlords, will be injured by the increase in the price of corn."[31] Ricardo wished to demonstrate that the landlord's interests are not the same as the people's interests, that what benefits a landowner does not benefit the nation as a whole. Ricardo argues that "the interest of the landlord is always opposed to the interest of every other class in the community. His situation is never so prosperous, as when food is scarce and dear: whereas, all other persons are greatly benefitted by procuring food cheap."[32]

A third kind of attack on the landlord came from the radicals, whose leveling rhetoric was suppressed as seditious by Tories and Whigs alike. Radical writers, sympathetic to the plight of the displaced and pauperized agricultural worker, questioned the landowners' right to inherit and to monopolize land. "Landlords, and landlords only," wrote Thomas Evans in 1816, "are the oppressors of the people.—The time has come that something must be done. . . . The easy process is to declare that the territory of these realms should be the people's farm; thus transforming all the lands, waters, mines, houses, and all feudal permanent property to the people." This attack on the landlord gathered momentum with the Anti–Corn Law League and with publications such as William Cobbett's *Legacy to Labourers: What Is the Right which Lords, Baronets, and Squires, have to the Lands of England?* which had chapters subtitled "Can they do what they like with our lands?" and "Can they use them so as to drive the natives from them?"³³

Civic Virtue and Patriotism

Amidst these attacks on the landed classes and against a background of great social unrest—the population explosion, the displacement of the agrarian laborer, the pauperization of the small farmer, the food riots of 1810, the Luddite rebellion of 1812, and the passage of the Corn Laws—Austen constructed the image of the ideal country gentleman.³⁴ With her portrait of Mr. Knightley, she participated in what the historian Harold Perkin calls "the remarkable revival of the paternal aristocratic ideal,"³⁵ a defense of the landed interests articulated in the late teens and twenties by High Tory journalists, who promoted the paternal system of government, revived the image of the landowner as chivalrous knight, and defended the Poor Laws by insisting on the right of the poor to receive the benevolence and protection of the rich. Writing in *Blackwood's,* Johnstone argued that true Tories "maintain that protection and support are the right of all. . . . As Tories we maintain it is the duty of the people to pay obedience to those in authority over them; but it is also the duty of those set in authority to protect those placed below them." "Those in authority," he asserts, "are not to sit in stately grandeur, and see people perish, nor, indeed, are they ever to forget that they hold their power and their possessions upon the understanding that they administer both more for the good of the people at large, than the people would do, if they had the administration of both themselves."³⁶

Austen's defense of the landed classes involves simultaneously idealizing the landlord and criticizing the monied status of the new gentry. In *Emma* Austen splits her gentry into two classes: the landed, represented by Mr. Knightley and his responsible stewardship of property, and the landless, represented by Emma and her inappropriate and ultimately irresponsible behavior. By laying the blame for misconduct at Emma's feet, Austen can describe the gentry's abuse of their powers and privileges, their selfishness and negligence, without indicting the paternalistic system of landownership and management. She makes it clear that it is the new gentry, not the real gentry, who are guilty of misconduct. Like Oliver Goldsmith in "The Deserted Village," Austen uses this conservative tactic of blaming the new monied gentry for not understanding the subtleties of the social formation of country villages, for neglecting their moral obligations to their communities, and for threatening to destroy the old society's feudal and communal social ties. Austen locates the source of corruption not in the landlord-tenant relation or in the system of paternal government, but in the bad taste, uninformed sensibilities, and selfishness of individuals not schooled in the responsibilities of owning land.

When Emma, landless, irresponsible, and fundamentally unattached to her community, marries Mr. Knightley, she gains access to a civic virtue that, for Austen, comes only with the responsibility inherent in owning and superintending an estate. Not only will Emma's character and conduct improve once she is tied to Mr. Knightley and his estate, her considerable fortune of thirty thousand pounds will, in his hands, be put to good use. As a result of this marriage, Emma's money, most likely originating in and still participating in the international credit system, is taken out of circulation and reinvested in property. Once invested in an English estate, her money is purified of any foreign and marketplace taint. Cleansed by this contact with the soil, her money can be used to rejuvenate the estate community. Liberated from the paper credit system and channeled into the local economy of the estate village, Emma's wealth will participate in the only economic system that, in Austen's eyes, is capable of bestowing virtue.[37]

Through her portrait of Mr. Knightley as the responsible

landholder, knowledgeable farmer, and useful, active member of his community, Austen defends the landed classes and their right to monopolize the land by stressing not just the utility of Mr. Knightley's stewardship but also the patriotic quality of his civic virtue. The patriotism that infuses Austen's portrayal of Mr. Knightley as the gentleman-cultivator is akin to Arthur Young's admiration for the marquis of Rockingham and his modern methods of agriculture. Young believes that the effects of the marquis' husbandry "are of the noblest and most truly national kind," arguing that "much does this neighbourhood owe to so patriotic a design, which was truly planned with judgment, and executed with spirit." "The senseless rabble," he writes, "may praise the military hero; it belongs to *the few* to venerate the spirited cultivator."[38] Mr. Knightley is Austen's "spirited cultivator," and his patriotism is evident in his conscientious stewardship of his estate and the surrounding community.

With an eye to events taking place across the channel, Austen underscores Mr. Knightley's patriotism by repeatedly using the adjective *English* to describe his language, manners, and activities. Unlike Frank Churchill and his French amiability, which consists of "smooth, plausible manners" (135), Mr. Knightley in all his interactions displays an "English delicacy towards the feelings of others" (134–35), Emma describing him as "so kind, so feeling, so considerate" (409) and as "good-natured, useful, considerate" (201). Even in his rather cool, matter-of-fact chats with his brother, he displays that characteristic "true English style" which buries "under a calmness that seemed all but indifference, the real attachment which would have led either of them, if requisite, to do everything for the good of the other" (90). Donwell Abbey, with its "old neglect of prospect," is "rambling and irregular," the appropriate "residence of a family of such true gentility, untainted in blood and understanding" (323), and the estate itself, including the Abbey-Mill Farm, is the best that England has to offer—"English verdure, English culture, English comfort" (325). For Austen, the true English gentleman is one who resides on his estate, supervises his farms' productivity, and superintends his community. Owning and caring for property responsibly is patriotic, for, as Austen was well aware, power and privilege divested of responsibility and consideration could lead to the disaffection of the middling classes and lower orders of society and could result, as in France, in revolution.

The Marriage of Land and Money

For the sake of my argument, I have stressed that Emma and Mr. Knightley represent the competing and antagonistic economies of money and landed property, perhaps at the risk of making Emma seem less attractive and less virtuous than she is and Mr. Knightley more virtuous than he is. Now I would like to complicate my description of these two characters by arguing that, though Emma is a member of the monied class, she is a gentrified member, and that Mr. Knightley, though represented as a paternalist, is a capitalist as well. Although Emma's fortune and country residence are of relatively recent acquisition, Emma is completely identified with the country gentry, sharing in their values as best she can. As an exemplary daughter, a kind sister, and an indulgent aunt, and as someone who desires to be useful to her community, she has all the right impulses. All she needs to assume her position as a member of the true gentry is a little education in self-control and a clearly defined role within her community.

Just as Emma is not some upstart, vulgar heiress, Mr. Knightley is not a pure paternalist, a kindly feudal lord who only engages in activities that promote his community's welfare. As a paternalist and a capitalist, he balances his paternal duties with his agricultural enterprise. As an efficient, successful farmer, he has adopted the capitalistic virtues of productivity and utility. His interest in scientific agriculture reveals his desire for higher yields, which, in turn, mean greater profits in the marketplace. Mr. Knightley's estate, though a source of civic virtue for Austen, is neither entirely free of capitalistic practices nor innocent of responsibility for the deterioration of the old society's feudal ties. The Donwell Abbey estate, as its name indicates, has its origins in the confiscation of church lands, a process that involved the expulsion of the hereditary subtenants and the confiscation of these subtenants' property rights, which had allowed them to share in the church's tithes.[39] Having only one tenant farmer who rents a very large farm, Mr. Knightley owns property that has benefited from farm engrossment and modern ideas about productivity. By combining "many small farms into a few of great size," Mr. Knightley, or probably his father, was consulting his "private advantage," to quote from Gisborne, behaving in a "sordid and ungenerous manner."[40] Mr. Knightley's "plan of a drain" (90) implies that he is engaged in reclaiming marshy wasteland, a process that frequently involved enclosing common land and claiming for private use land once used to support many. Enclosure meant expulsion and dispossession for self-supporting peasants who pastured cows, gathered firewood, and grew food on this so-called wasteland. Though Mr. Knightley demonstrates a sincere concern for his neighbors, the fact that his land has been engrossed and enclosed indicates that he has engaged in and continues to engage in practices that are motivated primarily by self-interest and a desire for material gain.

As someone who enjoys going over his land agent's accounts, Mr. Knightley is well aware of the economic dimensions of social relations. Whenever a marriage is discussed, it is Mr. Knightley, not Emma, who points out the financial rewards or drawbacks of the arrangement. He reminds Mr. Woodhouse, who laments Miss Taylor's marriage, that "every friend of Miss Taylor must be glad to have her so happily married." Though he recognizes how painful it is for Emma to lose such a companion, he is sure Emma knows "how much the marriage is to Miss Taylor's advantage; she knows how very acceptable it must be at Miss Taylor's time of life to be settled in a home of her own, and how important to her to be secure of a comfortable provision" (9). Discussing Martin's proposal to Harriet, Mr. Knightley says to Emma, "My only scruple in advising the match was on his account, as being beneath his deserts, and a bad connexion for him. I felt, that as to fortune, in all probability he might do much better" (55). Mr. Knightley certainly recognizes the value of Emma's fortune, a fortune he can anticipate using to improve his property, for as the typically cash-poor country gentleman, he has "little spare money," not even enough to own and maintain carriage horses (191). With this marriage he will gain access to the much-needed capital that will ensure his continued ability to balance productivity with civic responsibility. He also gains access to Hartfield, which, after all, as a "notch in the Donwell Abbey estate" (123), is a missing piece of what was once his family's property. By marrying a genteel member of the monied classes to a capitalistic paternalist, Austen bridges the gap between these two powerful groups and resolves on a fictional level economic, political, and social tensions produced by the antagonism between the landed and monied classes, an antagonism that threatened to erupt into open, even armed conflict.[41] As Asa Briggs points out, there was in the early nineteenth century widespread fear in Parliamentary circles that the mercantile and manufacturing classes would join forces with the working classes against the landed classes to push for reform, even revolution.[42] Both disenfranchised groups were angered by the arrogance and blatant self-interest of the landed classes when they passed the Corn Laws and felt the landowners had violated their trust and had abdicated their role as governors. Through this marriage Austen reconciles the competing claims of money and land as she upholds the efficacy and legitimacy of the paternal system of social relations while at the same time recognizing the value of the talents, energy, and capital of the monied classes. Emma's money, imagination, and enthusiasm will infuse new life into the paternal order, which is, like the bachelor Mr. Knightley, in danger of not reproducing itself. Austen's marriage of land and money in *Emma* mirrors what Gramsci calls the "suture" that took place in the early nineteenth century between the landowning and capitalist classes,[43] an ideological fusion that helped the upper classes to maintain their hegemonic control over England's economic, political, and social life.

CHAPTER FOUR

Mansfield Park, Hannah More, and the Evangelical Redefinition of Virtue

H AVING hinged my argument that Austen is a radical Tory on her portrait of Mr. Knightley as the ideal paternalist, I must now deal with the fact that almost all of her other portraits of the gentry and aristocracy are quite negative. In *Pride and Prejudice* Lady Catherine de Burgh is absurdly self-centered, rude, and bigoted, while her nephew Darcy is overly proud and reserved, the natural result of having been spoiled as the only son and heir of a great estate. *Northanger Abbey*'s General Tilney lacks civility and behaves disgracefully toward Catherine, while *Persuasion*'s Sir Walter Elliot is vain, selfish, and lacking in common sense, Austen representing him as "a foolish, spendthrift baronet" (234). In this chapter I focus on Austen's negative portrait of the Bertram family, paying particular attention to the way in which Austen's portrait of the Mansfield family resembles the Evangelical critique of the irresponsible and self-indulgent upper classes. I am suggesting neither that *Mansfield Park* is an Evangelical novel nor that Fanny is an Evangelical heroine. It is, however, important to understand why Fanny is so easily mistaken for the heroine of an evangelically inspired novel and to understand why the novel has led several critics to suspect Austen of sympathizing with the Evangelical movement. A comparison of *Mansfield Park* with Hannah More's *Coelebs in Search of a Wife* will help to explain the ideological and political significance of Austen's flirtation with and ultimate rejection of the Evangelical reformation of the manners and morals of the upper and lower classes.[1]

More's "Gay and Busy World"

Austen's portrait of the Bertram and Crawford families shares with Evangelical discourse in general and with Hannah More's work in particular a concern with the upper classes' pursuit of pleasure, its exhibitionism, and its obsessive consumption of material objects.[2] Typical of the Evangelical attack on the moral inadequacies of the upper classes is Hannah More's *Coelebs in Search of a Wife* (1808), a didactic novel filled with descriptions of the "gay world" of London's high society.[3] In chronicling the hero's search for the perfect helpmate, More represents the titled and the landed elite as morally lax and incapable of exercising self-restraint. Coelebs meets the "self-appointed queens" of London society, who "maintain an absolute but ephemeral empire over that fantastic aristocracy which they call the world" (190). Characters like Lady Denham, habituated to self-indulgence, have "grown old in the trammels of dissipation" (78). Mrs. Fentham, motivated by "vanity, ambition, [and] the hunger for applause," is doomed to suffer "disappointment and jealousy" which "poison the days devoted to pleasure" (72). Lady Melbury, "acknowledged queen of beauty," is, despite her good qualities, "extravagantly addicted to dissipation and expense." She is, for More, the quintessential upper-class woman whose generosity and liberality are negated by her inability to regulate her conduct: "She is one of those admired but pitiable characters, who, sent by Providence as an example to their sex, degrade themselves into a warning. Warm-hearted, feeling, liberal on the one hand; on the other, vain, sentimental, romantic, extravagantly addicted to dissipation and expense, and with that union of contrarieties which distinguishes her, equally devoted to poetry and gaming, to liberality and injustice" (101).

Lady Melbury's faults, according to More, are due to an improper education. Having lost her mother at an early age, she has grown up without proper guidance and restraint. Her mother, a "woman of sense and piety . . . would have formed the ductile mind" of her daughter for better things than gaming and extravagance (105). "Made for nobler purposes" (104), Lady Melbury suffers also from not having the kind of husband "who would prudently have guided and tenderly have restrained her." Her husband is "satisfied with knowing how much she is admired and he envied" and "never thought of reproving or restricting her" (104). Women like Lady Melbury are, in More's eyes, victims of a "fashionable education" (xi) that does not prepare them for domestic happiness. More argues that an education which "smothers a woman with accomplishments" renders her vain, selfish, lacking in self-restraint, and generally unfit for the domestic duties that fall to a wife and mother.[4] Coelebs is in search of a properly educated young woman whose training is not "made up of the shreds and patches of useless arts" but is a truly useful and Christian education that "inculcates principles, polishes taste, regulates temper, cultivates reason, subdues the passions, directs the feelings, habituates to reflection, trains to self-denial, and, more especially, that which refers all actions, feelings, sentiments, tastes, and passions, to the love and fear of God" (10).

"Errors in the Education of His Daughters"

An education that polishes manners and teaches accomplishments while failing to instill moral principles is a subject that occupies Sir Thomas Bertram's mind as he ruminates over his "errors in the education of his daughters."[5] He realizes too late that in distinguishing Maria and Julia for their "elegance and accomplishments," he has failed to direct his attention to "the necessity of self-denial and humility" (463). Though they "joined to beauty and brilliant acquirements, a manner naturally easy" (34), they have "never been properly taught to govern their inclinations and tempers, by that sense of duty which can alone suffice" (463). Sir Thomas also realizes too late that Mrs. Norris's "excessive indulgence and flattery" (463) have contributed to her beloved nieces' downfall. With counsel such as hers, "it is not very wonderful that with all their promising talents and early information, they should be entirely deficient in the less common acquirements of self-knowledge, generosity, and humility" (19).

In her portraits of the beautiful, accomplished, and well-mannered Maria and Julia, Austen makes it clear that each of them lacks a "higher species of self-command, that just consideration of others, that knowledge of her own heart, that principle of right" (91). Maria's appetite for flattery and attention leads her into a dangerous flirtation with Henry Crawford. Like More's Lady Denham, her "vanity, ambition, [and] hunger for applause" doom her to suffer "disappointment and jealousy." While Maria's conduct is driven out of control by "selfish passion" (464), Julia's "feelings, though quick, were more controulable." "Less the darling of her aunt," Julia escapes Maria's fate; her "education had not given her so very hurtful a degree of self-consequence" (466). Tom, too, suffers from not having a sense of higher duty and obligation to others. Though he has "easy manners, excellent spirits, a large acquaintance, and a great deal to say" (47), he is "careless and extravagant" (20) and is full of "cheerful selfishness" (24). He feels "born only for expense and enjoyment" (17) and shrugs off his huge gambling debts even though they must be paid with his brother's patrimony. Austen punishes these three Bertram children: Maria is expelled from polite society, Julia is doomed to spend her life with a fool, and Tom is deserted by his gaming partners when dangerously ill with fever. He, unlike his sisters, has a second chance. His near death from an illness brought on by carelessness and his long, slow convalescence change him, and he regains his health "without regaining the thoughtlessness and self-ishness of his previous habits" (462).

Just as More's town-bred gentry are deformed by London high life, so are Austen's Londoners, the Crawfords. As Edmund points out, Mary Crawford's moral lapses are the result of her tastes having been shaped by her urban associates. Attracted to Miss Crawford's "beauty, wit, and good humour" (64) but pained by her dissatisfaction with simple country living, Edmund believes that her "warm feelings and lively spirits" (63) have not received the proper influence. "We must suppose," Edmund says to Fanny, "the faults of the niece to have been those of the aunt" (64). Mary's avowed dislike of the clergy and refusal to take religion seriously pain him even more, and he again blames her aunt, her uncle, and her London acquaintance: "Yes, that uncle and aunt! They have injured the finest mind! I know her disposition to be as sweet and faultless as your own, but the influence of her former companions makes her seem, gives to her conversation, to her professed opinions, sometimes a tinge of wrong. She does not *think* evil, but she speaks it—speaks it in playfulness—and though I know it to be playfulness, it grieves me to the soul" (269). Edmund's infatuation with Mary Crawford comes to an end when she cavalierly dismisses as folly her brother's adulterous liaison with Maria Rushworth. Shocked by her lack of "feminine modesty," Edmund continues to blame others for her failings. "This is what the world does. . . . Spoilt, spoilt! . . . She was speaking only, as she had been used to hear others speak, as she imagined every body else would speak. . . . Her's are not faults of temper . . . . Her's are faults of principle, Fanny, of blunted delicacy and a corrupted, vitiated mind" (455–56).

Like his sister, Henry Crawford has spent his formative years in London under the tutelage of his less-than-virtuous uncle. His tastes and principles have been shaped by "early independence and bad domestic example" (467), making him "thoughtless and selfish from prosperity and bad example" (115). Henry Crawford's irregular conduct, especially his flirtation with the engaged Maria Bertram, leads Fanny to conclude that his actions are dictated by "selfish vanity" (194). She accuses him of "behaving so dishonourably and unfeelingly," of having a "corrupted mind" (225), and of feeling "nothing as he ought" (224). His marriage proposal and his promised perseverance she regards as "selfish and ungenerous." "Here was again," she says of his actions, "a want of delicacy and regard for others which had formerly so struck and disgusted her. . . . How evidently was there a gross want of feeling and humanity where his own pleasure was concerned" (328–29).

The language Austen uses to describe the Mansfield families echoes More's disapproval of the gentry and her attack on their idleness, extravagance, and selfishness. Austen makes it clear that in every activity, from sight-seeing to choosing a play to perform, the Crawfords and the Bertrams are motivated by a "selfishness which, more or less disguised, seemed to govern them all" (131). She portrays Tom, Maria, Julia, Mary, and Henry as having "known no principle to supply as a duty what the heart was deficient in" (329). Their habits of "selfish indulgence" (236) prevent them from curbing their desires, and their fashionable education deprives them of a proper sense of their duties and obligations as well as of an ability to enjoy the quiet pleasures of domestic life.

Domestic Femininity

Austen's use of the language and the ideology of the Evangelical movement is not limited to her depiction of the morally bankrupt Bertrams and Crawfords. Austen also employs the Evangelical discourse of domestic femininity to portray the virtues of her heroine, "my Fanny" (461). Fanny's meekness, her moral gravity, and quiet gratitude are qualities that, despite their power to repel twentieth-century readers, were requisite for the much-admired heroines of Evangelical tales.[6] Austen's Fanny is quite like More's Lucilla, the heroine of *Coelebs*. Both are gentle, quiet, and retiring young women who, unlike most fashionable young ladies who thrive on the bustle and commotion of the gay world, prefer the quiet pleasures of domestic life. While Lucilla is by nature "gentle, feeling, animated, modest," by education "elegant, informed, enlightened," and by religion "pious, humble, candid, charitable" (159–60), Fanny is "gentle tempered" (329), compassionate, and full of "kind-heartedness" (166) and wishes only to be useful to those whom she loves or to whom she feels gratitude. Edmund says to her, "You have good sense, and a sweet temper, and I am sure you have a grateful heart, that could never receive kindness without wishing to return it. I do not know any better qualifications for a friend and companion" (26). Later he says that she combines moral integrity with tenderheartedness and grateful dependence, making her "the perfect model of a woman" (347).

Lucilla's and Fanny's natural modesty makes them avoid any

display of personal charms and talents. Just as Lucilla's "graceful modesty" (347), "humility," and sense of "unworthiness" (307) prevent her from drawing attention to herself—"Contented to please, she had no ambition to shine" (125)—so does Fanny's modesty make her almost as "fearful of notice and praise as other women were of neglect" (198). Both young women are completely without vanity; they are, in fact, quite diffident about their merits. Neither of them is flattered by marriage proposals from handsome, wealthy, young men of property. Lucilla refuses "a young noble-man of clear estate, and neither disagreeable in his person or man-ner, on the single avowed ground of his loose principles" (326). Her reasons for rejecting his offer—she "feared his principles were not those of a man with whom she could venture to trust her own" (327–28)—are echoed in Fanny's rejection of Henry Crawford: "I cannot approve his character" (349).

Lucilla is More's example of the new domestic woman, one whose temperament and tastes are not driven by vanity, greed, or sexual desire, but are rather the product of a liberal education combined with the discipline of "Christian principle" (234). Lu-cilla is exactly the wife Coelebs has been searching for, the perfect woman to fill the role of wife as companion, helpmate, and friend. She is Coelebs's Eve, who, following Milton's prescriptions, has studied "household good" so that the home becomes the seat of peace, happiness, and virtue and conveys in the domestic arrange-ments a feeling of "order, regularity, and beauty" (2). As a "retired country gentleman . . . who loves home, and lives at home" (13), Coelebs, like the domestic husband in William Cowper's *The Task,* wants a wife for "his warm but simple home, where he en-joys / With her who shares his pleasures and his heart / Sweet converse,"[7] a wife whose "tranquillity, smoothness, and quiet beauty" (*Coelebs* 3) are matched by a "firm and regular character" (*Coelebs* 13) and an informed and elegant mind. Coelebs's father gives him this advice on choosing a bride: "The *exhibiting,* the *displaying* wife may entertain your company, but it is only the informed, refined, the cultivated woman who can entertain you; and, I presume, whenever you marry, you will marry primarily for yourself, and not for your friends: you will want a COMPANION; an ARTIST you may hire" (13).

Mary Crawford's harp playing, when seen in the context of More's disapprobation of performance, takes on added significance. Austen indicates that Miss Crawford's harp playing is disruptive and, along with the exhibiting and displaying of musical and theatrical performances, is at odds with the rhythms of a rural community. Mary is "untouched" by and "inattentive" to her natural surroundings (209) and sees "inanimate nature with little observation" (81). Because she is oblivious to seasons and the activities of farmers around her, Mary Crawford cannot understand why no one is willing to spare a cart or a wagon to transport her harp in the midst of a "very late hay harvest" (58). "Guess my surprise," she says to Edmund, "when I found that I had been asking the most unreasonable, most impossible thing in the world, had offended all the farmers, all the labourers, all the hay in the parish" (58). Mary's harp playing is disruptive also because it is linked to her sexuality: "A young woman, pretty, lively, with a harp as elegant as herself . . . was enough to catch any man's heart" (65). Mary's presence, along with her brother's, by introducing a sexuality associated with exhibition and display, disrupts the equanimity of the Mansfield domestic enclosure, making even Edmund dissatisfied with quiet family gatherings. After the sexually charged rehearsals of *Lovers' Vows,* the Bertram family cannot easily return to their old ways. Edmund and his siblings are miserable when their father returns and dismantles their theater, forbidding any more "noisy pleasures" in hopes of restoring "domestic tranquillity" (186). Edmund complains, "We are sometimes a little in want of animation among ourselves" (196), clearly wishing for Mary's presence.

Fanny, on the other hand, sympathizes completely with her uncle's desire for the quietness and "the repose of his own family circle" (196). She is happiest when at home surrounded by the people and the things she loves and is pleased when her uncle returns, restoring at least the semblance of family unity. Fanny's enthusiasm for the tranquility of domestic harmony is quite like Cowper's love of domesticity as expressed in *The Task,* a poem from which she often quotes:

> Now stir the fire, and close the shutters fast,
> Let fall the curtains, wheel the sofa round,

And, while the bubbling and loud-hissing urn
Throws up a steamy column, and the cups,
That cheer but not inebriate, wait on each,
So let us welcome peaceful evening in.[8]

This is the kind of evening Fanny wishes for and Sir Thomas desires when he requests nothing but tea and his "beloved circle" (181) the night of his homecoming.

While Mary Crawford's sexuality threatens to disrupt domestic tranquility, Fanny's modesty, gratitude, consideration, and tenderheartedness are qualities that make her the only female upon whom Sir Thomas and Edmund can rely. When Maria runs off with Henry Crawford and Julia elopes with the shallow Mr. Yates, Lady Bertram and Mrs. Norris are overwhelmed by confusion, while Mary Crawford's blasé attitude toward the whole affair repulses Edmund. Fanny calms her anxious Aunt Bertram and soothes Edmund by listening to him despair over Mary's "corrupted, vitiated mind" (456). Fanny's "good sense," "sweet temper," and "grateful heart" are qualities that not only are useful in maintaining peace in a household, but are, as Edmund states early in the novel, the highest qualifications for "a friend and companion" and, as it turns out, for a wife.

Fanny, as Edmund's companion, will make a far better wife than Mary ever would, for Mary does not share Edmund's values or even his tastes. Fanny is uniquely qualified to be his companion, as she has been raised "to think and feel" (113) as Edmund does. It is no wonder that they "enjoy . . . sweet converse," meeting frequently to share their thoughts and feelings, for Fanny is Edmund's pupil: "He recommended the books which charmed her leisure hours, he encouraged her taste, and corrected her judgment" (22). Fanny is Edmund's Eve; she will, like More's description of Adam's helpmate and unlike Mary, inspire his good works and support him in his chosen profession. With her love of domestic tranquility, her meek manner, and her sober judgment, Fanny will make a good wife for a conscientious clergyman. She even resembles a description of the wife of a famous Evangelical minister: "She had little sprightliness or vivacity; was not obtrusive in conversation, yet was not taciturn. . . . Her demeanour was grave, but by no means gloomy. Profoundly humble, and beautifully meek, she could never offend, and was rarely offended; . . . her prudence, sound good sense, sobriety of mind, and correctness of judgement were exemplary. All this was veiled by a delicate and invariable modesty, and sanctified by eminent piety."[9]

The Evangelical Redefinition of Womanhood

Do the traits and beliefs that many twentieth-century readers find unattractive in Fanny and therefore problematic have their origin in an Evangelical refashioning of womanhood? Passivity, modesty, physical frailty, shyness, moral seriousness, and love of nature[10]— do these characteristics of Fanny's suggest that Austen was participating in the new Evangelical discourse on feminine virtue? Fanny shares certain traits with Lucilla and in *Mansfield Park* Austen certainly seems to participate in the Evangelical critique of the gentry. And yet Fanny is not an Evangelical heroine.

Lucilla, More's ideal young woman, is a product of Christian discipline. Possessing a mind "habitually disciplined by Christian principle" (234) and "Christian vigilance" (241), Lucilla monitors her feelings and actions, daily practicing self-government and self-renunciation. Concerned that she finds too much satisfaction in her charitable activities for the neighborhood poor, she fears that "her virtues" sometimes "lose their character by not keeping proper place. They become sins by infringing on higher duties" (347–48). She worries that "an enjoyment which assumes a sober shape may deceive us, by making us believe we are practising a duty, when we are only gratifying a taste" (350). "The practice of self-denial and putting aside of self" characteristic, according to Leonore Davidoff and Catherine Hall, of Evangelicalism is demonstrated admirably by Lucilla when she announces to her mother that she must give up gardening because she is afraid that she loves it too much.[11] Her mother suggests that she limit her time gardening by "hanging up her watch in the conservatory to keep her within her prescribed bounds." Lucilla is "so observant of this restriction, that when her allotted time is expired, she forces herself to leave off, even in the midst of the most interesting operation." Proud of her daughter, Mrs. Stanley approves of this system, for "time is saved, self-denial is exercised, and the interest, which would languish by protracting the work, is kept in fresh vigour" (353).

The watch in the garden is emblematic of More's belief that everyone, even the pious, must vigilantly monitor the state of their souls and be continually on guard against sinful impulses. More argues that a serious Christian must practice a "habitual watchfulness."[12] It is the "daily business of a Christian," writes More, to avoid activities, however innocent in appearance, that "stir up in us improper propensities," that might "awaken thoughts which ought not to be excited" and create "those feelings, which it is his constant duty to suppress" (Knight 305). Lucilla practices daily "self-examination, that she may learn to watch against the first rising of bad dispositions, and to detect every latent evil in her heart" (306). More urges the reading of religious texts that will aid in this rigorous self-examination, texts that will "teach us to pull off the mask from the fairest appearances, and discover every hiding-place, where some lurking evil would conceal itself" and "show us not what we appear to others, but what we really are" (Knight 308). At the heart of More's urging of self-denial and self-government is a belief in original sin. More's Evangelicalism taught that because human nature is naturally sinful, people are in need of constant self-regulation. The "passive and self-denying virtues . . . are peculiarly the evangelical virtues," writes More in *Thoughts on the Importance of the Manners of the Great to General Society*. She observes that the gospel "enjoins the harder task of renouncing self, of living uncorrupted in the world, of subduing besotting sins, and of not thinking of ourselves more highly than we ought."[13]

An expert in the practices of self-denial and self-regulation, Lucilla is More's new domestic woman. Her enthusiasm for "household good," her pleasure in caring for her younger siblings, and her dutiful, happy compliance with her parents' directives make Lucilla an exemplar of domestic femininity. The new domestic woman, who, like Lucilla, practiced Christian discipline, was encouraged to apply the techniques of self-regulation to the apportionment of time, space, and resources. Again Lucilla's watch has significance, for the timepiece, used to discipline the self, is an emblem of mastery over time. Davidoff and Hall describe how clocks, mainly decorative objects owned in the eighteenth century primarily by the upper classes, became an essential item in the middle-class home, regulating work and time, giving method and order to daily activities. Evangelical writers urged their readers to manage their time carefully, to set aside a time to pray, to read the Bible, and to "watch over" (Knight 187) their thoughts and actions. The management of time, More remarks, is "moral arithmetic," and she urges her readers to "conscientiously regulate" time, to "accurately distribute it, appropriate the hour its due employment." This "habit of turning time to account," More writes, "will put us on a more strict *watchfulness* over our hearts and lives."[14]

Clocks, memorandum books, and account books, the paraphernalia used by Evangelicals for self-surveillance, became the new domestic woman's tools to govern time and resources, while cleaning and organizing her house became her way to manage space. Davidoff and Hall quote the first and last stanza of a poem (*Family Fortunes,* 88) which Jane Biddell inscribed on a blank memorandum book, a gift to her fifteen-year-old daughter; the poem reflects the Evangelicals' "scrupulous emphasis on diary keeping, on New Year's resolutions, on birthday books and the annual casting up of accounts before God" (ibid.):

> The Memorandum, brief yet clear
> The record of each hour so dear
> Spent as the conscience best can tell
> On which remembrance loves to dwell
> · · ·
> That the ensuing year may tell
> That thou has spent the period well
> Little will thou avail the time
> Allotted in this nether clime
> If true improvement marks each year
> And fits us for a nobler sphere.

The new domestic woman's exercise of self-restraint makes her a good manager of a household, "where strict attention" is paid to "order and regularity" for, as Ann Taylor, an Evangelical writer on domesticity, says, "To do everything in its proper time, to keep everything in its right place, and to use everything for its proper use, is the *very essence* of good management."[15]

Evangelical Redefinition of Virtue

Through her portrait of Lucilla, More achieves her double goal of positing a new kind of feminine virtue, one based on elaborate technologies of "self-government" (*Coelebs,* 346), while simultaneously attacking the upper classes for their moral inadequacies. Pious, obedient, kind, and organized, Lucilla stands in sharp contrast to the town-bred ladies that Coelebs had encountered earlier in the novel, women who are made unhappy by their inability to control the impulses that feed their vanity, greed, and sexual desire. More argues that these town ladies, who have been taught only to "paint, and play, and sing, and draw, and dress, and dance" (Knight 192) and who have not benefited from the techniques of Christian discipline, will not make good wives or mothers because they will be unhappy in fulfilling their domestic duties. In *Coelebs* when a "thorough-paced town-bred lady" marries a retired country gentleman, she discovers too late that with only her books, her "domestic employments and the sober society of her husband" the country not only held "no charms for her, but . . . was a scene of constant ennui and vapid dulness." She resents her husband and his way of living and languishes "for the pleasures she had quitted." She is unhappy, her husband is made unhappy by her dissatisfaction, and they become estranged from one another. More's point is that had she been taught early self-government and had she had "a fund of principle," this town-bred woman might have been able to come to accept and even to find satisfaction in her quiet life in the country (346).

More portrays upper-class women not only as lacking in self-control, but also as neglecting their duty to superintend and care for those who depend on them for their livelihood. More describes Lady Melbury's treatment of a flower girl whose father has died and whose mother is dying as a result of her careless attitude toward paying her bills. Moved to tears by the sight of the extreme poverty of the "sweet girl with the jonquils" (106), Lady Melbury orders twelve dozen flowers, never intending to pay for them. Though she is "warm-hearted," "liberal," and "sentimental" she is incapable of submitting to self-regulation, and as a result, her good qualities are negated by her thoughtlessness and selfishness. "Extravagantly addicted to dissipation and expense" (101), she gambles with the household funds and loses the money that was meant to pay the many small tradespeople who cater to her. "She was miserable because she durst not ask Lord Melbury to pay this woman, he having already given her money three times for the purpose, which she had lost at faro" (108).

More also attacks upper-class men for their careless, disinterested attitude toward those who could benefit from their superintendence. She is critical even of well-meaning and generous gentlemen like Sir John Belfield who take pleasure in performing acts of benevolence because they are "indolent in the proper distribution of money, and somewhat negligent of its just application" (293). Though in earnest "on the general principle of benevolence," Sir John had not regarded charity as "a matter demanding anything but money; while time, energy, discrimination, system, he confessed he had not much taken into the account" (292). In a tract titled "A Cure for Melancholy" More portrays the local gentry as "thoughtless, lavish, and indolent," people who would "subscribe with equal readiness to a cricket match or a charity school." The lord of the manor "had that sort of constitutional good nature" which inclined him to give a guinea whenever he came in sight of misery; "he had that selfish love of ease, which promoted him to give to undeserving objects, rather than be at the pains to search out the deserving."[16] More criticizes his careless largesse, saying that "it was his duty so to husband his wealth, and limit his expenses, as to supply a regular fund for established charity."[17]

In *Coelebs* Mrs. Stanley, voicing More's beliefs, argues that the gentry can help relieve the distresses of the poor only by taking the time to become "intimately acquainted with the worth and the wants" of the needy "within their reach" (289) and by establishing "systematic schemes of Charity" (292). To toss a coin to a beggarly looking man, woman, or child when moved by the sight of their distress does not help the deserving poor to better their lot in life. She argues that true charity must have at its core the goal "to make men better," and the way to do this is "by the infusion of a religious principle, which shall check idleness, drinking, and extravagance" and will put the poor "in the way to become healthier, and richer, and happier" (294). More argues in *Coelebs,* in "Estimate of the Religion of the Fashionable World," and in a few of the "Cheap Repository Tracts" that liberality and benevolence do not produce real good for either the giver or the receiver. The person who gives a little money to the poor out of pity is acting on impulse, relieving the tension produced by seeing something unpleasant, not on some well-thought-out plan of systematic relief that has as its goal the long-range good of the poor. This kind of spontaneous, idiosyncratic charity, More argues, is typical of the gentry, who are forever acting on impulse and are unwilling to submit to the rigors of Christian discipline. She argues that it is only the "conscientious Christian" who, because of his duty to "obey the whole will of God," can "subdue self-love," and he "who does not habituate himself to certain interior restraints, who does not live in a regular course of self-renunciation, will not be likely often to perform acts of beneficence, when it becomes necessary to convert to such purposes any of that time or money which appetite, temptation, or vanity solicit him to divert to other purposes."[18]

The careless and unsystematic charity typical of the upper classes contrasts with Lucilla's intense concern for the poor who inhabit the estate community. Rather than give alms to those who beg for them, she tries to teach the poor to help themselves. She runs the local Sunday school, teaching children to read the Bible, she instructs the girls in sewing and the boys in agriculture, she gives flowers she has raised to little girls so that they can sell them and use the money to buy shoes, and she gives as a wedding gift several fruit trees she has raised so that married couples can eventually have a supply of fruit to sell or to eat as they see fit. Lucilla also practices what her mother preaches about becoming acquainted with the poor's "worth and wants" by regularly visiting the cottages of the poor, where "she could get at their wants and their characters" (122). She spends one day a week sewing "caps, aprons, and handkerchiefs" to distribute on these charitable visits, makes her own medicine and sees that the sick take it regularly, and saves up her money to buy books to give to "her indigent neighbors" (122). Lucilla's ability to regulate herself enables her to devote a great deal of time and energy to activities that not only aid the poor but also function as a way to supervise and manage the dispossessed members of the estate community.

The Economy of Self-Regulation

Lucilla, More's example of the new domestic femininity, functioned as a powerful critique of the moral inadequacies of the upper classes. By equating virtue with self-regulation, More launched an attack on the selfishness and laziness of the pleasure-loving upper classes, linking their neglect of social and moral duties to their inability to control their impulses. The upper classes, unschooled in self-control and without any notion of economy, were, in More's eyes, incapable of performing their duties as superintendents of the poor and governors of the nation. By valorizing the regulation of self, time, space, and resources, More was engaged in a radical reconstitution of virtue that involved replacing the old aristocratic notions of public virtue, honor, and benevolence with new bourgeois notions of self-regulation and surveillance. The new domestic woman, who could conduct herself with prudence and efficiency, was a symbol, argues Kate Ellis, "for the stability that the middle class saw itself bringing to a society whose aristocrats (all the way up to the royal family) had lost the capacity for moral leadership and whose lower orders might at any moment become a Jacobin mob."19

Though Lucilla is a member of the gentry and More herself was descended from a landed family, More in her writings championed a new social order, one based on merit, self-discipline, and the management of time, space, and resources. More's values and the values of the Evangelicals became, as Davidoff and Hall argue, those of the nineteenth-century middle classes: "The zeal of the serious Christians played a vital part in establishing the cultural practices and institutions which were to become characteristic hallmarks of the middle classes."[20] More's economy of self-regulation and surveillance emerges in the next generation, secularized, shorn of its emphasis on original sin, as the middle-class work ethic used to promote the cause of the manufacturing and mercantile interests of the mid-nineteenth century. Dr. Andrew Ure's chapter the "Moral Economy of the Factory System" in his *Philosophy of Manufactures* (1835) owes much to More's notion of Christian discipline, the subordination of the will to a regular system. He urges "moral discipline" as a way to control workers, to make them "renounce their desultory habits of work, and to identify themselves with the unvarying regularity of the complex automaton."[21] Nancy Armstrong argues that women's "strategies of self-discipline" eventually provided "the liberal rationale for extending the doctrine of self-regulation and, with it, the subtle techniques of domestic surveillance beyond the middle-class home and into the lives of those much lower down on the economic ladder."[22] Domestic femininity with its powers of self-surveillance became, as Ellis argues, "a part of the ideology by which the bourgeoisie justified its moral and economic supremacy."[23]

Fanny and the Economy of Expenditure

Is Fanny, like Lucilla, an Evangelical heroine? She is not, though her sickliness is consistent with the denial of self and the self-immolation that Evangelicals admired; though her set speeches in praise of nature echo Cowper and Jane Taylor, two Evangelical poets; though her mention of the slave trade conjures up the debates on the abolition of slavery that were instigated by Evangelicals like More and William Wilberforce; and though Fanny's belief in the importance of the clergy and their duty to watch over the morals and manners of their parish echoes the Evangelicals' insistence on clergy residing in their parishes. Despite these similarities between Fanny's beliefs and Evangelical doctrine, she is not the heroine of an evangelically inspired novel because she does not participate in the economy of self-regulation that underlies More's beliefs.

Fanny's shyness, meekness, and modesty are not the attributes of a carefully controlled young woman who is vigilantly monitoring and checking her impulses. Fanny is naturally and constitutionally shy. She never exercises the kind of restraint that Lucilla engages in, and she does not consciously cultivate humility as does Lucilla. It takes no self-control for Fanny to disappear into the background of a family scene; in fact, the opposite is the case. On several occasions when she is called upon to speak or to display some accomplishment, she must struggle to put herself forward in an attempt to master her shyness and diffidence.

Fanny does not practice self-restraint; rather, she expends her energy, time, and emotions in the service of other people. Her dutifulness to her uncle, her forbearance of her Aunt Norris, and her attentions to her Aunt Bertram originate not in an economy of self-discipline but in a much older system that emphasizes service , exchange, and the social relations of "ruling-and-being-ruled."[24] Describing what he calls the "economy of expenditure," Georges Bataille argues that unlike the middle-class economy of production, the medieval and aristocratic social and economic system valued display and expenditure. In feudal societies expenditure, or "ostentatious loss," is required to "maintain rank" and social position. Bataille equates this medieval economy of expenditure with the potlatch of Northwest American Indians. In a potlatch ceremony the person who gives away the most is the most highly respected member of the tribe. Bataille writes, "*Potlatch* excludes all bargaining and, in general, it is constituted by a considerable gift of riches, offered openly and with the goal of humiliating, defying, and *obligating* a rival." Giving away one's goods creates obligation in the receiver, and this debt gives the donor power over the donee. Power is thus achieved by giving away one's goods, not by accumulating them as in capitalist societies, and "it is only through loss that glory and honor are linked to wealth."[25]

Fanny engages in an economy of expenditure not unlike the one Bataille describes, only instead of giving away all of her possessions or spending all her resources on display, she expends herself. Lacking material goods or access to monetary funds, Fanny freely and generously gives her energy, her time, and her affection to others. What little energy she has, she spends running errands for her aunts and cousins. What time she has, she spends in doing things for other people—she sews her Aunt Bertram's needlework for her, reads to her, and cuts roses for her as well as performing small tasks of assistance for just about anyone who asks her, including coaching Mr. Rushworth on his lines for the play, prompting the other players, and listening to Mary Crawford and Edmund rehearse their lines (however painful this might be to her).

Fanny also expends her feelings, and her liberality is reflected by the strength of her attachment to people, places, and things. Henry Crawford, an expert in making women desire him, is the only one who really understands what Fanny has to offer: "She had feeling, genuine feeling. It would be something to be loved by such a girl!" (235). Other characters cannot love the way Fanny does: Mary Crawford, though attracted to Edmund, cannot contemplate sacrificing for him the glamour and glitter of the fashionable world; Sir Thomas, too somber and restrained, cannot express his affection for his children as he ought; Lady Bertram, languid, enervated, and addicted to ease, cannot exert herself to feel intensely about those around her; and the others, Tom, Maria, Julia, and Henry Crawford, all of whom by focusing their energies on themselves and on taking care of their own needs and desires are unable really to love anyone other than themselves. Only Edmund comes close to Fanny in his willingness to expend himself for others. Only he, of all the characters in the novel, ever notices Fanny or thinks about how she is feeling.

Fanny, however, feels more intensely than Edmund can ever know. She is forever "feeling most strongly," and her emotions are the "quiet, deep, heart-swelling sort" (369) over which she has little control. Overpowered by her feelings when surprised by Sir Thomas's sudden return, she nearly faints: "Her agitation and alarm exceeded all that was endured by the rest." Trembling excessively, she experiences "compassion" for her uncle and "for almost every one of the party . . . —with solicitude on Edmund's account indescribable" (176). Once when Edmund had sat by her and had taken her hand and "pressed it kindly," she was so overwhelmed that without the cover which making tea afforded, "she must have betrayed her emotion in some unpardonable excess" (335). There are moments when she tries to restrain and censor her feelings for Edmund, knowing that she can have no romantic claim on him as his poor cousin, but she is a miserable failure at exercising any restraint over her affection. Feeling it "to be her duty, to try to overcome all that was excessive, all that bordered on selfishness in her affection for Edmund," Fanny tries to be "rational" about Edmund and Mary Crawford and tries "to do her duty" by making "resolutions on the side of self-government," but "having many of the feelings of youth and nature," she seizes the piece of paper on which Edmund has written "My very dear Fanny" and grows rhapsodic, practically swooning over these words (264–65). Because Fanny is always "feeling, thinking, trembling, about every thing" and is often "agitated, happy, miserable, infinitely obliged, absolutely angry" (302), she is far from being More's new domestic woman. She does not practice those strategies of self-discipline and self-denial that mark Lucilla as a member of a new social, economic, and political order.

Conserving the Paternal Order

In *Mansfield Park* Austen depicts the workings of three competing economies: the present economy of consumption that the Crawfords and Tom, Maria, and Julia Bertram participate in, a corrupt version of the older aristocratic economy of privilege and display that had been tempered with obligation and is now deformed by the forces of commercial enterprise and consumerism; the new bourgeois economy of surveillance and self-regulation; and the old economy of expenditure that is organized around hierarchies of service and obligation. Fanny and Edmund and Sir Thomas in his best moments represent this older economy because their actions are based on consideration and kindness.[26] They think about what other people need and want and try their best to oblige them. From the moment of Fanny's arrival at Mansfield Park, Edmund has been kind to her: "He was always true to her interests, and considerate of her feelings, trying to make her good qualities understood, and to conquer the diffidence which prevented their being more apparent; giving her advice, consolation, and encouragement" (21–22). She reciprocates by listening to him "with kindness and sympathy" (270), even when the topic is his affection for Mary Crawford. "You are all considerate thought!" (268) he says to Fanny; "You are a kind, kind listener" (268). Fanny loves Edmund because he has shown her consideration; he has taken time and energy to think about and address her problems of loneliness and isolation and has taught her how to think and feel with depth and sincerity. She says of Edmund, "There is a nobleness in the name of Edmund. It is a name of heroism and renown—of kings, princes, and knights; and seems to breathe the spirit of chivalry and warm affections" (211).

Austen associates this serving of other people with a chivalry characteristic of the old society's hierarchy of duty and deference. As Bataille argues, expenditure creates obligation. In *Mansfield Park,* expenditures of time, energy, and feeling in the service of others create feelings of debt and deference. As someone who receives the gift of her uncle's charity and as someone who serves out of deference and gratitude, Fanny has experienced daily the workings of a hierarchy based on obligation and gratitude and has practiced her role as the obedient and grateful dependent in the dynamic of ruling-and-being-ruled. She violates this code of duty and deference only once, when she tells her uncle that she will not marry Henry Crawford. She is devastated by Sir Thomas's anger at what he thinks is "ingratitude" (319) and by his accusation that she is behaving with a "willfulness of temper" and "without any consideration or deference for those who have surely some right to guide you" (318). Aware how serious it is to appear ungrateful, ingratitude being tantamount to breaking the ties that bind society together, Fanny is miserable: "Her heart was almost broke by such a picture of what she appeared to him. . . . Self-willed, obstinate, selfish, and ungrateful" (319). With the possible exception of Edmund, who, as a second son, has felt the effects of living in a hierarchy based on property and patronage, no other character has experienced like Fanny so completely the relations of obligation and gratitude that lie at the heart of the old society's paternal order. Because she has rehearsed daily the dynamic of gratitude and deference, she is the best qualified to inherit and carry on the society's traditions.[27]

Mary and Henry Crawford, Tom, Maria, and Julia represent the deterioration of the old order. They are arrogant, selfish, and thoughtless, thinking only of what they are owed by society, of what they can spend on themselves, and forgetting that with power and privilege come responsibilities.[28] Their selfishness represents for Austen a serious problem, one that, unlike More, Austen does not attempt to solve by substituting the new economy of self-discipline for the old paternal order. In fact, if any character resembles the new domestic woman and the enterprising middle classes, it is Mrs. Norris, who with her concern for "household good" and her obsession with domestic economy is a parody of the economy of self-restraint. She says, "I *am* of some use I hope in preventing waste and making the most of things" (141). Her inability to give anything away, her delight in driving hard bargains, and her pride in managing people's lives discredit the new economy of disciplined domesticity. Describing this new bourgeois economy, Bataille writes, "Everything that was generous, orgiastic, and excessive has disappeared. . . . The modern bourgeoisie is characterized by the refusal of this obligation" to display and expend. Mrs. Norris's horror at what she considers an indecently excessive number of dishes served at the Grants' dinner table is typical of her antipathy to anything "generous, orgiastic, and excessive."[29]

Austen's solution to the moral deterioration of the upper classes is quite simply to expel from society those who abuse their economic privilege. At the end of the novel, the selfish and negligent have been removed from the estate community, and the domestic circle is drawn tighter around those who deserve to inherit the estate, its traditions, and its responsibilities.[30] Those who behave with courtesy and consideration and those who act usefully, contributing to the well-being and happiness of those around them, remain at Mansfield to protect and nurture the old social order, which is defined by relations of duty and deference, obligation and gratitude, relations that Fanny, as an impoverished cousin dependent on her uncle's bounty, has had many years to rehearse.

Austen locates virtue not in self-discipline and technologies of surveillance, but in generosity and liberality, precisely those attributes that More attacked in "Estimate of the Religion of the Fashionable World." Charitable acts, acts of kindness and consideration originating in spontaneous feelings of pity or gratitude were, for More, rendered morally suspect because they did not originate in a disciplined duty to God. For Austen, however, such expenditure of genuine feeling is to be valued and nurtured, as it is the heart and soul of the old society's chivalric and paternal order.

Service

If in *Emma* and in *Mansfield Park* Austen is defending the old society's paternal order and its chivalric values of duty and deference, how do we explain Austen's apparent political and ideological about-face in *Persuasion*? Some critics have argued that Austen abandons the gentry, and in championing the navy is promoting the cause of the middle classes.[31] Certainly Austen is very critical of Sir Walter Elliot for his self-indulgent consumption of his patrimony and his negligent treatment of his estate, preferring the sensible superintendence of Kellynch by Admiral and Mrs. Croft to Sir Walter's spendthrift ways. Just as Maria and Julia Bertram are expelled from the estate community, so it seems that Austen is advocating the removal of a degenerate gentry, substituting in its place naval officers, men of merit, discipline, and energy. Is Austen, then, calling for the end of a system that privileges land and blood over merit and utility? I think not.

Austen's critique of the gentry for its self-absorption and rampant consumerism has all the earmarks of a radical Tory condemnation of the gentry for failing to perform their duty and to fulfill their obligations to society. She is not advocating the redistribution of property or the privilege that comes with property ownership;

rather she is suggesting that new blood be pumped into the old system, and it is important to note that this new blood does not come from the middle classes but from the professional classes, specifically the military. Captain Wentworth, Captain Harville, Captain Benwick, and Admiral Croft—these men are military heroes, not bankers or merchants or manufacturers. These naval officers have served their country, served in the sense that Fanny serves her aunts, expending themselves, generously sacrificing their health, happiness, and lives for the benefit of their country.

Austen uses the word *useful* and its variants over twenty times in this novel, employing it to describe Anne and to describe the activities of these military men. But we should not confuse Anne's "usefulness" or Captain Harville's "usefulness and ingenuity"[32] with Bentham's utilitarianism or with political economy's use-value or with middle-class notions of utility, for a great difference lies between being of use and using something. Being of use is to expend oneself in the service of another, while to use something is to manipulate an object (or person) for one's own benefit. The naval officers in this book are of use, and again Austen valorizes service, a behavior that has nothing to do with middle-class values of regulation and accumulation. The kind of reform that Austen is suggesting in *Persuasion* is profoundly conservative: that England return to ancient baronial days and award property to those who deserve it, those valiant warriors who have served their king and country. It is appropriate then that Admiral Croft is installed in Kellynch, replacing the degenerate (and effeminate) Sir Walter, and that Anne's hand in marriage is won by the most skillful and brave of warriors, Captain Wentworth.[33]

CHAPTER FIVE

Women, the Clergy, and the Battle for the Superintendency of the Poor

I N the early nineteenth century women writers of the middling classes used the evangelically inflected discourse of domestic femininity not only to discredit the moral authority of the landed upper classes, but also to criticize Church of England clergy for their self-indulgence, their neglect of pastoral duties, and their abdication of paternal authority and obligation. They attacked the clergy specifically for their neglect of the poor's physical, moral, and spiritual well-being. These women argued for the importance of teaching the poor to read the Bible and of instructing them in the rudiments of Christian doctrine, of offering the poor an education that the Church of England clergy was unwilling or unable to provide.

The conflict over the education of the poor that took place between charitable women and the orthodox Church of England clergy can be traced through a series of tracts and literary texts, ranging from early discussions of the Sunday school in Sarah Trimmer's *The Oeconomy of Charity* (1787) to the celebration of the Sunday school fête in Maria Louisa Charlesworth's *The Cottage and Its Visitor* (1860). My discussion of this conflict between women and clergy over the superintending of the poor focuses on three areas: the critique of clergymen in Austen's *Mansfield Park*, Elizabeth Gaskell's *My Lady Ludlow* (1859), Anne Brontë's *Agnes Grey* (1847), and Charlotte Brontë's *Shirley* (1849); Hannah More's defense in her letters and tracts of her Sunday school activities designed to educate the poor; and the social and political ramifications of teaching children self-discipline as revealed in Elizabeth Hamilton's *The Cottagers of Glenburnie* (1808), Mary Leadbeater's *Cottage Dialogues* (1811), and *Agnes Grey*. In all three areas women writers sought to redefine moral and spiritual authority as feminine and to extend women's sphere of authority and action beyond the private realm of the domestic enclosure into the political realm of public activity.

Two Types of Clergymen

In *Mansfield Park* Austen presents us with two types of clergymen: Mr. Grant, whose love of well-prepared dinners dominates his outlook on life and dictates his wife's daily labors, and Edmund, who realizes that he, as a member of the clergy, will be the guardian of the "religion and morals" of his parishioners (92). Mr. Grant's selfish indulgence of carnal appetites is represented as being typical of the regular clergy of the Church of England, who, as Mary Crawford points out, do nothing all the rest of their lives "but eat, drink, and grow fat" (110). Clergymen, she argues, are drawn to their profession more out of laziness than out of religious inspiration. Younger sons must seek their livelihood in commerce or the professions, and those who lack ambition and desire the fairly undemanding life of a private gentleman with but a few public duties are drawn to the church. Thinking of her brother-in-law, Mr. Grant, Mary Crawford says, "Indolence and love of ease—a want of all laudable ambition, of taste for good company, or of inclination to take the trouble of being agreeable, . . . make men clergymen" (110).

Though Edmund admits the justice of Mary's remark as it refers to the "indolent selfish bon vivant" (111) Mr. Grant, he insists that all clergy need not be lazy and self-serving. However, most rank and file clergy were, as the historian Elie Halevy points out, content to hold two or more livings and to collect tithes and income from their parishes without feeling the compunction to do more than deliver a monthly sermon to their parishioners, baptize, marry, and bury as the occasion arose.[1] It is Mary Crawford's hope that Edmund will be such a clergyman and will conduct himself as if he were "a man of independent fortune" (248) and ignore what she regards as rather demeaning pastoral duties. Thus, she is disappointed by Edmund's decision, which she regards as a most singular one, to reside in his parish so that he may give his parishioners "his constant attention" and prove "their well-wisher and friend" (248). Edmund's intention to reside in his parish rather than merely spending "three or four hours" (248) on Sunday to "read prayers and preach" (247), while surprising and frustrating the worldly Miss Crawford, implies a seriousness about the performance of pastoral duties that hints of Evangelicalism.

With her portrait of Mr. Grant, Austen was participating in a critique that drew on an older literary tradition that satirized the follies and foibles of the clergy, a tradition which had produced such characters as Fielding's Parson Adams, Goldsmith's Dr. Primrose, and Sterne's Yorick. Toward the end of the eighteenth century literary representations of parsons began to take on a harsher cast, and instead of caricaturing lovable but foolish parsons began to portray the clergy as selfish, negligent, and indifferent to their parishes' spiritual and material needs. Crabbe's "squarson" (a conflation of *squire* and *parson*) in "The Village," who is too busy hunting, dining, and card playing to attend to a dying pauper, became a type that figured frequently in novels, poems, short stories, and tracts well into the mid–nineteenth century.[2] This critique of the clergy gained a new emphasis and an added significance when produced by women. Jane Austen and Hannah More in the early part of the century and Elizabeth Gaskell and Anne and Charlotte Brontë in the middle of the century wrote narratives that critically portrayed a type of clergyman More called worldly. This discourse sought to undermine the authority of the hunting, drinking, and eating "top-booted" squarson[3] with portraits of a new kind of clergyman. Not the kindly, fatherly figure of Frances Burney's *Evelina* and Goldsmith's *Vicar of Wakefield,* this new style of clergyman, in showing concern for his parishioners' spiritual and temporal well-being, displayed what had by the nineteenth century become characteristically feminine traits. He expressed sympathy for the poor and weak, felt a desire to soothe and nurture the afflicted, and demonstrated a willingness to sacrifice material comfort, health, and peace of mind for the good of others. In criticizing the selfishness and negligence of the worldly clergy and in valorizing the good works of the sincere clergy, writers like Austen, More, Gaskell, and the Brontës were participating in a discourse that had as its subtext a sexual politics. These writers used gendered traits to establish moral categories, linking masculine behaviors—hunting, smoking, drinking, swearing—with the worldly, self-indulgent High Church clergy and associating feminine traits with clergymen who were conscientious and devout and in some cases explicitly Evangelical.

Orthodox and Evangelical Clergy

In *My Lady Ludlow* Gaskell's narrator, recalling her youth, describes in a gently mocking tone the vicar, Mr. Mountford, who was not "a bad clergyman, as clergymen went in those days."[4] He had been chosen for the living of Hanbury on account of "his excellent horsemanship" (14). His riding days had ended, however, when hunting received the disapproval of his bishop, and having to forgo his favorite exercise he became very stout, for "he liked good eating as much as any one" (14–15). "He ate so much and took so little exercise" that his parishioners often heard of "his terrible passions with his servants, and the sexton and clerk" (15). His gluttony and ill temper, reminiscent of Mr. Grant's love of good food and sour moods when disappointed in a meal, are matched by his love of ease, which prevents him from visiting the sick and the unhappy: "He was afraid of being made uncomfortable; so, if he possibly could, he would avoid seeing any one who was ill or unhappy; and he did not thank anyone for telling him about them" (15). Kind in his own way, Mr. Mountford would send his ill parishioners "plates from his own dinner of what he himself liked best; sometimes of dishes which were almost as bad as poison to sick people" (15). He played cards on Sunday, was "true blue," hated dissenters and the French, and "could hardly down a dish of tea without giving out the toast of 'Church and King, and down with the Rump'" (16).⁵ When he died, he left "some of his property (for he had a private estate) to the poor of the parish, to furnish them with an annual Christmas dinner of roast-beef and plum-pudding, for which he wrote out a very good receipt in the codicil to his will" (16).

When Gaskell's narrator introduces the new vicar, Mr. Gray, she hints that there are those in the parish who, because he performs his pastoral duties with diligence and sincerity, suspect him of being not a "Church and King" member of the clergy, but a "Moravian Methodist" (17). Mr. Gray, as it turns out, is not a Methodist, but he is very unlike Mr. Mountford. Taking his pastoral duties seriously, Mr. Gray exhausts himself in visiting the sick and poor, reading them the Bible, and trying to comfort them with whatever pecuniary assistance he can. Like most Evangelicals, Mr. Gray is interested in building a Sunday school, and for most of the narrative he tries to persuade the local gentry of the importance of teaching the poor to read so that they might learn how to conduct themselves as good Christians. In one of his interviews with the imperious and intimidating Lady Ludlow, the widow of Lord Ludlow and chief landowner in the Hanbury parish, Mr. Gray displays his intense commitment to the children of the parish: "The evil of the world is too strong for me. I can do so little. . . . The evils do exist, and the burden of their continuance lies on my shoulders. I have no place to gather the children together in, that I may teach them the things necessary to salvation. . . . I cannot rest, while children whom I could possibly save are being left in their ignorance, their blasphemy, their uncleanness, their cruelty" (142). He worries that the boys are "growing up to be men fit for, and capable of any crime" (141). Lady Ludlow replies that in "Mr. Mountford's time, I heard no such complaints" about the village children, and because she is afraid of change, she continues to thwart Mr. Gray's plans to do "something to alter their condition" (139).

His brave exchange with Lady Ludlow notwithstanding, Mr. Gray is a very shy, nervous, physically weak, small-framed, and easily agitated young man. He blushes when flustered and trembles when emotionally excited. While discussing the dire need for Sunday schools with Lady Ludlow, he speaks "in an agitated, nervous kind of way" (141), and "his eyes were dilated, and . . . they were full of tears with his eagerness" (140). A coughing fit interrupts his speech, "after which he trembled all over" and "sat, a little panting, a little flushed, trying to recover his breath" (141). "Too weak, exhausted, and nervous," Mr. Gray grows dizzy as he stands to take his farewell (145).

Gaskell's portraits of Mr. Mountford and Mr. Gray are highly gendered, ascribing to Mr. Mountford masculine habits of hunting, cursing, and eating with gusto and to Mr. Gray feminine traits of physical frailty, nervousness, sensibility, and the desire to nurture and comfort the sick and the poor. In contrast to Mr. Mountford, whose bodily appetites motivate his actions, Mr. Gray is tenderhearted, and this quality colors his feelings, thoughts, and activities. Even when Mr. Gray performs a heroic action—saving the life of a little boy who has fallen into an abandoned mining pit— Gaskell describes his actions in feminine terms, stressing not physical strength and ability, but his tenderness and nurturance: "He lifted the poor lad, as if he had been a baby . . . ; and laid him soft and easy on the wayside grass, and ran home and got help" (51). In spite of or perhaps because of his feminine characteristics, Mr. Gray overcomes the parish's initial wariness to his new doctrines and becomes deeply involved in the lives of his parishioners, both rich and poor. The people of Hanbury held an affection for the "good, jovial Mr. Mountford,—and his regrets that he might not keep a pack, 'a very small pack,' of harriers, and his merry ways, and his love of good eating" (204), but "everyone, rich and poor" (205), loved, honored, and reverenced Mr. Gray for his kind ways, his intense interest in their moral and physical well-being, and his devotion to his pastoral duties.

Like Gaskell, Anne Brontë pairs up two very dissimilar clergymen in *Agnes Grey*, and like Gaskell, she uses gendered traits to highlight their religious and political differences. Mr. Hatfield, the rector, a High Church Tory and a top-booted parson, harangues his congregation with sermons on Church "rites and ceremonies, apostolic succession, the duty of reverence and obedience to the clergy, the atrocious criminality of Dissent, . . . and the necessity of deferential obedience from the poor to the rich."[6] He performs pastoral duties with dispatch in an eagerness to get on to more pleasant pastimes, such as hunting with the local squirarchy and flirting with the daughters of the gentry. He dismisses the poor's claim on his attention as an annoying nuisance. When Nancy Brown, a widow and the mother of a field laborer, asks Mr. Hatfield to help her understand sin and repentance, he dismisses her worries with an abrupt and scornful reply: "Oh, it's all stuff! You've been among the Methodists, my good woman" (147). Though Nancy Brown understands that the rector is "rich an' young, and such like cannot right understand the thoughts of a poor old woman such as me" (148), she is hurt when he refuses to speak with her after church: "I've nothing to say to you but what I've said before . . . take the sacrament, of course, and go on doing your duty; if that won't serve you, nothing will. So don't bother me any more" (149). She is especially mortified when she overhears him call her "a canting old fool" (149). Nancy Brown is not the only poor parishioner who has received unkind treatment from Mr. Hatfield. "Us poor bodies," she says, "are fair feared on him," for when he comes into a cottage, "he's sure to find summit wrong" and begins to criticize the household "as soon as he crosses the doorstuns" (146). "He thinks," she concludes, "it his duty to tell 'em what's wrong" (146).

Mr. Weston, Reverend Hatfield's curate, on the other hand, is very sincere about taking care of the spiritual needs of his flock. In addition to being a man of "strong sense, firm faith, and ardent piety," Mr. Weston is a man of "true benevolence and gentle, considerate kindness" (156), capable of "sincere good will, and even deep, touching, unobtrusive sympathy" (218). His visits to "a poor labourer who was in the last stages of consumption" are appreciated by the dying man, who says, "Maister Westin 'ull pray with me quite in a different fashion [from Mr. Hatfield], an' talk to me as kind as owt'; an' oft read to me, too, an' beside me just like a brother" (154); whereas Mr. Hatfield's occasional and hurried visits, consisting of hastily reading over a "part of the service for the sick" and "some harsh rebuke to the afflicted wife," served to increase rather than "diminish the troubles of the suffering pair" (154). When Weston visits Nancy Brown, he patiently listens to her worries about salvation and sin, and explains biblical passages carefully so that she may understand the complexities of the Scriptures. "He listened to me as steady an' patient as could be, an' never a bit o' scorn about him," says Nancy Brown (150). He keeps her company, reads to her whenever her eyes fail her, and even rescues her cat from the gamekeeper's gun. The cat, like all animals in both Charlotte and Anne Brontë's stories, becomes a test of a man's character. Ellen Nussey remarked after a visit to the Brontës in 1834, "The Brontës' love of dumb creatures made them very sensitive of the treatment bestowed upon them. For any one to offend in this respect with them was an infallible bad sign, and a blot on the disposition."[7] When Mr. Hatfield pays an impatient visit to Nancy Brown, he kicks her cat, irritated by its desire to sit in his lap. Mr. Weston, on the other hand, pets the cat as it curls up on his lap while he chats with its mistress.

The kindness and consideration of Gaskell's Mr. Gray and Brontë's Mr. Weston are also attributes of Austen's Edmund in *Mansfield Park*. Part of Austen's project in *Mansfield Park* is to redefine chivalry, to disassociate it from the masculine realm of violence and action and realign it with the Christian virtue of charity. Edmund, whose very name "breathes the spirit of chivalry" (211), rescues Fanny from loneliness and feelings of worthlessness not with bold acts of physical prowess, but rather with small, quiet acts of kindness and consideration. Edmund's good qualities, including his kindness to Fanny, are feminine. He never hunts, as does Henry Crawford, or gambles, as does his brother. Yet despite his virtues, Edmund is not as good as Fanny: he lacks the resolve to resist rehearsing *Lovers' Vows* and flirting with Mary Crawford. Fanny, not Edmund, is the moral center of the novel, and her moral strength lies in her timidity, her passivity, and her resistance to temptation, qualities whose construction as feminine can be traced to Richardson's *Pamela* and *Clarissa*.[8]

By associating masculine pursuits such as hunting, drinking, and smoking with paternal negligence and feminine traits such as sympathy and kindness with the responsible care of the poor, writers sought to destabilize traditional male moral authority and to erect in its place a new, feminine version of moral authority. By locating virtue within the feminine, Austen, Brontë, and Gaskell sought to extend feminine authority beyond the hearth and home and into the public realm. This movement to extend women's sphere of activity into the public realm can also be seen in the tracts and didactic fictions of Hannah More, Mary Leadbeater, and Elizabeth Hamilton.[9] These writers justified women's participation in public affairs by portraying them as naturally capable of assuming with grace and skill paternal duties long neglected by overworked or indifferent clergy.[10] Hannah More's letters and tracts on Sunday schools convey with clarity this tension between capable charitable women (and feminized men) and the negligence of a top-booted and high-flying clergy.

"High Church Bigots" and More's Sunday Schools

In letters about her efforts to establish Sunday schools in the Mendip district, More represents the area as being "sunk in a deplorable state of ignorance and vice." More attributes this regrettable state of affairs to the absence of paternal authority.[11] The parish of Cheddar, the site of her first Sunday school, had no resident gentry; and it did not have a resident clergyman: "No clergyman had resided in it for forty years. One rode over, three miles from Wells, to preach once on a Sunday, but no weekly duty was done, or sick persons visited, and children were often buried without any funeral service" (*Memoirs* 1:389). Ruling in place of proper authority were "a dozen wealthy farmers, hard, brutal, and ignorant" (*Memoirs* 1:389). More describes how the neighborhood was dominated by a farmer, a "chief despot, . . . very rich and very brutal," who protested her plan to educate the poor, for he said "it makes them lazy and useless."[12] Threatened by her plan to reform the manners of the poor, "these petty tyrants" resisted until she persuaded them that her plan would "secure their orchards from being robbed, their rabbits from being shot, their game from being stolen, and which might lower the poor rates."[13]

To run her school More chose a woman "of excellent natural sense, great knowledge of the human heart, activity, zeal, and uncommon piety" (*Memoirs* 1:390). More tells how she provided this "excellent woman" with money so that when she visited the sick in the parish she could bestow medicine and small gifts of money on the ill. In this way she gained "access to the houses and hearts of the people," soon gaining "their confidence." More confesses that she provided her agent with money for the ill purposely with a "view to their spiritual concerns; but we concealed the true motive at first" (*Memoirs* 1:390). More describes with pride how this woman read and prayed with the poor and "in all respects did just what a good clergyman does in other parishes" (*Memoirs* 1:390). More's excellent woman fills most capably the gap left by negligent clergy, absent gentry, and greedy farmers.

Vulnerable to accusations that her Sunday schools represented an interference in parish affairs, More insisted that she always chose parishes that did not have resident clergy, or if the parish did have resident clergy, she would ask them their permission to open a school: "Not one school here did I ever attempt to establish without the hearty concurrence of the clergyman of the parish" (*Memoirs* 2:72). She carefully defends herself from the charge of usurping the role of the clergy by arguing that her actions supplemented the clergy's work, aiding the vicar and his curates in the moral supervision of the poor. In More's tract "A Cure for Melancholy," Mr. Simpson, the vicar of the village of Weston, encourages the widow Mrs. Jones, once the wife of a wealthy merchant but now living on "a very narrow income,"[14] to forget her once-magnificent past and her present sorrows by busying herself in charitable work. By "going about and doing good . . . in a subordinate way," she will "greatly promote . . . the labours of the parish minister" (*Works* 2:177–78). One of Mrs. Jones's charitable projects is the resurrection of the parish girls' school, which had "fallen into neglect; for though many would be subscribers, yet no one would look after it" (*Works* 2:188). More interrupts her narrative to say that "many parishes are quite destitute of schools, because too many gentry neglect to make it part of the duty of their grown-up daughters to inspect the instruction of the poor" (*Works* 2:188). Laying the blame for this negligence at the feet of the gentry, More is careful to avoid the appearance of censuring the vicar: "It was not in Mr. Simpson's way to see if girls were taught to work. The best clergyman cannot do every thing. This is ladies' business" (*Works* 2:188), a statement reiterated in *Coelebs*: "Charity is the calling of a lady; the care of the poor is her profession. Men have little time or taste for details" (289).

In "A Cure for Melancholy" More manages simultaneously to criticize the gentry for abdicating their paternal duty to govern the poor, to forgive the clergy for their neglect of charity, and to open up a space for middle-class women to perform an important public function. She also endows her middle-class women with "talents" (*Works* 2:177) consisting of intelligence, energy, an ability to organize people into associations, an understanding of the art of economy (*Works* 2:178), and perhaps most important, an ability to relate, because of their middling status, to both the rich and the poor (*Works* 2:179). More's aim in this tract for the "Middle Ranks" is to encourage women to expand their charitable activities from an occasional spontaneous charitable gesture to a regular system of charity, involving the setting up of a public institution such as a charity school, a Sunday school, or even a "Friendly Society" for poor women, an organization that functioned a bit like a savings and loan association and that, she says, provided "great relief to the sick and lying-in, especially in the late seasons of scarcity" (*Memoirs* 2:73).

Though More represented her activities as merely filling a void left by the gentry and clergy, her charitable activities, especially her Sunday schools, threatened a great many people. As her biographer M. G. Jones writes, the Sunday school, "an implied criticism of the lives and religion of the orthodox clergy and laymen, [was] deeply resented by them," and it was also "an open challenge to the monopoly exercised by the big farmers and the little gentry over the bodies and souls of the children of the rural poor."[15] More's Sunday schools offended the clergy by presuming to prescribe codes for moral conduct and religious belief. Irritated by her assumption of the role of spiritual authority, William Cobbett, in his High Tory phase, declared her a "Bishop in Petticoats," saying, "It is a fearful thing to think of, that this woman had under her tuition the children of a large portion of England"[16] while another critic, a clergyman, attacked her for her presumption: "You, madam, now, and on other occasions, have assumed the high office of a *censor morum,* and a censor also of religious practices and religious beliefs" (*Memoirs* 2:148). Sharing Cobbett's indignation and sympathizing with the *Anti-Jacobin*'s High Church party attack on More's activities, the historian Ford K. Brown expresses his sense of outrage at the notion of a woman presuming to preach to the poor: "She had no cure of souls, was not the Established Church incumbent of the parish or an ordained priest of any kind, and had assumed moral and spiritual authority by self-bestowed credentials of good intent and superior merit" (192).

Brown is correct that More had, in establishing Sunday schools and benefit clubs, assumed moral and spiritual authority over the poor. She indeed felt authorized not only to prescribe to the poor but also to instruct and to judge the performance of the parish clergy. For instance, in her correspondence with the curate of Axbridge she does not limit herself to praising him for his support of her Sunday school; she also encourages him to continue his evangelical style of preaching, telling him that the schoolmistress had reported to her of the "good effect your exhortation at Christmas" had on many of his parishioners. She says that "their value for you seems to have increased in proportion as your preaching has been more strict and evangelical." She believes that "it will be generally found that no men are so loved or respected as strict gospel ministers." "Worldly clergy," on the other hand, "lose their great aim, and do not even please worldly people; so far, I mean, as to be respected and venerated by them, however they may like to associate with them in their parties of pleasure or their schemes of dissipation" (*Memoirs* 2:64).

More describes in her letters how she supports the clergy who conduct themselves as Evangelicals and how she undermines activities of those she perceives to be her enemies, "the worldly clergy" (*Memoirs* 2:29) and "the high church bigots" (*Memoirs* 1:400). Patty, Hannah's sister, tells how "our favourite Mr. Jones had, through active interference and perseverance of Hannah, been presented to the living of Shipman by the Dean and Chapter of Wells."[17] Writing to Wilberforce, Hannah recounts what she calls a "small victory": "I must tell you that we have kept possession of the pulpit at Wedmore ever since, and sent one of our own clergy every Sunday to keep up the attention of our plan" (*Memoirs* 2:23). In spite of opposition to the building of a school in Wedmore, she went ahead with the project, only later on to be accused by the farmers of "teaching the poor without a license." She reports that the farmers at Wedmore say "they will never rest till they have worried me out of the parish; and as they have employed an attorney of bad character, they will, I fear, be able to give me a good deal of trouble." She adds that she suspects the work of "two bad clergymen" to be "at the bottom" of this trouble in Wedmore (*Memoirs* 2:80). Writing to John Newton, a fellow Evangelical, she complains that in some of the parishes "we dare not do all we wish, by reason of the worldly clergymen, who are now quiet and civil, but who would become hostile if we attempted in *their* parishes what we do in some others. In some of the most profligate places we have had the most success; and where we chiefly fail, it is with your *pretty good kind of people,* who do not see how they can be better" (*Memoirs* 1:476–77)

Hostility toward More's activities exploded in the parish of Blagdon when the curate, Thomas Bere, accused her schoolmaster there of being a Methodist and her schools of promoting subversion against the Established Church and the constitution. Bere, she writes, attacked her schools as "seminaries of fanaticism, vice, and sedition" (*Memoirs* 2:69) and described her goal as the corruption of "the principles of the community" (*Memoirs* 2:67). She writes, "It is circulated among the worldly and Socinian clergy that I have been in the constant habit of praying for the success of the French in my schools" (*Memoirs* 2:81). In a letter to Wilberforce More represents Bere's attack on her schools, her politics, and her religious principles as "an atrocity," and she wonders that Dr. Moss, Bere's bishop, could be so "ignorant of the general worthlessness of his character." "I pity those men in high stations for not being more in the way of ascertaining the real characters of their clergy . . . , but there is a sort of *esprit de corps,* which makes them support each other in public, even when (as in the present case) their private language is different" (*Memoirs* 2:78).[18]

Bere's attack on Hannah More's Sunday schools and the viciousness of the *Anti-Jacobin*'s championing of his cause are explained by Ford K. Brown as the regular church's defense of its parishes from the influence of Methodism and a kind of Evangelicalism that while it professed to uphold the Church of England in reality fostered a doctrine and a practice that undermined the Church's authority. What is missing from Brown's explanation is an explicit discussion of gender.[19] Brown's portrait of More is laced with snide remarks that pivot on the idea of More being a woman, his misogyny barely masked by his mocking tone. When he asks what right she had to preach to the poor—"She had no cure of souls, was not the Established Church incumbent of the parish or an ordained priest any kind"—he is outraged not so much by her transgressing the boundaries between lay and clergy, but by her transgressing gender boundaries to assume the role of an ordained priest, a role reserved for men. More's building of Sunday schools threatened the high church bigots because her activities threatened to delegitimate and marginalize the orthodox clergy in their own parishes. She also threatened the Established Church by professing a "religion of the heart,"[20] which was something better suited to women and their newly constructed feminine graces of sympathy and kindness than to men.

In her battle with the regular clergy for women's rights to superintend the poor, More contrasts the empty ritual and meaningless forms of the Established Church with the Evangelical's personal apprehension of God. Christianity, she argues in *Practical Piety,* is "not a religion of forms, and modes, and decencies," or "a religion consisting of a mere code of laws" and "an external conformity to practices" (2–3). Christianity, as she sees it, is "an inward religion" (13), a "religion of the heart" (11), requiring a "thorough renovation of the heart" (8). Producing "a new heart and a new life," Evangelical Christianity transforms a person, changing his "temper and disposition" (55), so that "his rebellious will is subdued, his irregular desires are rectified; his judgments is informed, his imagination is chastised, his inclinations are sanctified; his hopes and fears are directed to their true and adequate end" [*sic*] (4). Being a good Christian does not, she insists, consist of "outward observances" (71), of "general decency of behavior," or of "an attendance on public worship" (53). She argues that decent behavior "without any internal change of disposition, is not Christian reformation," for there is "no complete reformation in the conduct effected without a revolution in the heart" (61). For these reasons, she rejects orthodox religion and its "cold compliment of ceremonial attendance" (71), believing that a "religion which sinks Christianity into a mere conformity to religious usages, must always fail of substantial effects" (76). "The ineffectiveness of such a religion," a religion that does not touch the heart and reform the disposition of its practitioner, "will be obvious" (77).

To combat the popularity of Evangelicalism and the failure of the regular church to capture the hearts of the lower classes, the High Church faction resurrected Christian symbolism and Church ritual, giving birth in the 1830s to the Anglo-Catholic movement. The High Church party felt that ritual, symbolism, church art, architecture, and music could be used to draw the poor back to the Anglican church, providing "the poorer worshippers," as the bishop of Exeter said in 1851, "solace to that poverty to which the providence of God had consigned them."[21] The Anglo-Catholic movement tried to reassert Church authority by stressing the Apostolic Succession, the transmission of authority and grace through the ordained ministry that was said to stretch down through the ages from the Church of the First Century. This emphasis on the ministry as a sacred institution entrusted with the preparation and the perpetuation of the holy Eucharist was a reaction against Evangelicalism's emphasis on the individual's relation to God and the individual's personal apprehension of the Scriptures. This movement was also an attempt by High Church clergy to wrest away from women the moral and spiritual authority they had gained in their communities by performing what were essentially pastoral duties. As the historians Davidoff and Hall remark, the Tractarians "were deeply hostile to the Evangelical mobilization of lay women" and believed in "the sinfulness of allowing non-clergy to interfere in spiritual matters" (99).[22] By redefining the ministry as an institution entrusted with the Sacrament, the Anglo-Catholic movement redefined the clergy's duties as having to do with the sacred rather than with the charitable parish work that by the 1830s had become women's work.

Superintending the Poor

Although portrayed by her accusers as a dangerous, destabilizing, radical force, More saw herself and her schools as supporting rather than undermining the authority of Church and State and as pacifying rather than inciting the poor. Her schools, she argued, were, in the words of the bishop of Wells, "calculated to improve the morals of the lower classes" and for this reason were "entitled to the approbation and support of every friend to religion and good order" (*Memoirs* 2:76). "My object," wrote More, "is not to make fanatics, but to train up the lower classes in habits of industry and piety" (*Memoirs* 2:72). "I had so fully persuaded myself, that I had for many years especially in the late awful crisis [French Revolution], been devoting my time and humble talents to the promotion of loyalty, good morals, and attachment to church and state among the poorer people" (*Memoirs* 2:67).

Whether her schools did promote good order among the lower classes is a question not easily answered, but both Hannah More and her sister Patty argued that the schools were effective in changing the general character of the people in many parishes.[23] To illustrate the efficacy of their Christian pedagogy, they both recount the reduction in the number of warrants issued for arrests and criminal charges brought to trial. More tells how even Curate Bere (before he turned against her) declared that "since the institution of the schools, he could now dine in peace, for that where he used to issue ten warrants, he was not now called on for two" (*Memoirs* 2:73). She quotes from a letter written by Mrs. Bere (again, written before the Blagdon controversy): "The school goes on well. There seems to be a serious spirit working for good among the common people. . . . Two sessions and two assizes are past, and a third of each nearly approaching, and neither as prosecutor nor prisoner, plaintiff nor defendant, has any one of this parish, once so notorious for crimes and litigation, appeared. And, moreover, warrants for wood-stealing, pilfering, &c., are quite out of fashion" (*Memoirs* 2:71–72).

More used the promise of better-behaved working classes to persuade the gentry and the farmers to support her schools. In her tract "The Sunday School" More portrays her fictional counterpart, Mrs. Jones, arguing with a rich farmer over the efficacy of education for the laboring classes. Mrs. Jones says, "To teach good principles to the lower classes is the most likely way to save the country. Now, in order to this, we must teach them to read." The Bible, she argues, teaches the "duties of children, of servants, of the poor," and the "knowledge of that book, and its practical influence on the heart, is the best security you can have both for the industry and obedience of your servants." To placate the farmer's fear that his workmen "will think themselves too good to work" and will "fly in my face," challenging his authority, she insists that a boy who is taught that stealing is a sin is less likely "to rob a hen-roost or an orchard, than one who has been bred in ignorance of God's law." "Your property," she contends, will be more secure by "teaching the boys in the school" than by the threat of the "stocks on the green" (*Works* 2:200–03).

An assumption running throughout More's letters and tracts on Sunday schools is that the rural poor and even the poor of the new industrial towns, like Nailsea, are morally depraved and living in a state of sin and ignorance as bad and as "dark as Africa" (*Memoirs* 1:395). More implies that the reason for the deplorable state of morals and manners of the poor is that the men in charge of the moral and social well-being of these communities are either absent or negligent. Her solution to what she saw as a politically dangerous situation was to institute schools to train the poor in Christian discipline, to make the poor obedient, grateful, and pious. More portrays women, primarily those of the middling classes, as possessing the time, talent, and self-discipline that would enable them to run a school and teach children and to perform duties that the clergy would not or could not do. More represents the clergy who resist her work as "bad clergymen" who fail to perform their duties out of bigotry or selfishness; she portrays the schoolmistresses and herself as far more capable of restoring to the countryside a moral order based on reciprocal ties of duty and deference, a paternal order that the traditional keepers of the paternal system, the clergy and the gentry, were incapable of enforcing.

More's juxtaposition of "stocks on the green" with her Sunday schools captures the conflict between older forms of social control based on the threat of physical punishment as a deterrent to deviant behavior and a newer form of social control based on self-discipline and the internalization of the mechanisms of control. More believes that the threat of the stocks, the fear of the law's power to punish, and even the specter of the Australian penal colony of Botany Bay were ineffective and that the old forms of punishment were no longer and perhaps never were very efficacious in making the laboring poor obedient and deferential. If anything, the threat of physical punishment encouraged the lower classes merely to pretend to conform to their betters' wishes and the confines of the law, producing only the appearance of compliance while never really touching the heart of the sinner. External forms of deference, doffing of caps and dropping of curtsies, do not, More insists, mean that the working poor are truly obedient and humble. Only religion, with "its practical influence on the heart" (*Works* 2:202), can ensure true deference. More sought to secure the nation by influencing the hearts of the potentially rebellious poor and believed Christian discipline and the inculcating of Christian principles to be the most effective way to achieve this end.

More's Evangelical belief in a personal relation with an all-knowing and all-seeing God is central to the kind of Christian discipline she propounded in her schools. Though she told farmers that she was planning to teach the duties of the poor as outlined in the Bible, More really meant to construct for the children of the poor the image of an all-powerful, all-knowing God who would see into the hearts of these children, watch their daily actions, and monitor their every thought. More knew that the idea of an omniscient God who would take a personal interest in even the seemingly least significant child could be used as a powerful tool of social control. Functioning like Bentham's model prison, the Panopticon, More's God, "whose eye is on the heart" (*Piety* 71), creates in the believer the feeling that he or she is being watched continually. The believer (or the prisoner), imagining himself to be watched, soon begins to watch himself and thereby makes himself into an object of observation and thus control.

More's notion of Christian discipline is quite like what Michel Foucault has called "disciplinary power," which operates through "its invisibility" and "at the same time it imposes on those whom it subjects a principle of compulsory visibility."[24] Foucault explains that "it is the fact of being constantly seen, of being able always to be seen, that maintains the disciplined individual in his subjection" (187). More's Evangelical God, with his invisibility, his omniscience, and his personal regard (*regarder*) for every sinner, functions like Bentham's panoptic institutions. Analyzing the disciplinary power of the Panopticon, Foucault writes, "He who is subjected to a field of invisibility, and who knows it, assumes responsibility for the constraints of power; he makes them play spontaneously upon himself; he inscribes in himself the power relation in which he simultaneously plays both roles; he becomes the principle of his own subjection. By this very fact, the external power may throw off its physical weight; it tends to the non-corporeal; and, the more it approaches this limit, the more constant, profound and permanent are its effects" (202–03).

More's Evangelical God was, as she argued, a powerful instrument of social control, more powerful than the stocks and emblems of physical force. No wonder she takes great pride in claiming for her schools the power of reducing the number of warrants for arrests and transportations to Botany Bay. Her schools replace physical punishment and external force with the regulation of the self. She proudly describes how her schools transform communities, reducing pilfering and poaching and reforming leisure time activities, eradicating excessive drinking in taverns, the singing of lewd songs, and children playing on Sunday. More's Sunday schools, in tandem with the charitable work of other benevolent women, may have begun as a way of filling the gap left open by negligent or absent authority, but within a few decades these new institutions had become a powerful disciplinary tool that was to compete with and eventually replace the "residual forms of feudal power" and its "local mechanisms of supervision."[25]

Feminine Forms of
Social Control

According to More, women of the middling classes were especially well suited to teach the poor about "the religion of the heart" (*Piety* 11) not only because they had the time, talent, and self-discipline, but because they were expert at touching the hearts of the poor. Like her schoolmistress at Cheddar, the women More represents as model schoolmistresses knew how to work their way into the homes of the laboring poor. "In order to procure them access to the houses and hearts of the people, they were furnished, not only with medicine, but with a little money, which they administered with great prudence. They soon gained their confidence, read and prayed to them; and in all respects did just what a good clergyman does in other parishes" (*Memoirs* 1:390). Lucilla in *Coelebs in Search of a Wife* dispenses sympathy and gifts, cementing ties of duty and deference and positioning herself so that she can measure their need against their desert. When More writes about her own charitable activities, she stresses the efficacy of kindness in manipulating the poor:

> I have devoted the rest of my life to the poor, and those that have no helper; and if I can do them little good, I can at least sympathize with them, and I know it is some comfort for a forlorn creature to be able to say, "there is something that cares for me." That simple idea of being cared for has always appeared to me a very cheering one. Besides this, the affection they have for me is a strong engine with which to lift them to the love of higher things: and though I believe others work successfully by terror, yet kindness is the instrument with which God has enabled me to work. (*Memoirs* 1:400)

Her pedagogical technique was to mingle kindness with tangible rewards while avoiding threats and punishments. She distributed Bibles, prayer books, and tracts to reward her industrious pupils, "those who have given some evidence of loving and deserving them" (*Memoirs* 1:391), and organized annual Sunday school feasts to celebrate the accomplishments of her students, rewarding "each young person" with "some articles of dress" (*Memoirs* 1:392), stockings, caps, aprons, even shoes.[26]

More's teaching techniques involved a combination of surveillance and coercion. As Mrs. Crew, the schoolmistress of the *Cheap Repository* tract on Sunday schools, says, a teacher must watch her pupils not only at school but in everyday life to see if they have really learned the lessons of Christian discipline: "I must therefore watch whether those who are diligent at church and school, are diligent in their daily walk. Whether those who say they *believe* in God, really *obey* him. Whether they who profess to *love* Christ keep his *commandments*" (*Works* 3:49). Mrs. Jones, the Hannah More figure in the story, gives a sermon at the annual Sunday school fête, saying, "I . . . like to see you deny your appetites" (*Works* 3:57). More made surveillance an integral part of the Sunday school festivities. She describes how even though she did not live in the villages where her schools were established, she and her sister would "collect all the facts we can as to the conduct of the villagers" during the past year. She would gather information about "whether the church has been more attended, fewer or more frauds, less or more swearing, scolding, or Sabbath-breaking," and then during the annual festivities "in a little sort of sermon," she would use this information "in a battle array . . . of praise, censure, and exhortation" (*Memoirs* 1:391–92). During one such sermon addressed to a congregation of three hundred pupils and "half a dozen clergy," More attacked the "gross conduct" of a few young women. The attack was efficacious: "I had the pleasure of witnessing the most becoming gravity and exact decorum in that part of my audience which I most feared, when I excluded from the pale of our establishment a female offender" (*Memoirs* 1:399).

Perhaps the most explicit discussion of More's ideas on the role middle-class women can have in educating the poor in the technologies of self-regulation can be found in her *Cheap Repository* tract "The History of Hester Wilmot." In this short story More charts the reforming effect of Sunday school on Hester and her family. Hester's parents, "both ungodly and unhappy," maintain themselves "by their labour" (*Works* 3:36). Her father, a man of "no fixed principle" (3:39), spends most of his time drunk in the tavern, and her mother, a house-proud tyrant with a "violent, ungovernable temper" (3:36), refuses at first to send Hester to school because she needs her to stay home to scrub floors and to take care of the younger children. Hester's mother is finally persuaded by Mrs. Jones that Sunday school will not make Hester "proud, lazy, and dirty" but will teach her "to fear God" (3:41) and to respect her parents. Once at school Hester learns a far more important lesson than just to read the Bible; she learns to understand the catechism. Her teacher, Mrs. Crew, had "deep insight . . . into the corruption of human nature," and, says More, "I doubt if anyone can make a thoroughly good teacher of religion and morals who wants this master key to the heart" (3:43). Mrs. Crew knew that "out of the heart proceed lying, theft, and all that train of evils which begin to break out in young children" (3:44). Equipped with patience and the knowledge of the human heart, Mrs. Crew transforms her pupils into Christians, turning Hester, who was "by nature peevish and lazy" (3:49), into a quiet, helpful, hardworking girl. Through Mrs. Crew's efforts, Hester became "acquainted with her own heart, and with the Scriptures," and her "evil tempers were, in a good measure, subdued, for she had now learnt to imitate, not her violent mother, but *him who 'was meek and lowly'*" (3:50).

Mrs. Crew credits her success in transforming her pupils into good Christians to her having taught the children not just to memorize the catechism, but to understand it. Patiently she broke "this fine summary of the Christian religion" into digestible bits: "Those who teach the poor must give line upon line, precept upon precept, here a little and there a little, as they can receive it" (3:46). She believes that this is the only way to activate reflection and effect a reformation of the heart and that "those who had learned the Catechism in the common formal way, when they were children, had never understood it when they became men and women, and it remained in the memory without having made any impression on the mind" (3:46). The implication is that the clergy who were responsible for religious training had failed to make their pupils understand Christian principles, had focused, as was their wont, on the formal features of the ritual, and had demanded compliance only with external forms, never thinking to impress the meaning of the words on the hearts of their pupils. Religious training that emphasized the "heartless homage of formal worship" (*Piety* 71) could not therefore hope to transform behavior.

Through Hester's story More demonstrates the superiority of feminine and Evangelical forms of social control. The "once pert" Hester, thanks to Mrs. Crew's religious instruction, had grown "as mild as a lamb," and her good behavior, in turn, transformed her father, who had begun to see that "there must be something in religion, since it can change a heart" (3:55). His good behavior—coming home to read and avoiding the tavern—works a change on Hester's ill-tempered mother: "She had observed, that since her husband had grown religious he had been so careful not to give her any offense." Her mother becomes a considerate wife, her father a hardworking husband, and More concludes that "both these changes arose from the same cause, the growth of religion in their hearts" (3:64–65).

Combining surveillance with kindness, women of the middling ranks sought to teach the poor what they themselves had mastered: self-discipline and techniques for managing time, space, and resources. Women like Hannah More, Mary Leadbeater, and Elizabeth Hamilton believed that the poor's misery and destitution were the result of ignorance and improvidence and that if they could be taught to control their appetites and passions (a Malthusian wish) they could then begin to apply their energies to making the best of their limited resources by learning household economy. Both Mary Leadbeater in *Cottage Dialogues* (1811) and Elizabeth Hamilton in *The Cottagers of Glenburnie* (1808) provide their readers with a combination of moral precepts on self-discipline and tips on household management, including advice on how to not waste money on tea, tobacco, or whiskey, how to save scraps for a pig and waste for a compost heap, how to clean out milk cans thoroughly, to brew ale at home, and to spin yarn and sew clothes. Leadbeater and Hamilton provide their working-class readers with several examples of how self-control can lead to an improved quality of life. For instance, Leadbeater and Hamilton each depict arguments between a good housewife and her slovenly neighbors over how to make butter. The thrifty, hardworking woman stresses the importance of cleaning out the milk cans and the butter churner while the slovenly neighbors moan and groan about how tiresome it is to wash and scrub the heavy milk pans. The good housewife argues that sour milk will spoil the taste of butter, and stray hairs and little bits of dirt will bring down the price of the butter, but her neighbors are too lazy to follow her advice. She proceeds to market with her clean, sweet butter, getting twice as much as her neighbors get for their sour, dirty butter. She can then apply that extra money to purchase cloth for winter coats for her children while her neighbors' children will shiver in the winter's cold.[27]

Assuming the role of instructress, Mary Leadbeater preaches through her dialogues lessons for the laboring poor on moral conduct and household economy. Her topics range from respecting parents to helping care for younger siblings, from learning how to grow a garden to learning how to read and cipher, and from avoiding the dissolute habit of drinking tea to refraining from teasing and torturing animals. The publisher of a Dublin edition of *Cottage Dialogues* notes in the preface that he knows "a benevolent lady, who declares that her 'Rose and Nancy' [Leadbeater's book] has become 'as black as her shoe' by frequent thumbings of her poorer neighbours."[28] Leadbeater represents the opinions and lives of two young women, one good, one bad, and two young men, also one good and one bad. Nancy and Thady, the naughty ones, are really not so much bad as they are too lazy to make themselves do unpleasant or boring but necessary tasks, while Rose and Martin are able to practice good household economy because they can control their impulses. Thady, for instance, thinks he has bad luck when it is clear that he is not capable of controlling himself. He does not have the patience to learn to read, and so for recreation he plays cards, drinks punch, and loses his wages. He cannot control his temper either, knocking down a man, almost killing him in a rage. "Sure I could as well quiet the raging sea, as rule myself when I'm vexed. I wish I was not born so passionate" (166), he says, trying to excuse his destructive behavior. His friend Martin says, "Depend on it, Thady, that we can govern our passions if we mind ourselves; but the oftener we are angry, the harder it is to keep from it" (167).

Nancy, like Thady, cannot control her temper or her appetites. "It's my nature to be hasty and I can't help it," Nancy says after quarreling with her neighbor. Her friend Rose cautions her: "We must try to get the better of our bad inclinations, and pray against them, and not let them grow into bad habits" (53). Nancy's inability to control her appetite leads her down the path of ruin. Her love of tea makes her quit a good job as a servant because her mistress forbids her the beverage except on Sunday evenings and washing days. Rose defends Nancy's employer's wise policy, saying that tea drinking is "a bad fashion": "What would you do in a house of your own? you could not afford to drink tea, and you would be hankering after it when you got the way of it" (23). Eventually Rose's prediction that Nancy's tea drinking would cause trouble comes true when Nancy marries and sets up her own household. Her passion for tea depletes her husband's meager wages, and stressed by poverty, he flees to the public house and eventually, weakened by drink, dies. Nancy too, now a widow with several children, ignores her responsibilities and turns to whiskey for comfort, eventually drinking herself to death. Rose explains that Nancy suffered this fate "because she did not exert herself under her troubles, but looked for comfort to what was not comfort" (122). Leadbeater's message to the poor was to learn self-regulation and to bear trouble "quietly and humbly" and "not to look for comfort any where but in [their] own heart[s] and endeavours" (122–23).

Like More and Leadbeater, Elizabeth Hamilton preached self-control to the poor and submission to their appointed lot in life. Her protagonist in *Cottagers of Glenburnie,* Mrs. Mason, is reminiscent of Mrs. Jones and Mrs. Crew, teaching the poor of Glenburnie efficient management of their scanty resources and bringing to bear on them the microtechniques of socialization. The minister of Glenburnie urges his parishioners "to listen to her advice," for "she will instruct you in the art of governing your children's passions, and of teaching them to govern themselves; and thus, by the blessing of God, she may eventually be the means of rescuing them from a sentence of condemnation—more awful than the most awful that any human tribunal can pronounce."[29] Mrs. Mason assumes the role of instructor for the girls in the local charity school, and "at first several children were refractory, and many symptoms of a mutinous disposition appeared; but by patience and perseverance, all were so completely brought into subjection" (385). Teaching the girls three simple rules—"to do every thing in its proper time; to keep every thing to its proper use; and to put every thing in its proper place" (348–49)—she encourages them to apply these precepts to their own homes. The result is that the village is "a picture of neatness and comfort," for "the girls exerted themselves with no less activity, to effect a reformation within doors" (395). Through her charitable activities, Mrs. Mason succeeds in "improving the hearts and dispositions of the youth of both sexes, and in confirming them in habits of industry and virtue" (397).

The Failure of Feminine Benevolence

Confident that the poor's distress and depravity could be rectified by female surveillance and instruction sweetened with kindness and sympathy, women writers like More, Leadbeater, and Hamilton produced narratives that, as Mitzi Myers has pointed out, are "fantasies of benevolent female power."[30] For this generation of writers, women's domestic virtues were "the grand means of saving the nation" (*Memoirs* 2:59), as men in their roles as clergy and landlords had failed to teach deference and duty to the laboring classes. These women writers were confident that women of the middling classes, who had mastered the microtechnologies of self-regulation, could change the hearts of the poor, teaching them to accept with humility and gratitude their place in the paternal order.

Less confident of women's ability to transform the hearts of the poor and thus to ameliorate their distresses were the writers of the next generation who, like Anne and Charlotte Brontë, had experienced the economic and social turmoil of the "hungry forties."[31] In her novel *Agnes Grey* Anne Brontë depicts the unsuccessful efforts of her heroine, a governess and daughter of an impoverished clergyman, to socialize her charges, to teach them how to control their impulses. One of the combat zones in Agnes's battle to reform the hearts of her charges is the treatment of animals. As the historian Harriet Ritvo has pointed out, the anticruelty to animals movement linked kindness to animals with the "exercise of self-control" and "the need for compassion . . . with the need for discipline." "The treatment of animals," Ritvo argues, was used "as an index of the extent to which an individual had managed to control his or her lower urges." The Royal Society for the Prevention of Cruelty to Animals (RSPCA), as Ritvo observes, chose to locate the problem of cruelty to animals in the "uneducated and inadequately disciplined lower classes" and turned a blind eye to upper-class bloodsports like fox hunting: "The identification of cruelty as a lower-class propensity implied a rhetoric of moral distinction which potential patrons found comforting and attractive."[32] The RSPCA's move to locate cruelty in the lower classes while ignoring upper-class cruelty to animals was, as Ritvo contends, motivated by a desire to keep the organization's aristocratic patrons from withdrawing their support. Middle-class anticruelty reformers, like other evangelically supported movements, however, criticized both the upper and lower classes for their cruelty, representing the lack of compassion for animals as a failure in self-discipline, a failure that was common to both upper and lower classes.

Before beginning her first job as a governess, Agnes Grey had felt confident of her ability to know intuitively how to educate the hearts and minds of her charges, "how to win their confidence and affections; how to waken the contrition of the erring; how to embolden the timid, and console the afflicted; how to make Virtue practicable, Instruction desirable, and Religion lovely and comprehensible."[33] Once engaged as a governess, she soon learns, however, that her powers to effect any change on the behavior and dispositions of her charges are extremely limited. Shocked by her pupil's cruelty to animals, she "hoped in time to be able to work a reformation" (77). The "little tyrant" Tom, the son of a newly gentrified merchant, recounts with delight how his father gave him a nest "full of young sparrows, and he saw me pulling off their legs and wings, and heads, and never said anything, except that they were nasty things" (78). Agnes endures patiently the wild behavior of this boy and his sister, believing that if she "could struggle on with unremitting firmness and integrity, the children would, in turn, become more humanized" (91). She hopes to teach the boy to curb his propensity for violence and the girl to overcome her ill temper and sullen obstinacy by "unshaken firmness, devoted diligence, unwearied perseverance, unceasing care" (107). Her attempts to reform the boy fail as he persists in treating animals cruelly, robbing yet another nest of baby birds and planning torments for them "with fiendish glee" (104). His uncle, looking on this scene with approval, is pleased to see that the boy is "beyond petticoat government" (105) and cannot be influenced by Agnes's efforts to touch his heart.

Agnes also fails to civilize her pupil at her next placement, the family of a "genuine, thorough-bred gentleman" (112). Agnes cannot persuade Miss Matilda, who delights in riding, hunting, swearing, and imitating her father, a "blustering, roystering, country squire" (119), that her behavior is insufficiently feminine. While taking a walk with Agnes, Matilda runs off after her dog who is chasing a rabbit, only to return later with "the lacerated body of the young hare in her hand" (208). She tells Agnes with excitement about the dog's pursuit, asking her, "Wasn't it a noble chase? . . . Didn't you hear it scream? . . . It cried out just like a child" (208–09).

Agnes's failure to transform the hearts of her pupils sounds a negative note in the literature on women's ability to socialize the rebellious classes. Being a governess is an impossible task, she argues, the name "a mere mockery" (84). Brontë suggests that female "instruction and surveillance" (84) cannot control or transform the violent tempers and irregular, capricious behavior of children, "a set of mischievous, turbulent rebels" (93). Without access to any real power to punish, a governess cannot exact obedience from her charges and cannot hope to shape their thoughts and feelings. The only check on the children's wild behavior was the fear of their father's anger: "The habitual fear of their father's peevish temper, and the dread of the punishments he was wont to inflict when irritated, kept them generally within bounds in his immediate presence" (84). Agnes's failure signals the failure of feminine forms of social control that rely on internalization of norms and codes and the need for a return to paternal authority, which relies on compliance with external forces of control. Women's mastery of the techniques of self-regulation does not mean, for Anne Brontë at least, that women are qualified or able to transfer these disciplines to other classes and to the opposite sex.

In *Shirley,* Charlotte Brontë depicts the failure of not only women but also the clergy to effect any change in the violent nature of the upper and lower classes. She attacks the clergy for failing to turn their energy "into the channel of the pastoral duties," for failing to expend it "in the diligent superintendence of the schools, and in frequent visits to the sick of their respective parishes."[34] Her portraits of the three litigious and gluttonous curates and the fighting-mad, Methodist-hating Tory rector, who should have chosen the military for his profession, are shot through with ridicule. She trivializes their disputes over Church politics and their jealousy of the Methodist and dissenting clergy and their battle over control of their parishes. She also indicates that the only conscientious and hardworking clergyman, Mr. Hall, an Evangelical Anglican, no matter how hard he tries, cannot change the conditions under which the rural poor live and work. Neither can all the charitable ladies who devote long hours to sewing for the poor and visiting the sick effect any significant change in the social and economic conditions of the laboring poor. Brontë's sarcastic tone belittles some of the ladies' charitable efforts:

> It ought perhaps be explained . . . [that] the 'Jew-basket' and 'Missionary-basket' . . . are . . . a good-sized family clothes-basket, dedicated to the purpose of conveying from house to house a monster collection of pincushions, needle-books, cardracks, work-bags, articles of infant wear, &c.&c.&c., made by the willing or reluctant hands of the Christian ladies of a parish, and sold perforce to the heathenish gentlemen thereof, at prices unblushingly exorbitant. The proceeds of such compulsory sales are applied to the conversion of the Jews, . . . or to the regeneration of the interesting coloured population of the globe. Each lady-contributor takes it in her turn to keep the basket a month, to sew for it, and to foist off its contents on a shrinking male public. (112)

Brontë conveys a sense of futility when describing women's charitable efforts.[35] She portrays women's domestic virtues as being incapable of saving the nation; domestic tasks are trivialized as busy work that traps women in an endless round of mindless tasks. In her depiction of the Luddite strike and attack on the mill, Brontë conveys a sense in which economic problems had grown too large and complicated to be resolved by setting up a Sunday school or by teaching rural women how to clean milk cans or by scolding boys for torturing baby birds.

By the 1840s the first generation of middle-class women reformers had died, and with them the belief in and enthusiasm for the power of women's benevolence to work a transformation in people's lives.[36] Women's domesticity, once credited with the power to save the nation, had subsided into the practice of dull routine, and belief in the power of feminine forms of social control had waned. The clergy, too, had been trivialized, marginalized by their in-house disputes over surplices and crucifixes, leaving yet another void which could not, in the eyes of Charlotte Brontë or Thomas Carlyle, be filled by the lazy, self-indulgent, inbred gentry, the "Joe-Manton Captains of Idleness."[37] To solve the social and economic ills that plagued England, Charlotte Brontë created out of her imagination a new-age paternalist who combines business acumen and strength of character bordering on ruthlessness with a sense of social responsibility, inspired by his loving wife, for a displaced and pauperized laboring population. Robert Moore, this new species of paternalist who combines masculine power with feminine sympathy and surveillance, describes to his wife how he hopes to resolve the economic and social problems that face manufacturers and their workers: "I have seen the necessity of doing good: I have learned the downright folly of being selfish. . . . If I succeed as I intend to do, my success . . . will line yonder barren Hollow with lines of cottages, and rows of cottage-gardens. . . . The houseless, the starving, the unemployed shall come to Hollow's mill from far and near; and Joe Scott shall give them work, and Louis Moore, Esq. shall let them a tenement and . . . such a Sunday-school as you will have, Cary!" (643–44).

In *Shirley* Brontë's trivializing of women's charitable work and her valorizing of the industrialist's paternalism reinforce the demarcation between women's and men's spheres of influence. Brontë rejects More, Leadbeater, and Hamilton's promotion of "benevolent female power" and their project to extend women's sphere of authority beyond the confines of the domestic enclosure and into the political realm of public action. Brontë's two heroines, despite their creative, restless energies, are firmly reinscribed within the domestic sphere when the novel closes. Cary is content to sit quietly by her husband's side and gently and subtly guide him toward a more sympathetic (and feminized) treatment of the poor, while Shirley relinquishes to her new husband her role as landlord and paternalist, a position she unexpectedly and freakishly inherited, and sinks with some confusion and relief into the role of the lady of the house and wife of the lord of the manor.[38]

The Cottage Visitor, the Housekeeper, and the Policeman: Self-Regulation and Surveillance in *Bleak House*

CHARLOTTE BRONTË's depiction of women's charity as futile and self-serving is echoed in Charles Dickens's *Bleak House,* especially in his portraits of Mrs. Jellyby, the philanthropist with an African mission, and Mrs. Pardiggle, the cottage visitor. Like Brontë, Dickens trivializes the charitable activities of women by showing how little they accomplish. Dickens's attitude toward philanthropic women may be explored through his portraits of three beneficent visitors, Mrs. Pardiggle, Ada, and Esther, and the effect of their visit on a brickmaker's family.

The visit to the cottage of a poor family is a standard scene in the short stories of nineteenth-century women's magazines, in Evangelical tracts, in pamphlets distributed by charitable organizations, and in such novels as Austen's *Emma,* Maria Edgeworth's *The Absentee* and *True Charity,* Brontë's *Shirley,* Gaskell's *North and South,* and George Eliot's *Middlemarch.* In the chapter entitled "Covering a Multitude of Sins" Dickens introduces his cottage visitor Mrs. Pardiggle, an active member of many ladies' benevolent societies. Boasting to Ada and Esther, Mrs. Pardiggle announces in her "loud, hard tone," "I am a School lady, I am a Visiting lady, I am a Reading lady, I am a Distributing lady; I am on the local Linen Box Committee, and many general Committees."[1] Among many of Mrs. Pardiggle's self-imposed duties are distributing religious tracts and dispensing advice to the poor in their homes. Proud of the way she conducts her campaign against the dirt and atheism of the poor, she drags Ada and Esther along to witness her in action during a visit she makes to a brickmaker's cottage. The brickmaker's family consists of "a woman with a black eye nursing a poor little gasping baby by the fire; a man, all stained with clay and mud, and looking very dissipated, lying full length on the ground, smoking a pipe; a powerful young man, fastening a collar on a dog; and a bold girl, doing some kind of washing in very dirty water" (99). Despite the family's indifference, even hostility, to her efforts, Mrs. Pardiggle is pleased with herself and proud of her energy and determination. Referring to her charitable activities, Mrs. Pardiggle says, "I am so accustomed and inured to hard work that I don't know what fatigue is. . . . This gives me a great advantage when I am making my rounds. . . . If I find a person unwilling to hear what I have to say, I tell that person directly, 'I am incapable of fatigue, my good friend, I am never tired, and I mean to go on until I have done.' It answers admirably" (97).

Mrs. Pardiggle represents one kind of cottage visitor, the evangelically inspired philanthropic woman, who was a common figure in magazine stories and novels as well as religious tracts. Cottage visiting became the rage following publication of Hannah More's portraits of the charitable Lucilla Stanley and Lady Belfield in *Coelebs in Search of a Wife* and continued to be a very popular charitable activity throughout the century. Handbooks like *The Ladies' Companion for Visiting the Poor* (1813) and *The Female Visitor to the Poor* (1846) were published to prepare the cottage visitor for her task.[2] Benevolent societies were established to organize, monitor, and inspire the lady visitors. Such organizations as the Friendly Female Society, the Society for Bettering the Condition of the Poor, and The Ladies' Royal Benevolent Society for Visiting, Relieving, and Investigating the Condition of the Poor in their own Habitations encouraged women to visit the homes of the poor, to offer comfort to the dying, to dispense medicine to the ill, to provide mothers with information on hygiene and food preparation, and to instruct the ignorant in the tenets of the Christian faith. Mrs. Pardiggle's gift to the brickmaker's family of a "little book . . . fit for a babby" (100), typical of the kind of tracts distributed by visitors, is designed, as the Ladies' Royal Benevolent Society asserts, "for the purpose of instilling, at a very inconsiderable cost to the Society, moral and religious principles in conformity with the doctrines of the Church of England, into the minds of the poor at a time of sickness and calamity."[3] Mrs. Pardiggle's style of cottage visitation would have been approved of by the London City Mission: "This visiting from house to house and room to room is the chief, indeed the staple, work of the society. . . . The evangelization of London depends upon the penetrating power of reasoning with men and women individually—meeting their difficulties in friendly conversation, and in the beseeching of them to be reconciled to God."[4]

The Business of Charity

Mrs. Pardiggle is Dickens's middle-class charitable woman: the inveterate dispenser of tracts, Bibles, and pamphlets on prayer, prudence, and cleanliness; the busybody who pokes her head into other people's business (99). Dickens explicitly links Mrs. Pardiggle's method of dispensing charity with business. Esther points out that Mrs. Pardiggle's voice when speaking to the cottager's family is "too business-like and systematic" (99) and that "she certainly did make, in this, as in everything else, a show that was not conciliatory, of doing charity by wholesale, and of dealing in it to a large extent" (101). Mrs. Pardiggle boasts of her energy and capacity for hard work: "I am a woman of business. I love hard work; I enjoy hard work. The excitement does me good." Pleased with the way she conducts her campaign against the poor, she is eager for Esther and Ada to witness "her capacity" for "doing charitable business" (95).

Not only is Mrs. Pardiggle's manner brusque and businesslike but her charitable activities are systematized and organized much along the same lines as factory work with its division of labor. Mrs. Pardiggle has "rounds" (97); she visits her clients in a "regular order" (101); and she is responsible for visiting only those poor in her district.[5] Benevolent societies like the ones Mrs. Pardiggle belongs to divided areas into districts and assigned ladies to be

responsible for visiting the poor on a regular but limited basis.
Every society had different rules, but in general visitors to the poor
met weekly to discuss their cases, and they also submitted to the
board of directors reports that were compiled into quarterly and
yearly reports.[6]

Middle-class charitable ladies like Mrs. Pardiggle were proud
of their societies with their committees, their districts and their
rounds, their cases and their quarterly reports. They felt they were
effective because they were organized. More efficacious than the
gentry with their sentimental gifts of food and coal, these middle-
class charitable ladies were giving the poor the opportunity to learn
a set of morals that included thrift, prudence, and industry. Unlike
the gentry, whose misplaced, haphazard generosity kept the poor
dependent on their bounty, they were helping the poor to help
themselves morally and economically.[7]

Mrs. Pardiggle fails to change the dirty, angry, drunken brickmaker into a clean, pious, grateful member of the laboring poor. In
contrast, Mrs. Pardiggle's equally energetic and pious counterparts
in the pamphlets published by benevolent and religious organizations always succeed. In "The Influence of Pious Women in
Promoting the Revival of Religion," a pamphlet published by the
Religious Tract Society, Mrs.—visits a poor family, gives them a
psalter, "the first sacred book they ever possessed," and returns a
week later to find a young person reading it. Taking the psalter
from the young man, she then reads aloud, and eventually neighbors, hearing her voice, drift into the room: "Another and another
followed, until seventeen persons were sitting or standing around
her, listening to the words of eternal life." After reading, she seizes
the opportunity to explain to the people in the crowded room "the
nature of divine forgiveness" and how to obtain it. A woman, listening to her words, begins to weep and to walk away. "Stop," calls out
Mrs.—, "stop: remember that our Lord Jesus Christ shed tears
over the sins of others. . . . Come back and hear more about it."
The weeping woman returns while Mrs.—continues to lecture on
the subject of forgiveness and sin "until the place became a Bochim
'a place of weepers'; everyone was in tears: and when she arose to
come away, they asked her, with much solicitude, 'When will you

come to see us again?'" The pamphlet tells us that this very same Mrs.—not only made numerous visits to the poor, but also sold in one month "more than *one thousand five hundred* Bibles, Testaments, and Psalters."

When Mrs. Pardiggle reads from the Bible to the members of the brickmaker's household, things do not go nearly so well. The poor, uneducated, and irreligious family Mrs. Pardiggle visits resists her proselytizing first with silence and sullen looks and then with sarcasm and angry protest. The brickmaker, seeing Mrs. Pardiggle about to begin her usual attack, says, "I wants a end of these liberties took with my place. I wants a end of being drawed like a badger. . . . No, I an't read the little book wot you left. There an't nobody here as knows how to read it; and if there wos, it wouldn't be suitable to me. . . . No, I don't never mean for to go to church."[8] Ignoring his warning, Mrs. Pardiggle "pulled out a good book, as if it were a constable's staff, and took the whole family into . . . religious custody; . . . as if she were an inexorable moral Policeman carrying them all off to a stationhouse" (100). They barely listen to Mrs. Pardiggle; the older man tells her to get out and leave them alone. She replies, "I am never fatigued. I shall come to you again, in your regular order" (101).

Dickens's Mrs. Pardiggle provides a sharp contrast to usual nineteenth-century portraits of the visiting lady. In almost every description of the cottage visit the charitable lady leaves knowing that she has succeeded in guiding the benighted poor onto paths of righteousness. Stories of the cottagers' gratitude and the visitor's efficacy are commonplace in charitable and Evangelical societies' quarterly and yearly reports. A typical description of a destitute family whose spiritual and material needs are met by a visiting lady is reported in the pamphlet "The Nature, Design, and Rules of the Benevolent or Stranger's Friend Society; Instituted for the Purposes of Visiting and Relieving Sick and Distressed Strangers, and other Poor at their Respective Habitations" (1804). The family of a Joseph Connel "was discovered in great distress by a visitor, who had scarcely ever witnessed such a scene of affliction." The report continues, "Connel and two young children lay together in a bad fever. His eldest son (a young man of twenty-two) was pining away in an opposite corner of the room. Around the fire-place, were three small children, crying to their distracted mother for victuals, but she was destitute, both of food and money, and expected to perish by famine." The Stranger's Friend Society immediately relieved them with pecuniary assistance, and "under the blessing of Almighty God, the family were all restored to health again." Even more satisfying for the society is their success with this family's morals: "The instructions they received of the visitors have made good impressions upon their minds. They are now determined by the assistance of God, to live to his glory, who has so graciously delivered them in the time of their greatest affliction."

Dickens reverses the standard scene of affliction relieved and gratitude expressed: his cottagers are sullen, sulking, and openly hostile; his visiting lady does not succeed in bringing "the man out of darkness into a marvelous light."9 By juxtaposing Mrs. Pardiggle's reception with that of the charity society's tracts, Dickens ridicules the tracts' idealized portraits of the cottage visitor while underscoring Mrs. Pardiggle's failure to aid the poor.

Dickens's attack on charitable women is not limited to Mrs. Pardiggle. His portrayal of Mrs. Jellyby is savage in its ridicule. He repeatedly links Mrs. Jellyby and her charitable activities with dirt and chaos. Her house is filthy, her servants drunk, her husband ignored, and her children's health and happiness neglected. Mrs. Jellyby regards her family and their needs as "petty details" that threaten to interfere with her concentration on her "public duties" (309), which at this particular moment is focused on Africa. Mrs. Jellyby spends all day long writing letters and planning meetings to further her scheme to settle the "superabundant home population" in Africa, where they will cultivate coffee berries and Christianize the natives (32). She has neither time for her family nor interest in household matters. When Esther and Ada visit the Jellyby household, they cannot help noticing that the bedrooms have "such a marshy smell" (37); "the windows were so encrusted with dirt, that they would have made Midsummer sunshine dim" (43); and the parlor, "which was strewn with papers and nearly filled by a great writing-table covered with similar litter, was . . . not only very untidy, but very dirty" (35). Mrs. Jellyby's person is likewise unkempt: "In truth Mrs. Jellyby required a good deal of attention, the lattice-work up her back having widened considerably since I first knew her, and her hair looking like the mane of a dustman's horse" (389). Caddy, Mrs. Jellyby's daughter, upset by the "bills, dirt, waste, noise, tumbles downstairs, confusion, and wretchedness" (172), tries to put her mother's house in order but fails in this overwhelming task, saying, "I have tidied and tidied over and over again; but it's useless. Ma and Africa, together, upset the whole house directly. We never have a servant who don't drink. Ma's ruinous to everything" (391).

Throughout *Bleak House,* Dickens ridicules "the Women of England, the Daughters of Britain, the Sisters of all the Cardinal Virtues separately, the Females of America, the Ladies of a hundred denominations" (93–94): the phrase mocks the titles of Sarah Ellis's conduct books. Dickens's disdain for these women is so strong that his sarcastic, angry voice displaces Esther's usually diffident, modulated voice.[10] Among the charitable ladies Esther describes is "an extremely dirty lady, with her bonnet all awry, and the ticketed price of her dress still sticking on it, whose neglected home, Caddy told me, was like a filthy wilderness, but whose church was like a fancy fair" (393). "The great object" of these charitable ladies is, according to Esther, "to form themselves into committees for getting in and laying out money. . . . They threw themselves into committees in the most impassioned manner, and collected subscriptions with a vehemence quite extraordinary. . . . They wanted everything. They wanted wearing apparel, they wanted linen rags, they wanted money, they wanted coals, they wanted soup, they wanted interest, they wanted autographs, they wanted flannel, they wanted whatever Mr. Jarndyce had—or had not" (93).

Middle-class women who staff charitable organizations are, in Dickens's world, not very effective in helping anyone but themselves. Mr. Jarndyce, Esther recalls, had remarked once that there are "two classes of charitable people; one, the people who did a little and made a great deal of noise; the other, the people who did a great deal and made no noise at all." Mrs. Pardiggle, Esther suspects even before meeting her, is "a type of the former class" (94). Mrs.

Pardiggle, Mrs. Jellyby, and their set are motivated not by genuine feeling or by sympathy or even pity for the poor cottagers or natives of Africa, but by the feeling of self-importance they gain from their so-called charitable activities. Mrs. Pardiggle thrives on baiting the poor brickmaker; she enjoys her position of moral authority and derives pleasure from bullying those she deems morally inferior (100). Dickens's representation of charitable women reveals an egotism that motivates women like Mrs. Pardiggle, a selfishness that makes their charitable visits in reality inappropriate, inconsiderate, and ultimately unkind.

The Tears of a Gentlewoman

Ada's response to the brickmaker's family is quite different from Mrs. Pardiggle's "mechanical way of taking possession of people" (101). Mrs. Pardiggle is too busy fighting the good fight with the master of the household to notice the quiet suffering of the mother, who sits by the fire shielding her "poor little child" from the "noise and violence and ill-treatment" (101). Ada, on the other hand, is drawn to this scene and inquires if the infant is ill. As Ada approaches the mother and infant, Ada sees that the baby has died and bursts into tears, crying, "O Esther, my love, the little thing! The suffering, quiet, pretty little thing! I am so sorry for it. I am so sorry for the mother. I never saw a sight so pitiful as this before! O baby, baby!" (102)

Ada's response to this cottager's distress, her spontaneous tears and outburst of genuine feeling, are not original with Dickens. He is making use of a character and a scene that were featured in many novels and short stories of the late eighteenth and early nineteenth centuries: a sweet, innocent young lady happens upon a lonely cottage, hears a tale of distress, sheds tears, and expresses sympathy and then leaves the cottager, promising to return to do what she can to help. An important feature of this scene is the class of the young woman: she is always upper class, often the daughter of the local squire or lord, a visiting cousin, or friend of the family. An example of such a scene is in Maria Edgeworth's *True Charity*. Walking through the forest one day, Laura, a young lady in her late teens, happens upon a small boy crying because, as she soon learns, his father is "gone to the wars," his sister is dying, and his mother is ill, unable to work and provide the family with bread. "So," he concludes, "we must all die for hunger. I should not mind anything, if it was not for poor Susy [his sister]" (136). Laura is moved by the boy's story and asks if she can help. He suggests she come home with him to speak to his mother. The scene that she is greeted with upon entering the cottage "riveted" her attention: "The dying sister, . . . a child of nine years of age, was lying on a humble pallet, with very few signs of animation; while the parent, who was gently supporting her head, seemed little less exhausted by penury and suffering, than the child whose wants she was administering" (137). Laura listens to the mother's story, and when the poor woman speaks of the "inevitable death" of her daughter, Laura, "too young, and too much affected herself to offer consolation," offers instead her tears. "She could . . . only blend her tears with those of the mourner; but those tears spoke volumes to the heart of the disconsolate parent; they told her that, there was one being who still sympathises in her misfortunes, and she was comforted" (138).

Ada's tears, like Laura's, are spontaneous and genuine, and Ada's tears, like Laura's, are well received: "Such compassion, such gentleness, as that with which she bent down weeping, and put her hand upon the mother's, might have softened any mother's heart that ever beat. The woman at first gazed at her in astonishment, and then burst into tears" (102). Ada, like Laura, returns later to the cottage, bringing "some little comforts" (103). Ada's and Laura's tears are emblems of "the sympathies of a compassionate heart," which according to *The Young Ladies' Faithful Remembrancer of Obligations, Responsibilities, and Duties* are even more efficacious in touching the hearts of the poor and afflicted than giving them "worldly goods": "In your intercourse with the afflicted you will soon discover that the balm of genuine pity, flowing from a tender heart, and the rays of sensibility, beaming from an expressive countenance, are often more effectual in allaying human misery than any gift or service you could render."[11]

Ada's and Mrs. Pardiggle's response to the brickmaker's family are clearly quite different, and this difference is marked by class. Ada is the ward of Chancery, an heiress in waiting, and cousin to Mr. Jarndyce. Her class is as distinct from Mrs. Pardiggle as her manner. Ada's heart is kind and gentle; her manner graceful, innocent, and fresh; her person very pretty and delicate, all that a young lady should be. Mrs. Pardiggle, on the other hand, is the middle-class tract dispenser and evangelical saver of souls. Far from being refined and delicate, she is coarse and ugly, with "choking eyes" (95) and spectacles, and has the brusque, businesslike manner of a wholesale grocer.

Upper-class Sympathy

Ada's tears, used by Dickens to illustrate the emotional poverty of Mrs. Pardiggle's mechanical style of charity, are the characteristic response of gentlewomen (and gentlemen)[12] to the distresses of the poor. Tears, pity, and the expression of genuine concern are the hallmark of the old society's paternalistic treatment of the poor. The rich and the poor of eighteenth-century rural England had been bound together in a system of reciprocity, a system ideally of obligation and duty on the part of the aristocracy and gentry and deference and gratitude on the part of the laboring poor. In the late 1780s, an era of political unrest, Sarah Trimmer published *The Oeconomy of Charity*, urging the renewal of the "practice of reciprocal benevolence and gratitude" as a way to restore social harmony. England's "welfare and happiness" depend on the "mutual interchange of good offices," which means that those in "superior stations" must exercise "justice, condescension and charity" while the poor display "honesty, diligence, humility and gratitude."[13] J. S. Mill argued that this paternal system depends on the myth or ideal of "dependence and protection," which promotes the idea that the rich's relation to the poor is one of "affectionate tutelage" and depicts the relation as "only partly authoritative" and as "amiable, moral, and sentimental."[14] This form of paternalism was an extremely effective means of social control, especially in the predominately agricultural eighteenth century. To ensure the laboring poor's cooperation with this system, which was based on an extreme inequality of property distribution, the gentry deflected the poor's hostility and preempted any attempts at organizing against the one very visible common enemy, the lord of the manor, with benevolence, usually in the form of small gifts of food, clothing, and coal distributed by the landlord's wife, daughter, or sister. Such gifts were emblematic of the master's personal concern. Paternalism, when it successfully disguised its inherent despotism, used kindness and personal, face-to-face contact to disarm the laboring poor's resentment of a system that made their oppression a requirement of its existence. As the historian Jessica Gerard argues, the landowner's wealth and power required of the agricultural laborer not only his poverty and powerlessness but also his endorsement of the system that oppressed him: "The right to rule and the enjoyment of land, privilege, and wealth carried moral obligations of public service and benevolence toward their dependents, whose gratitude, deference, and submission legitimized the existing social order."[15]

Ada's tears and small gift, then, are typical of the gentry's paternalistic response to the poor, a paternalism that presumed the kind of intimacy that living in close proximity over an extended period of time produces. As noted in chapter 1, Howard Newby argues that paternalism is "most effective on the basis of face-to-face contact" and that it is a form of social control that is reinforced by charity, but that this charity, to be most effective, must be bestowed personally "in a voluntary and uninstitutionalized relationship between giver and receiver."[16] More important than Ada's tears, then, is the spontaneity of her response and the fact that she happens upon this family, that her visit is not connected with a routinized system of charity.[17]

There are several examples in *Bleak House* of this kind of personal, emotionally intense, and spontaneous paternal benevolence. Lady Dedlock's adoption of Rosa as her servant and companion bears all the marks of a paternal relation. Lady Dedlock provides Rosa with a home and accepts Rosa's devotion in return for this condescension. Lady Dedlock feels an almost irrational affection for Rosa and keeps her near her at all times, especially when she needs the comfort of Rosa's sweetness and innocence. Lady

Dedlock, "standing beside the village beauty, smoothing her dark hair with that motherly touch, and watching her with eyes so full of musing interest," says to Rosa, "'Listen to me, child. You are young and true, and I believe you are attached to me.'" Rosa replies, "'Indeed I am, my Lady. Indeed there is nothing in the world I wouldn't do, to show how much,'" and "kneels at her feet and kisses her hand" (371).

Sir Leicester's relationships with Mrs. Rouncewell and her son George are also deeply paternal. Mrs. Rouncewell feels the devotion and gratitude that a trusted servant should feel for her master. Even her ironmaster son recognizes that she is so tied to Sir Leicester and Chesney Wold that to ask her to move with him to his northern industrial town would be "to sever this strong bond," and that "would . . . break her heart" (368). The son says, "She is one of those examples—perhaps as good a one as there is—of love, and attachment, and fidelity in such a station, which England may well be proud of; but of which no order can appropriate the whole pride or the whole merit, because such an instance bespeaks high worth on two sides; on the great side assuredly; on the small one, no less assuredly" (368).

Dickens at once ridicules and idealizes the Dedlocks' paternalism: he recognizes the despotism that lies at its heart and yet admires the depth of feeling between master and servant as well as the comfort that can be derived from this reciprocal relationship. The narrator comments sarcastically on Sir Leicester's qualifications as a master: "He supposes all his dependents to be utterly bereft of individual characters, intentions, or opinions, and is persuaded that he was born to supersede the necessity of their having any. . . . But he is an excellent master still" (78). Dickens, however, dignifies Sir Leicester's rather archaic paternal feelings for Mrs. Rouncewell. Sir Leicester really is a good master because he respects Mrs. Rouncewell. She knows that he trusts her and that he feels that "his dignity . . . [is] safer with her than with anybody else" (78). It is she who cares for Sir Leicester after he is incapacitated by his stroke: "His favourite and faithful housekeeper stands at his bedside. It is the first act he notices, and he clearly derives pleasure from it" (708). Sir Leicester is confused, agitated, and unable to speak; Mrs. Rouncewell is the only one who can understand his attempts at communication. After hearing the terrible news that Lady Dedlock has vanished, he swoons, "and it is an hour before he opens his eyes, reclining on his faithful and attached old servant's arm. The doctors know that he is best with her" (709). Mrs. Rouncewell and her son George take care of Sir Leicester, Mr. George helping him to sit up and get about. The dignity and formality of the exchanges between Mr. George and Sir Leicester are shot through with deep feeling. Sir Leicester "looks at the trooper until tears come into his eyes. . . . 'I ask your pardon, Sir Leicester,' says the trooper, 'but would you accept of my arms to raise you up?' . . . The trooper takes him in his arms like a child, lightly raises him, and turns him with his face more towards the window." Sir Leicester thanks George: "You have your mother's gentleness . . . and your own strength. Thank you" (737). Their relationship with the baronet is physically intimate and emotionally intense, the baronet saying to George, "You are another self to me" (738). Together Mrs. Rouncewell and her son maintain what is left of Sir Leicester and Chesney Wold after Lady Dedlock's death.

Dickens, however, is not recommending paternalism as a solution for the ills of his society. Mrs. Rouncewell's fidelity and Sir Leicester's attachment are no longer applicable to mid-nineteenth-century England and its social relations. Paternalism, an outmoded form of social control, can exist successfully only in an agricultural setting, on the country estate, and in the closed estate villages; it cannot be transferred to the city or the manufacturing town, for as Mrs. Rouncewell says, there is "a world beyond Chesney Wold that I don't understand" (80). It is also a world her master does not understand, or rather it is a world he refuses to recognize as existing.

More involved with the world beyond the estate but not very well equipped to deal with its chaos and pathos is Mr. Jarndyce, who, like the Dedlocks, employs the paternal mode of benevolence. Unlike Mrs. Pardiggle, Mr. Jarndyce has no system, so that when he bestows money he does so haphazardly, without examining the result of his charitable activity. Mr. Skimpole, a frequent recipient of Mr. Jarndyce's charity, is an opportunist whose life-style of refined self-indulgence is supported by Mr. Jarndyce. Esther worries that Skimpole is not the frivolous, carefree, and pleasure-loving "child" he pretends to be, and eventually she decides that he is cunning, supremely selfish, and very destructive, especially in his introducing of Richard to Mr. Vholes and his encouraging Richard to live as if he will inherit a fortune. In Mr. Skimpole's case, Mr. Jarndyce's spontaneous, personal charity is ill considered and perhaps partly responsible for Richard's destruction. Some of his beneficent projects do, however, fare better; Esther, for instance, owes her position in his household to his bounty and kindness. Without his intervention and aid, Esther might never have grown into the generous, loving woman that she becomes.

According to middle-class moralists like Hannah More, spontaneous and highly idiosyncratic benevolence, like Mr. Jarndyce's, is typical of upper-class charity. As noted in chapter 4, More complains that the gentry are too unused to system and organization and too self-indulgent to examine carefully the objects of their benevolence or to follow through on their progress or decline. Describing the "thoughtless, lavish, and indolent" Sir John (*Coelebs* 169), More declares that "had he lived much within the sight of misery," he would have been "liberal." Not unlike Mr. Jarndyce, Sir John gave "to undeserving objects, rather than be at the pains to search out the deserving. He neither discriminated between the degrees of distress, nor the characters of the distressed" (170).

System and Sympathy

Dickens's middle-class visiting lady, the systematic and heartless Mrs. Pardiggle, is ineffectual in aiding those whom she endeavors to convert and save. His upper-class lady, the sympathetic Ada, is unable to do anything to improve the lives of the brickmaker's miserable family. Dickens juxtaposes these two types of beneficent women not only to discredit the work of women's charitable organizations and to highlight the inadequacies of sentimental paternalism. His larger aim is to provide a workable solution to the problems created by poverty. His solution is embodied in Esther, a model of feminine domestic virtue, someone who can combine system and feeling to produce useful activity.

Unlike Mrs. Pardiggle and Ada, Esther is supremely useful. As housekeeper to Mr. Jarndyce, Esther has made herself indispensable to everyone connected to Bleak House. In charge of the house, she is very busy making sure that everything is homey, cheerful, and tidy. "Being generally a methodical, old-maidish sort of foolish little person," she says of herself, "I was so busy" (86). "I was very busy indeed, all day, and wrote directions home to the servants, and wrote notes for my guardian, and dusted his books and papers, and jingled my housekeeping keys a good deal, one way and another" (223). To make herself worthy of Mr. Jarndyce's kindness to her she says to herself, "I should be busy, busy, busy— useful, amiable, serviceable, in all honest, unpretending ways" (569). She is useful because, unlike Mrs. Pardiggle, she consciously consults the wishes of those she aims to aid, and she employs her energy and skill for organization in satisfying their needs. Ada says to her after their brief stay at Mrs. Jellyby's house, "You are so thoughtful, Esther, . . . and yet so cheerful! and you do so much, so unpretendingly! You would make a home out of even this house" (40). Mr. Boythorn notices "Miss Summerson's forethought for every one about her" (112). She does not just service people; she uses her intuition and her intelligence to analyze their motives, desires, and needs, and then she does what she can for them. Recognizing her considerate and disinterested kindness,[18] Mr. Jarndyce says of her, "But we must take care, too, that our little woman's life is not all consumed in care for others" (168) and tells her to rest: "These are late hours for working and thinking. You do that for all of us, all day long, little housekeeper" (221).[19]

Combining method with empathy, Esther is useful in a way that neither Mrs. Pardiggle nor Ada can be. Esther's usefulness is derived in part from her ability to organize details, to "tidy" messy and dirty things, like Mrs. Jellyby's house. On her first visit to the Jellybys', she occupied herself "in making our room a little tidy" (39), and in preparation for Caddy's wedding day, she, along with Caddy and Mr. Jellyby, tackles the chaos of Mrs. Jellyby's closets and their contents—"bits of mouldy pie, sour bottles, Mrs. Jellyby's caps, letters, tea, forks, odd boots and shoes of children, . . . nutshells, the heads and tails of shrimps, dinner-mats, gloves, coffee-grounds, umbrellas" (391). It takes several days, but Esther is able "to establish some order among all this waste and ruin" (391). Esther teaches Caddy housekeeping: "I showed her all my books and methods, and all my fidgety ways. You would have supposed that I was showing her some wonderful inventions, by her study of them" (388). Mr. Skimpole notices Esther's "capacity for the administration of detail" (405) and her "talent for business" (406). He says to her, "You appear to me to be the very touchstone of responsibility. When I see you, my dear Miss Summerson, intent upon the perfect working of the whole little orderly system of which you are the centre, I feel inclined to say to myself . . . *that's* responsibility!" (494). His veiled sarcasm notwithstanding, he recognizes that her busyness and organizational skills are useful, especially as he benefits from them directly.

When Esther visits the cottage of the brickmaker, her reaction to the family is quite different from both Mrs. Pardiggle's and Ada's. First of all, Esther understands the political and emotional problems of visiting the poor. She explains why she feels inadequate to the task: "I was not sure of my qualifications. That I was inexperienced in the art of adapting my mind to minds very differently situated, and addressing them from suitable points of view. That I had not that delicate knowledge of the heart which must be essential to such a work. That I had much to learn, myself, before I could teach others, and that I could not confide in my good intentions alone" (97). She recognizes that a gulf exists between herself and this family: "Between us and these people there was an iron barrier" (101). Unlike Mrs. Pardiggle, Esther respects their right to be who they are. She does not judge them; she even doubts her own ability (which is prodigious) to keep clean under these conditions: "I doubted if the best of us could have been tidy in such a place" (99). Unlike Ada, she does not weep; instead, she does something practical, useful, and kind: "Presently I took the light burden from her lap; did what I could to make the baby's rest the prettier and gentler; laid it on a shelf, and covered it with my own handkerchief" (102). In caring so tenderly for the dead baby, she performs a ritual that both expresses her sympathy for the baby and honors the mother's grief.

Unlike Mrs. Pardiggle and Ada, Esther belongs to neither the middle nor the upper classes. Though she is the daughter of a gentlewoman, because she is illegitimate she cannot enter the world of the gentry as an equal. In fact, as the object of Mr. Jarndyce's charity, she is dependent on his bounty and goodwill in a way that Richard and Ada are not, and as his housekeeper, she is shut out from ladylike activities and is constricted by her housewifery duties. She must be up before breakfast to get the household ready for the day—"I had only to rise a little earlier in the morning, and keep my accounts, and attend to housekeeping matters" (633). Esther's duties often prevent her from going on outings with Ada and Richard: "As it was the day of the week on which I paid the bills, and added up my books, and made all the household affairs as compact as possible, I remained at home while Mr. Jarndyce, Ada, and Richard, took advantage of a very fine day to make a little excursion" (113).

As the daughter of Lady Dedlock and as Mr. Jarndyce's housekeeper, Esther's social class is ambiguous; she is neither lady nor servant. As housekeeper, she is positioned within a class hierarchy that extends downward to the lesser servants beneath her and upward to Ada and to Mr. Jarndyce. Like Austen's Fanny, Esther is well practiced in the paternal dynamics of duty and deference, and like Fanny, she serves others out of gratitude. Grateful to Mr. Jarndyce for his benevolence, Esther says, "How could I ever be busy enough, how could I ever be good enough, how in my little way could I ever hope to be forgetful enough of myself, devoted enough to him, and useful enough to others, to show him how I blessed and honoured him" (564). When Esther agrees to marry Mr. Jarndyce but keeps her place as his housekeeper, she remains embedded in hierarchical relations; her dependency and gratitude are doubly ensured by her class and gender positions.

Esther represents Dickens's ideal woman. She is feminine because properly dependent and grateful, and she is useful because she can practice self-denial. Like Lucilla in More's *Coelebs in Search of a Wife,* Esther is an expert manager of time, space, and resources, and like Lucilla, Esther's management ability is dependent on her ability to suppress her own desires. Functioning like

Lucilla's watch in the garden, Esther's mind monitors her self, watching and regulating her thoughts and feelings. When upset over the loss of her "old face" and reluctant to look in the mirror, she scolds herself as if she were speaking to another person, viewing herself from a position outside herself (468, 498). As many critics have noted, she also exercises heroic self-control as she works hard to suppress her romantic desires, censuring her fantasies about Alan Woodcourt and reminding herself of her deep obligations to Mr. Jarndyce.[20] When Woodcourt finally speaks of his love for her, she says to herself with uncharacteristic passion: "O, too late to know it now, too late, too late. That was the first ungrateful thought I had. Too late" (775). She tells him that she is "not free" to think of his love, that she is "bound by every tie of attachment, gratitude, and love" (777) to Mr. Jarndyce. After this painful interview, she cries, but it is difficult to believe her statement that "they were not tears of regret and sorrow" (778) because she must pray and repeat the words of Mr. Jarndyce's proposal to calm herself down and to steel herself for a life of gratitude and duty.

Esther's exceptional powers of regulation are confined to a narrow sphere: herself and her home. Unlike Lucilla, whose powers of regulation extend out from herself into the community surrounding her where she superintends the impoverished and needy, Esther exercises her regulatory talents in a much-reduced arena. Esther cares for those in her immediate family—Ada, Richard, and Mr. Jarndyce. She extends her domain of concern to include Mr. Jarndyce's friends and acquaintances—Mr. Boythorn and Mr. Skimpole, Mrs. Jellyby's family, and in particular Peepy and Caddy—and Mr. Jarndyce's charitable projects—Charlie and her siblings. And she concerns herself with the welfare of those whom she meets by chance—Miss Flite and Jo. All of her charitable gestures come from her heart. Esther's charity is personal and private and is quite unlike Mrs. Pardiggle's impersonal and systematized charity work. Esther does not do "charitable business" (95), and her movements are not part of a routine orchestrated by an impersonal organization with a set agenda. Whereas Hannah More locates in the public sphere a space in which her heroine can exercise her "female benevolent power,"[21] Dickens limits his heroine to the domestic sphere. Esther says, "It is right to begin with the obligations of the home, sir; and that, perhaps, while those are overlooked and neglected, no other duties can possibly be substituted for them" (60). Dickens refuses to bestow his approbation on any woman who extends her realm of influence beyond these boundaries.[22]

Through his portraits of Mrs. Pardiggle and Mrs. Jellyby, Dickens dismisses the work of middle-class women's philanthropic organizations as meddlesome nonsense. Esther says of Mrs. Jellyby, "It struck me that if Mrs. Jellyby had discharged her own natural duties and obligations, before she swept the horizon with a telescope in search of others, she would have taken the best precautions against becoming absurd" (499). Jo becomes a litmus test for those who profess charitable intentions, and when the likes of Mrs. Pardiggle and Mrs. Jellyby ignore his presence, they discredit themselves as true philanthropists. Because Jo is "not one of Mrs. Pardiggle's Tockahoopo Indians; he is not one of Mrs. Jellyby's lambs, being wholly unconnected with Borrioboola-Gha," he holds no interest for them. "He is not softened by distance and unfamiliarity; . . . he is the ordinary home-made article" (595). Esther, on the other hand, takes the sick boy into her home and cares for him without any regard for the danger she puts herself in by nursing the feverish child. Dickens presents Esther's disinterested kindness as exemplary. In contrast to the useless busyness of Mrs. Pardiggle and Mrs. Jellyby, Esther's actions are truly beneficial because they do not invade the public realm in an aggressive manner. Esther says, "I thought it best to be as useful as I could, and to render what kind of services I could, to those immediately about me; and to try to let that circle of duty gradually and naturally expand itself" (97–98). Esther's "circle of duty" sounds a retreat for women into the domestic sphere and a retirement from public activity and from participating in institutional solutions to social ills.

Surveillance

Esther's retreat into the private sphere does not, however, mean that Dickens abandons the public realm to corrupt, self-serving institutions like Chancery and the depredations of malevolent forces of greed and self-interest represented by characters like Mr. Vholes and the Smallweeds. While Esther manages the private sphere, Mr. Bucket, the police detective, checks the destructive forces that threaten the public arena through a unique blend of surveillance and intimidation.[23] Mr. Bucket seems to have everyone under his surveillance, watching the motions of characters as disparate as Mr. George, Jo, the Smallweeds, Hortense, Gridley, and even Esther. He operates by "keeping his man in sight" while "dodging and lurking about in the gloom" (713). He brings "his keen eyes to bear on every slinking creature whom he passes in the midnight streets" (712). His powers of observation are almost supernatural: "He mounts a high tower in his mind, and looks out far and wide. Many solitary figures he perceives, creeping through the streets; many solitary figures out on heaths, and roads, and lying under haystacks. . . . Other solitaries he perceives in nooks of bridges . . . ; and in shadowed places down by the river's level" (714). As an object of Bucket's supervisory talents, Jo believes that the detective is "everywhere, and [is] cognizant of everything" (594), for Mr. Bucket has threatened Jo by saying, "Don't let me ever see you nowheres within forty mile of London, or you'll repent it," and Jo is convinced that "he'll see me if I'm above ground" (590). Not only can Mr. Bucket locate people and hold them in his gaze, he can also see into their hearts and minds. This gives him the power to anticipate people's actions and prevent them from succeeding in their less-than-honorable plans. He knows that old Mr. Smallweed plans to sell for a high price what might be papers of value to Mr. Jarndyce and coerces the old man into giving them to Jarndyce. Describing Mr. Bucket's ingenuity in orchestrating this maneuver, Esther marvels at "the cunning of Mr. Bucket's eye, and the masterly manner in which he contrived . . . to let us know" how matters stood (781).

Mr. Bucket's considerable talents of observation and his vast knowledge of human nature are important qualities for a man in his profession. At the time Dickens was writing *Bleak House* the police was a relatively new institution, and as such was an object of constant discussion and redefinition. Pamphlets, tracts, and handbooks enumerated and defined the duties of the police. Tracts like

"Preventive Police" (1829) by Sir Edwin Chadwick and manuals like "The Constable's Guide" (1843) sought to clarify the role of the policeman, stressing his importance in a society that is urban, anonymous, and indifferent, a society in which "men live for years, often during their whole lives, without knowing their next-door neighbours."[24] Chadwick argues that social problems, including criminal activity, arise in this kind of environment. In the absence of a community-based society in which "every individual is known, and his acts are subjected to the observation of his neighbours," troubles grow because "opportunities for observation diminish."[25] The policeman's job, according to many of these pamphlets, is to watch everyone, and to do so openly, so that everyone knows they are being watched. *The Constable's Guide* asserts that the police constable has the "power *ex officio* to keep a watch" for the purpose of detecting robberies and observing "suspicious persons" and "night walkers" and to search the homes of "suspicious persons" and those who "ride and go armed," and that "it is in his power to hold such watches as often as he pleases."[26] One pamphlet, "Observations on the present state of the Police," urges the police to watch suspected criminals, particularly those who receive stolen goods. Complaining that it is not easy to apprehend receivers of stolen goods, the author contends, "It is very difficult to convict them; but we may know them, we may become acquainted with their habitations and their hiding places; let us watch them, follow them, mark them down, wherever they rest; they must know that we do so: let them constantly feel this observance, and we need not legislate against them; they will quickly vanish: the eye of the police will be shunned, though the arm of the law may not be dreaded." By surveying suspected criminals and suspicious persons, the police force "produces practical good, at the expense, when rightly administered of no political inconvenience."[27]

The role of the police, according to Patrick Colquhoun, magistrate, reformer, and disciple of Bentham, is to preserve order and to protect "the peaceable inhabitants at all times against every species of injury, fraud, depredation" by "checking and preventing those offenses in particular which lead to the corruption of morals."[28] In *A Treatise on Indigence* Colquhoun criminalizes poverty, focusing on vagrancy, mendicancy, and theft, and offers the police, a "watchful and superintending agency," as a solution to these economic and social problems. He envisions a police force "in the shape of a *systematic superintending police*" that is "calculated to check and prevent the growth and progress of vicious habits, and other irregularities incident to civil society." He argues that the best way to secure peace, check "idleness and vagrancy," and encourage "industry" is to have a police force that uses "intelligence, labour, and investigation, aided by a thorough knowledge of facts."[29]

Colquhoun, Chadwick, and the author of the pamphlet "Treatise on the Police" portray the police's ability to gather and organize information as exemplary and crucial in preventing crime. Among England's "blessings" is her "well-regulated, and energetic police," who conduct themselves with "purity, activity, vigilance, and discretion."[30] A well-regulated police is one that gathers, records, and organizes as much information as it can: "1st, that at each watch-house, a book should be kept for entering all informations of the offenses committed within the district . . . ; 2ndly, that the keeper of the watch-house . . . should make copies of all such entries, and forward them on the day they are made to the chief of public office . . . ; 3rdly, that the whole of the copies of these informations be . . . methodized."[31]

Dickens's portrait of the police in *Bleak House* reflects this same admiration for their tidiness, accuracy, and systematic use of information. Esther notes the well-regulated quality of police work when Mr. Bucket brings her to a "watch-house": "two police officers, looking in their perfectly neat uniforms not at all like people who were up all night, were writing at a desk" (716). These officers write up a description of Lady Dedlock that "was very accurate indeed" (716), check with her for accuracy, copy it, and then dispatch it: "As soon as the paper was sent out upon its travel, the two officers resumed their former quiet work of writing with neatness and care" (716).

Energetic and well organized, the police, Dickens would have us believe, are an important force of order in a society that has shifted from small, face-to-face communities to large, anonymous metropolises. Mr. Bucket functions as a force of moral order. As a police detective expert in the techniques of surveillance, Mr. Bucket acts in a supervisory position, filling the void left by the "abdication of the governors." Dickens does not attribute moral decay to the failure of the gentry to take a leadership position in solving society's problems. Dickens's gentry are not negligent like the gentry in *Mansfield Park, Persuasion,* and *Coelebs*; rather they are incompetent and unable to cope with a world they find bewildering and incomprehensible. Unable to understand how an ironmonger can be elected to Parliament, Sir Leicester says, "It is a remarkable example of the confusion into which the present age has fallen; of the obliteration of landmarks, the opening of floodgates, and the uprooting of distinctions" (365). Because his knowledge of the world is obsolete and his rules are outmoded, Sir Leicester and his set are incapable of dealing with the likes of Jo and the problems presented by places like Tom-All-Alone's, for in these "tumbling tenements" vermin appear, "sowing more evil in its every footprint than Lord Coodle and Sir Thomas Doodle, and Duke of Foodle, and all the fine gentlemen in office, down to Zoodle, shall set right in five hundred years—though born expressly to do it" (204).

Dickens gives us the police state and the housewife to deal with the vagrancy and poverty generated by the agricultural and industrial revolutions. Empowered by techniques of surveillance, Mr. Bucket is authorized by the State to fill the gap left by the failure of both the gentry and middle-class charitable ladies to effect any change in the lives of the poor. Mr. Skimpole, nobody's fool, offers a telling analysis of Mr. Bucket: "He is the knowing man. . . . Skimpole deems it essential, in its little place, to the general cohesion of things, that he *should* think well of Bucket. The State expressly asks him to trust to Bucket. And he does" (773). And so does Esther, which in the world of *Bleak House* is another important endorsement. Trusting him completely, she relinquishes herself to his care while they search the wide world for her mother. "I knew he was far more capable than I of deciding what we ought to do" (731), Esther says in response to Mr. Bucket's "You can trust me" (730). Their journey together in search of the wayward Lady Dedlock—Esther safely enclosed in the carriage while Mr. Bucket alternates between walking and riding on top—represents Dickens's solution to the destructive forces that threaten society's cohesion. Each in his or her own way and in his or her own sphere acts as a force for order, Mr. Bucket by spying on people and coercing their compliance with the law and Esther by keeping account books, nursing the sick, and teaching Caddy to clean closets. Because they remain firmly in their own sphere of activity, their functions are complementary, not conflictual, and together they move through the muck and fog of London's streets bringing order to the lives of the people they touch.

Notes

INTRODUCTION

1. Raymond Williams traces this transition from feudal and "post-feudal arrangements" (60) to agrarian capitalism in *The Country and the City* (New York: Oxford University Press, 1973), esp. chaps. 7–11. Williams writes: "What really happened was that in the economically dynamic areas a capitalist social system was pushed through to a position of dominance, by a form of legalised seisure enacted by representatives of the beneficiary class. . . . But it cannot be isolated from the long development of concentration of landholding, from the related stratification of owners and tenants, and from the increasing number of the landless, which were the general consequences of agrarian capitalism" (98). E. P. Thompson describes this transition from a paternal order to a capitalist order as "the breakdown of the old moral economy of provision" and " the breakthrough of the new political economy of the free market" (136). See "The Moral Economy of the English Crowd in the Eighteenth Century," *Past and Present* 50 (1971): 76–136. See also the discussion of enclosure and the laborer's loss of property rights in chap. 5 of Philip Corrigan and Derek Sayer, *The Great Arch: English State Formation as Cultural Revolution* (New York: Basil Blackwell, 1985). "The great catastrophe which above all pervades the eighteenth century is the acceleration of that great 'freeing' of labour (and thus making of labour-power) that divides wage-labouring from generalized poverty; the long movement from service to employment, from provision to production / consumption, from political theatre to the individualism (and special associationism) of the vote: enclosures" (96).

2. J.H. is most probably the Reverend John Howlett, the author of several tracts on the poor, including *Examination of Mr. Pitt's Speech* (1796) and *Enclosures*. See *Lady's Magazine* 20 (1790): 367–68.

3. I use eighteenth-century terminology to describe class. As Asa Briggs points out in his article "The Language of 'Class' in Early Nineteenth-Century England," such phrases as *middle class* and *working class* did not come into regular usage until after 1815. In the eighteenth century writers referred to ranks and orders more often than they did to class. See Briggs, id., in *Essays*

in Labour History, ed. Asa Briggs and John Saville (London: Macmillan, 1960), 43–73. But when they did use *class,* they used the plural form—*the lower classes.* I like the eighteenth-century phrase *middling classes* because it conveys a sense of the variety of people who occupied the ranks between the gentry and the poor, also a rather large and amorphous category.

4. Michel Foucault, *Discipline and Punish: The Birth of the Prison,* trans. Alan Sheridan (1975; New York: Random House, 1979), 216–25.

5. Bruce Robbins, "Telescopic Philanthropy: Professionalism and Responsibility in *Bleak House,*" in *Nation and Narration,* ed. Homi K. Bhabha (London: Routledge, 1990), 226.

CHAPTER ONE. *THE MAN OF FEELING*

1. Oliver Goldsmith, "The Deserted Village," in *Collected Works of Oliver Goldsmith,* 5 vols. ed. Arthur Friedman (London: Oxford University Press, 1966), 4:287–304, ll. 385–88.

2. See Jonathan Swift, *Gulliver's Travels,* for an example of this linking of consumption of luxury items, imperialism, and moral corruption: "I assured him [Gulliver's Houyhnhnm master], that this whole Globe of earth must be at least three Times gone round, before one of our better Female Yahoos could get her Breakfast, or a Cup to put it in. . . . In order to feed the Luxury and Intemperance of the Males, and the Vanity of the Females, we sent away the greatest Part of our necessary Things to other Countries, from whence in Return we brought the Materials of Diseases, Folly, and Vice, to spend among ourselves." See Jonathan Swift, "A Voyage to the Country of the Houyhnhnms," *Gulliver's Travels* (1726: New York: Oxford University Press, 1990), 256.

3. See John Sekora's study of luxury as an important moral and political concept: *The Concept of Luxury in Western Thought, Eden to Smollett* (Baltimore: Johns Hopkins University Press, 1977).

4. Robert Southey, *Sir Thomas More; or, Colloquies on the Progress and Prospects of Society,* 2 vols. (London, 1829), 2:224–25.

5. Thomas Carlyle, "Chartism" (1839), in *The Works of Thomas Carlyle,* 30 vols. (1897; reprint New York: AMS Press, 1974), 29:156.

6. It is important to stress the difference between commerce and capitalism. Wallerstein defines *capitalism* as "that concrete, time-bounded, space-bounded integrated locus of productive activities within which the endless accumulation of capital has been the economic objective or 'law' that has governed or prevailed in fundamental economic activity." See Immanuel Wallerstein, *Historical Capitalism* (New York: Verso, 1983), 18, and id., *The Modern World System III: The Second Era of Great Expansion of the Capitalist World-Economy, 1740s-1840s* (New York: Academic Press, 1989). I take a more orthodox position and argue that money generated by high finance and merchant trade does not create capitalist relations. In other words, there is a difference between money and capital. As Elizabeth Fox-Genovese and Eugene Genovese argue, it is a mistake to see "capitalism as identical with large-scale commerce," for commerce "could not create capitalist social relations or a new system of production," and merchant capital remained "subservient to existing systems of production," existing as "parasites on the old order." See *Fruits of Merchant Capital: Slavery and Bourgeois Property in the Rise and*

Expansion of Capitalism (New York: Oxford University Press, 1983), 4–5. Capitalist social and economic relations are created when human effort is turned into "a commodity, and, as such, an article of trade," to quote from Edmund Burke, "Thoughts on Scarcity," *The Works of the Rt. Hon. Edmund Burke* (London: Oxford University Press, 1927), 4:10. David McNally is in agreement with the Genoveses, arguing that "capitalism was the product of an immense transformation in the social relationships of landed society." Merchants and manufacturers were incapable of "fundamentally transforming the essential relations of precapitalist society. Rather, the changes in agrarian economy, which drove rural producers from their land, forced them onto the labour market as wage labourers for their means of subsistence, and refashioned farming as an economic activity based upon the production of agricultural commodities for profit on the market, established the essential relations of modern capitalism" (xi–xii). See David McNally, *Political Economy and the Rise of Capitalism* (Berkeley: University of California Press, 1988), in particular the introduction and chapter 5. R. S. Neale also describes the landowners and landed aristocracy as agrarian capitalists who, playing the part of the "big" bourgeoisie, "led the transformation of England in the eighteenth century" (78). See R. S. Neale, *Writing Marxist History: British Society, Economy and Culture since 1700* (Oxford: Basil Blackwell, 1985), chap. 4.

7. Henry Mackenzie, *The Man of Feeling,* ed. Brian Vickers (1771; reprint New York: Oxford University Press, 1987), 87. Subsequent references are to this edition and appear in parentheses following the quotation. For a general discussion of Mackenzie's place in the development of the novel, see J. M. S. Tompkins, *The Popular Novel in England 1770–1800* (1932; reprint Lincoln: University of Nebraska Press, 1961), and for an understanding of the novel of sensibility, see Marilyn Butler, *Jane Austen and the War of Ideas* (Oxford: Oxford University Press, 1987); Janet Todd, *Sensibility: An Introduction* (New York: Routledge, 1986); John K. Sheriff, *The Good-Natured Man: The Evolution of a Moral Ideal, 1660–1800* (Tuscaloosa: University of Alabama Press, 1982); Stuart Tave, *The Amiable Humorist: A Study in Comic Theory and Criticism of the Eighteenth and Early Nineteenth Centuries* (Chicago: University of Chicago Press, 1960); R. F. Brissenden, *Virtue in Distress: Studies in the Novel of Sentiment from Richardson to Sade* (New York: Barnes and Noble, 1974); John Mullan, *Sentiment and Sociability: The Language of Feeling in the Eighteenth Century* (Oxford: Clarendon Press, 1988), chap. 3, "The Availability of Virtue," 114–46. See Mullan's interesting treatment of class in Mackenzie's novels: "The unlikely appearance of land-ownership in Mackenzie's novels as a basis for the operation of fellow-feeling is a literary device eschewing political projection. As a general fact, it is not possible to identify the virtue of feeling as represented in the novel of sentiment with any particular social class, nor yet with antagonism to any class" (132).

8. Farms are described not in terms of acreage, but in terms of the rental price. In the appendix of the fourth volume of *The Farmer's Tour through the East of England* (1771) Arthur Young constructed an elaborate table correlating rent with acreage. Usually the rent of good farmland would be a pound per acre—a three-hundred-acre farm would thus rent for three hundred pounds. Of course, if the land was poor and not fit for farming, it would be let for much

less—perhaps two acres a pound; some very rich land could be let for more as well.

9. I have found the following historians' accounts of paternalism most helpful: Howard Newby, *Country Life: A Social History of Rural England* (London: Weidenfeld and Nicholson, 1987); id., "Deferential Dialectic," *Comparative Studies in Society and History* 17 (1975): 139–64; id., *The Deferential Worker: A Study of Farm Workers in East Anglia* (Madison: University of Wisconsin Press, 1979); id., "Paternalism and Capitalism," in *Industrial Society: Class, Cleavage and Control*, ed. Richard Scase (New York: St. Martin's Press, 1977); Howard Newby et al., *Property, Paternalism, and Power: Class and Control in Rural England* (Madison: University of Wisconsin Press, 1978); D. C. Mills, *Landlord and Peasant in Nineteenth-Century Britain* (London: Croom Helm, 1980); G. E. Mingay, *English Landed Society in the Eighteenth-Century* (London: Routledge and Kegan Paul, 1963); id., *The Gentry: The Rise and Fall of a Ruling Class* (London: Longman, 1976); G. E. Mingay, ed. *The Victorian Countryside*, 2 vols. (London: Routledge and Kegan Paul, 1981); David Roberts, *Paternalism in Early Victorian England* (New Brunswick, N.J.: Rutgers University Press, 1977); E. P. Thompson, *The Making of the English Working Class* (New York: Random House, 1964); id., "The Moral Economy of the English Crowd in the Eighteenth Century," *Past and Present* 50 (1974): 76–136; F. M. L. Thompson, *English Landed Society in the Nineteenth Century* (London: Routledge and Kegan Paul, 1963).

10. See Harold Perkin, *Origins of Modern English Society* (1969; reprint London: Routledge and Kegan Paul, 1985), 49. I have found Perkin's discussions of the "old society" with its "bonds of patronage and dependency" (179) and of the landed classes' abdication of paternal responsibilities in chaps. 2, 6, 7 very useful.

11. J. G. A. Pocock, *Virtue, Commerce, and History* (New York: Cambridge University Press, 1988), 48.

12. William Cobbett was very concerned about the dissolution of paternal ties between farmers and their laborers. Attacking the shift from moral to political economies and the creation of what he called the "farming aristocracy, who now mix with attorneys, bankers, jews, jobbers, and all sorts of devils," he fears that "the link in the connection, the community of feeling, between the farmer and the labourer is broken" (*Cobbett's Weekly Political Register*, April 7, 1821, 10). Nathaniel Kent, agricultural expert, wrote that laborers who have been treated well by their masters will display an "attachment to their masters that is exemplary." Such a man will have "a stake in the common interest of the country," and "he is a strong link in the chain of national security." See Kent, "On the Poor," Essay XXXI, *Georgical Essays* 6 (1804): 468–71.

13. Nathaniel Kent, *Hints to Gentlemen of Landed Property* (London, 1775), 259, 240; Robert Southey, *Sir Thomas More; or, Colloquies on the Progress and Prospects of Society*, 2 vols. (London, 1829), 2:224–25; William Marshall, *On the Management of Landed Estates* (London, 1806), 374. Marshall's book, meant to be used by "professional men," is a condensed, single-volume version of his huge *Treatise on Landed Property* (London, 1804).

14. Newby, *Country Life*, 15.

15. For a discussion of John Locke's contribution to the concept of private

property, see David Rose et al., "Ideologies of Property: A Case Study," *Sociological Review* n.s. (1976): 699–730, esp. 699–709.

16. Newby, *Country Life*, 15, 8–16.

17. Marshall, *On the Management of Landed Estates*, 373.

18. William Marshall, *The Rural Economy of Yorkshire*, 2 vols. (London, 1788), 1:23, 36; Marshall, *On the Management of Landed Estates*, 378.

19. Marshall, *The Rural Economy of Yorkshire*, 1:36, 37; Marshall, *On the Management of Landed Estates*, 377–79.

20. Marshall, *On the Management of Landed Estates*, 378–79.

21. Thompson, "The Moral Economy of the Crowd," 94–107.

22. Kent argues that the decline in open markets is very destructive to the small farmer: "While the great farmer and miller are allowed to settle large bargains in a private room, from the exhibition of a mere pocket sample, a country may at any time be kept in the dark as to the real quantity of corn in it, and little farmers, by this means, must be quite ruined. I wish, therefore, to see fairs encouraged, and private markets revived" ("On the Size of Farms," *Georgical Essays* 5 [1803], 285).

23. For a discussion of the role of accounting in Young's effort to represent the farm as "a production unit" (73), see Keith Tribe, *Land, Labour and Discourse* (London: Routledge, 1978), chap. 4, "The Agricultural Treatise, 1600–1800." For a study of England's greatest landowning family and their policies on estate management, see J. R. Wordie, *Estate Management in Eighteenth-Century England: The Building of the Leveson-Gower Fortune* (London: Royal Historical Society, 1982). For nineteenth-century estate management, see David Spring, *The English Landed Estate in the Nineteenth Century: Its Administration* (Baltimore: Johns Hopkins University Press, 1963).

24. Twentieth-century social, economic, and agricultural historians have been debating the economic and social effect of enclosure on the small yeoman farmer and laborer. The spectrum of interpretation runs from J. L. and Barbara Hammond, *The Village Labourer* (London: Longmans, Green, and Co., 1927), a one-sided account that stressed the small farmer's and laborer's loss of access to open fields and their consequent impoverishment and eventual displacement, to more recent statistical accounts by economic historians, notably G. E. Mingay and J. D. Chambers, who, like Arthur Young, celebrate enclosure and the agricultural revolution. See Chambers and Mingay, *The Agricultural Revolution 1750–1880* (New York: Schocken Books, 1966). See also Mingay, "The Eighteenth-Century Land Steward," in *Land, Labour and Population in the Industrial Revolution,* ed. E. L. Jones and G. E. Mingay (London: Edward Arnold, 1967). For an interesting assessment of this debate, see John Barrell, *The Idea of Landscape and a Sense of Place 1730–1840* (Cambridge: Cambridge University Press, 1972), 189–215.

25. Arthur Young, *A Six Weeks Tour, through the Southern Counties of England and Wales* (London, 1768), 21–22.

26. Arthur Young, *The Farmer's Tour through the East of England,* 4 vols. (London, 1771), 2:161.

27. Arthur Young, *The Farmer's Letters to the People of England* (London, 1767), 286–87.

28. Kent, *Hints to Gentlemen,* 205.

29. Kent, *Hints to Gentlemen,* 205, 227; Kent, "On the Size of Farms," *Georgical Essays,* 5:281. See also his impassioned attack on engrossment in *Hints to Gentlemen of Landed Property*: "Those who contribute towards the destruction of small farms, can have very little reflection. If they have, their feelings are not to be envied. Where this has been the practice, we see a vast number of families reduced to poverty, and misery, the poor rates much increased, the small articles of provision greatly diminished in quantity, and number, and consequently augmented in price" (210–11).

30. Newby, *Country Life,* 11.

31. Young, *A Six Weeks Tour,* 54. As a second son, Arthur Young did not expect to inherit his father's modest estate, so he embarked on a mercantile career, taking a position in his uncle's countinghouse (*Dictionary of National Biography* [London: Oxford University Press, 1921–22], 21:1272–73).

32. The following potato crop table is representative of the many tables and charts that fill Young's agricultural narratives:

EXPENSES	£	s.	d.
Four ploughings, at 5 s.	1	0	0
Three harrowings, at 6s.		1	6
Twelve loads of dung, half price 1s. 6d.	0	18	0
Carriage of ditto		6	0
	2	5	6

[next page]

BROUGHT OVER	£	s.	d.
Dung, filling and spreading	2	5	6
Planting, men and women	0	2	0
Seed, 30 bushels, cut, &c.	2	0	0
Rolling	0	0	6
Skim-hoe twice	0	2	0
Hand-hoe	0	3	6
Earth up twice	0	2	0
Weeding	0	1	6
Gathering Tops	0	2	0
Taking up and pying	2	0	0
Rent	1	7	0
Taxes	0	6	0
	9	8	8
PRODUCE			
480 bushels worth, in feeding bullocks young cattle, horses, &c. 8d. a bushel	16	0	0
EXPENSES	9	8	8
	6	11	4

General View of the Agriculture of the County of Lincoln (1799), 143–44.

33. Young, *Farmer's Letters,* 294.

34. John Mordant, *The Complete Steward, or the Duty of a Steward to his Lord. Containing several new methods for the improvement of his Lord's estate,* 2 vols. (London, 1761), 2:382.

35. Leonore Davidoff and Catherine Hall, *Family Fortunes: Men and Women of the English Middle Class, 1780–1850* (Chicago: University of Chicago Press, 1987), 202.

36. Arthur Young, *Rural Oeconomy and Farmer's Kalendar* (1770), quoted in Newby, *Country Life,* 27.

37. Newby, *Country Life,* 14.

38. Max Weber, *On Charisma and Institution Building,* ed. S. N. Eisenstadt (Chicago: University of Chicago Press, 1968), 140–42.

39. Newby, *Country Life,* 25; Mingay, "The Eighteenth-Century Land Steward," 27.

40. See Raymond Williams's treatment of the effect of enclosure on rural communities in his chapter "Enclosures, Commons and Communities," *The Country and the City,* 96–107.

41. Brian Vickers, ed., "Introduction," *The Man of Feeling* (1771; reprint New York: Oxford University Press, 1987), vii.

42. Letter from Lady Louisa Stuart to Sir Walter Scott, quoted in ibid., viii.

43. Karl Marx, *Capital: A Critique of Political Economy,* vol. 1, trans. Ben Fowkes (1867; reprint New York: Random House, Vintage Books, 1977), 166–67.

44. Newby, "Paternalism and Capitalism," 70.

45. Marshall, *On the Management of Landed Estates,* 377.

46. John Throsby, *Select Views of Leicestershire,* 2 vols. (Leicester and London, 1791), 2:217.

47. Joseph Arch, quoted by F. M. L. Thompson, "Landowners and Rural Community," in *Victorian Countryside,* 2:457–58.

48. Thompson, "Landowners and the Rural Community," 458.

49. John Stuart Mill, *Principles of Political Economy, Books IV and V* (1848; reprint New York: Penguin, 1985), 119.

50. Newby, "Paternalism and Capitalism," 70–72; id., "The Deferential Dialectic," 143.

51. Perkin, *Origins of Modern English Society,* 51. Newby notes that "effective paternalism is therefore related to size, for above a certain size, personal, traditional modes of control break down" ("Paternalism and Capitalism," 73).

52. F. M. L. Thompson asserts that England "remained down to 1914, or more precisely until 1922, not merely an aristocratic country, but a country of a landed aristocracy" (quoted in Newby, *Property, Paternalism and Power,* 32). See Raymond Williams's discussion of the way in which the traditional system used pity and sympathy for a lost past as a way of displacing present abuses of the system: "The English landowning class, which had changed itself in changing its world, was idealised and displaced into an historical contrast with its own real activities. In its actual inhumanity, it could be recognized only

with difficulty by man linked to and 'dependent on it'. . . . The real ruling class could not be put in question so they were seen as temporarily absent, or as the good old people succeeded by the bad new people—themselves succeeding themselves" (*The Country and the City*, 83). Williams argues that it is the landowning class that engages in this regret for the old days as a way to disguise its power, while I am arguing that the middle class also participated in this discourse as a way to insert themselves into powerful positions in the rural economy.

53. Quoted from Sir Walter Scott's journal by Vickers, "Introduction," viii–ix.

CHAPTER TWO. ECONOMIC MAN AND CIVIC VIRTUE

1. For an interesting treatment of the history of the portrayal of the hero in eighteenth-century literature, see Robert Folkenflik's collection of essays *The English Hero, 1660–1800* (Newark: University of Delaware Press, 1982), in particular, J. Paul Hunter's "Fielding and the Disappearance of Heroes," 116–42, Arthur Lindley's "Richardson's Lovelace and the Self-dramatizing Hero of the Restoration," 195–204, and Howard Anderson's "Gothic Heroes," 205–21.

2. One conduct book writer cautions mothers against indulging their children's appetites: "It is doubtful whether the bodies or the minds of children sustain the greatest injury from the inordinate gratification of their appetites . . . ; sometimes in consequence of early indulgence . . . , the habit of self-denial is very difficult to form, perhaps is never acquired; and a life of disease is endured for want of it." See Ann Taylor, *Practical Hints to Young Females on the Duties of a Wife, a Mother and a Mistress of a Family* (London, 1815), 51.

3. Samuel Richardson, *Pamela, or Virtue Rewarded* (1740; reprint New York: Penguin, 1980), 278.

4. Jane Austen, *Pride and Prejudice* (1813; reprint New York: Oxford University Press, 1989), 328.

5. Robert Bage, *Mount Henneth* (1782; reprint New York: Garland, 1979), 1:70. Subsequent references are to this edition and appear in parentheses following the quotation.

6. William Godwin, *Things as They are or the Adventures of Caleb Williams* (1794; reprint New York; Penguin, 1988), 19. Subsequent references are to this edition and appear in parentheses following the quotation.

7. For a discussion of both Godwin and Bage as critics of the landed aristocracy, see Marilyn Butler, *Jane Austen and the War of Ideas* (Oxford: Clarendon Press, 1987), chap. 3; Gary Kelly, *English Jacobin Novel 1780–1805* (Oxford: Clarendon Press, 1976), chap. 4; and Mona Scheuermann, *Social Protest in the Eighteenth-Century Novel* (Columbus: Ohio State University Press, 1985), chaps. 6, 8. See also Peter Faulkner's biography of Bage for a discussion of *Mount Henneth* as a novel in which "middle-class values are shown to be superior to those of the aristocracy" (*Robert Bage* [Boston: Twayne, 1979], 38).

8. See John Barrell's discussion of the rural professional class in *The Idea of Landscape and the Sense of Place 1730–1840* (Cambridge: Cambridge University Press, 1972).

9. Young, *Farmer's Letters*, 293–96.

10. Marshall, *The Rural Economy of Norfolk, Comprising the Management of Landed Estates and the Present Practice of Husbandry*, 2 vols. (London, 1788), 2:201.

11. Newby, *Country Life*, 25–26.

12. Marshall, *On the Landed Property of England, an elementary and practical Treatise; containing the Purchase, the Improvement, and the Management of Landed Estates* (London, 1804), 349.

13. Mordant, *The Complete Steward*, 2:266–68.

14. Ibid., 207.

15. Marshall, *On the Landed Property of England*, 338–39.

16. Arthur Young, *A General View of the Agriculture of the County of Lincoln* (London, 1799), 20.

17. Marshall, *On the Landed Property of England*, 346–49.

18. Davidoff and Hall, *Family Fortunes*, 205. Davidoff and Hall argue, "The valuation of actions and materials in monetary terms . . . was an essential part of the middle-class challenge to the aristocratic male whose skills lay with gambling, duelling, sporting and sexual prowess" (205). With their ability to regulate "spatial, temporal, and social, as well as financial categories (319), the new middle classes could claim superiority to the upper classes and thus challenge "the earlier aristocratic hegemony" (30). For a detailed and comprehensive discussion of middle-class masculinity, see Davidoff and Hall, *Family Fortunes*, esp. chaps. 4, 5.

19. Newby, *Country Life*, 25.

20. For a more extensive treatment of Godwin's politics, see Marilyn Butler, *Romantics, Rebels and Reactionaries; English Literature and Its Background 1760–1830* (Cambridge: Cambridge University Press, 1981), and H. T. Dickinson, *British Radicalism and the French Revolution 1789–1815* (Oxford: Blackwell, 1985).

21. For a perceptive analysis of Falkland and his quest for masculine virtue, see Kate Ferguson Ellis, *The Contested Castle: Gothic Novels and the Subversion of Domestic Ideology* (Urbana: University of Illinois Press, 1989).

22. While not particularly sophisticated artistically, *Mount Henneth*, an extremely rich text in terms of verbalizing ideological and political positions, is only now receiving the attention it merits. In "Bluestockings in Utopia" Ruth Perry examines Bage's representation of educated women and how the text relocates them within traditional class and gender hierarchies by reinscribing them within the domestic realm. See Perry's essay in *History, Gender, and Eighteenth-Century British Literature*, ed. Beth Fowkes Tobin (Athens: University of Georgia Press, forthcoming). In a paper delivered at MLA (1990) titled "The Native and the Nabob: Representations of Indian Experience in Eighteenth-Century Literature," Renju Juneja examines the portion of the novel that treats British imperialism in India. She argues that in having Mr. Foston, an East India merchant and moneylender, invest his enormous capital in a British estate, Bage counters contemporary images of the greedy, vulgar nabob by making his Mr. Foston a model of civic virtue. In "India in the Novels of Robert Bage," a paper also delivered at MLA in 1990, Chaman L. Sahni delineates Bage's anticolonial stance. Another part of this heterogenous narra-

tive that would prove fruitful to inquiry is Bage's fascination with America and the revolutionary war.

23. The Stanleys and another family, the Caradocs, into which the Stanleys eventually marry, are represented as being obsessed with their family's genealogy and heraldry. The Caradoc estate contains a museum devoted to the collection of armor worn by their warrior ancestors. On display is their genealogy, "the lineage of this august house, ascending, descending, and collateral," inscribed in a book "wherein the or, the argent, the gules, the ermine, and the azure, were displayed in rich emblazonry" (2:81–2). Bage also represents these rank-conscious gentry as being greedy and very interested in accumulating money, and he is quite critical of the methods they use to acquire this liquid asset. Employing the only "honorable" means available to the gentry who desire to accumulate wealth, Robert Stanley tries to marry his son into the Foston fortune, even though it means marrying down, and he tries to marry Laura Stanley to an old miser worth ten thousand pounds. Bage cleverly transposes stereotypes, representing the merchant as generous and benevolent and the gentleman as avaricious and selfish.

24. Daniel Defoe, *Roxana, the Fortunate Mistress,* ed. David Blewett (1724; reprint New York: Penguin, 1982), 150–51.

25. Ibid., 210.

26. Joseph Addison, *The Spectator,* no. 69, Saturday, May 19, 1711, in *Addison and Steele: Selections from The Tatler and The Spectator,* ed. Robert J. Allen (New York: Holt, Rinehart and Winston, 1970), 213.

27. Ibid.

28. Richard Steele, *The Conscious Lovers* (1722), in *British Dramatists from Dryden to Sheridan,* ed. George H. Nettleton et al. (New York: Houghton Mifflin, 1969), IV.ii.

29. Addison, *The Spectator,* no. 69, 213.

30. George Lillo, *The London Merchant; or, The History of George Barnwell* (I.i.19–21) (1731), in *British Dramatists from Dryden to Sheridan,* 601.

31. Ibid., III.i.14–23.

32. Adam Smith, *The Wealth of Nations, Books I-III* (1776; reprint New York: Penguin, 1986), 507–08.

33. As Ruth Perry ("Bluestockings in Utopia") points out, each of these deserving young men marries an equally deserving young woman. However, the men occupy the realm of commerce and manufacture while the women stay indoors reading, sewing, and waiting for the men to return from work so that they can do their work of soothing their tired men with music and pleasant chat.

CHAPTER THREE. THE MORAL ECONOMY OF PROPERTY
IN *EMMA*

1. Readers will recognize that I have borrowed and modified more than the title of E. P. Thompson's article "The Moral Economy of the English Crowd."

2. J. S. Mill, *Principles of Political Economy,* 121.

3. See Alistair Duckworth, *The Improvement of the Estate* (Baltimore: Johns Hopkins University Press, 1971), and Marilyn Butler, *Jane Austen and*

the War of Ideas (Oxford: Clarendon Press, 1975). Beginning with Duckworth's discussion of Austen in terms of Edmund Burke and Butler's treatment of her novels as politically motivated fictions, there has been a growing movement to counteract the idea that Austen "does not involve herself in the events and issues of her time" (Butler, 294). Among those arguing for the presence of the political in Austen's novels are the Marxist literary critics Raymond Williams, *The Country and the City*, and James Thompson, *Between Self and World* (University Park: Pennsylvania State University Press, 1988); the historians R. S. Neale, "Zapp Zapped: Property and Alienation in *Mansfield Park*," in *Writing Marxist History: British Society, Economy and Culture* (Oxford: Blackwell, 1985); David A. Spring, "Interpreters of Jane Austen's Social World," in *Jane Austen: New Perspectives*, ed. Jane Todd (New York: Holmes and Meier, 1983); and Warren Roberts, *Jane Austen and the French Revolution* (New York: St. Martin's Press, 1979); the sociologist Terry Lovell, "Jane Austen and Gentry Society," in *Literature, Society, and the Sociology of Literature*, ed. Francis Barker (Essex: University of Essex, 1976); and the feminists Nancy Armstrong, *Desire and Domestic Fiction: A Political History of the Novel* (New York: Oxford University Press, 1987); Mary Evans, *Jane Austen and the State* (London: Tavistock, 1987); Claudia Johnson, *Jane Austen: Women, Politics, and the Novel* (Chicago: University of Chicago Press, 1988); Judith Newton, *Women, Power, and Subversion: Social Strategies in British Fiction, 1770–1860* (1981; reprint New York: Methuen, 1985); Mary Poovey, *The Proper Lady and the Woman Writer: Ideology as Style in the Works of Mary Wollstonecraft, Mary Shelley, and Jane Austen* (Chicago: University of Chicago Press, 1984); and Lillian Robinson, "Why Marry Mr. Collins?" in *Sex, Class, and Culture* (New York: Methuen, 1986). Basically there are two camps of historically minded Austen critics: those like Duckworth and Butler, who see Austen as a conservative, and those like Poovey and Johnson, who see Austen as subversive and therefore radical. I agree with Butler, who writes that Austen's "novels belong decisively to one class of partisan novels, the conservative" (3). However, my approach differs from Butler's (as well as from Poovey's and Johnson's), for instead of limiting my discussion of Austen's historical context to novels, I place her text within a discourse on political economy. I have found Duckworth's discussion of stewardship invaluable. However, he uses the idea of the estate as a "metonym for other inherited structures—society as a whole, a body of manners, a system of language—and 'improvements,' or the manners, in which individuals relate to their cultural inheritance" (ix), while my goal is to demonstrate that Austen's treatment of the stewardship of the estate is a political act that locates her text in a discourse on land and power.

4. Jane Austen, *Emma* (1816; reprint New York: Oxford University Press, 1988). Subsequent references are to this edition and appear in parentheses following the quotation.

5. Although Mr. Knightley is very perceptive when it comes to Frank Churchill, he is not always so clear-sighted when it comes to understanding Emma's feelings and motivations. Just as much an "imaginist" (302) as Emma, Mr. Knightley misreads her relationship with Churchill, misconstruing her depressed looks after the announcement of the Fairfax-Churchill engagement and misinterpreting her injunction to remain silent when he is about to propose to her.

6. Thomas Gisborne, *An Enquiry into the Duties of Men in the Higher and Middle Classes of Society* (London, 1795), 384.

7. Sir James Caird, *The Landed Interest and the Supply of Food* (1878; reprint London: Cass, 1967), 56–57.

8. Gisborne, *Duties of Men,* 403. Gisborne is quite explicit about a landlord's duties to his rural community. A landlord must set an example for his tenants, dependents, and laborers "by reproving the idle, and restraining the vicious: by checking discontent, and discouraging turbulence and sedition, and pointing out the benefits resulting from subordination in society, and the blessing secured even to the poorest subject under the British constitution: by making his alms and charities subservient, as far as the urgency of distress will permit, to the interests of virtue and industry, in common cases by distinguishing with particular liberality those who lead exemplary lives, and are remarked for a careful discharge of relative and domestic duties" (406).

9. Mr. Knightley's knowledge of scientific agriculture is demonstrated by his mention of crop rotation and his desire to plant turnips. Planting turnips, advocated by Turnip Townshend, was a new farming method used to reclaim nonarable grassland by replenishing the nutrient-starved soil with vital nitrates. See G. E. Mingay, *Enclosure and the Small Farmer in the Age of the Industrial Revolution,* Economic History Series (London: Macmillan, 1968), 18–19. Clearly Mr. Knightley is unlike J. S. Mill's landowner, who has never studied the principles of "scientific agriculture," for, as Mill contends, "great landlords have seldom seriously studied anything" (*Principles of Political Economy,* 383).

10. David Davies, *The Case of Labourers in Husbandry* (London, 1795), 75.

11. The rural poor are mentioned three times in this novel: when Emma visits the sick cottager's family, when Harriet is plagued by begging gypsies, and when the Woodhouses' chicken coop is broken into by a thief, who could be, although it is not stated, a hungry vagrant. In all three instances, the poor are curiously anonymous, and the focus is all on Emma and her reactions to the cottager's sickness and poverty, on Harriet's hysteria and Frank Churchill's rescue, and on Mr. Woodhouse and his fear of burglary.

12. Mrs. Elton, though an outsider, is welcomed into the community as the wife of the vicar. She quickly becomes an intimate of the Highbury gossip scene, regularly visiting the Coles, Perrys, and Bateses and discussing local affairs. Emma, on the other hand, keeps herself removed from these "Highbury gossips!—Tiresome wretches!" (52).

13. *The Lady's Companion for Visiting the Poor* (London, 1813), v.

14. *The Friendly Female Society for relieving Poor, Infirm, and Aged Women of Good Character* (London, 1803), 3.

15. *Friendly Female Society,* 3.

16. For a similar argument about Emma's style of bestowing charity and its relation to her status as new gentry, see Jane Nardin, "Charity in *Emma,*" *Studies in the Novel* 7 (1975): 61–72.

17. H. T. Dickinson, *Liberty and Property: Political Ideology in Eighteenth-Century Britain* (New York: Holmes and Meier, 1977), 170–71. Pocock describes this "renewed (or neo-Harringtonian) assertion of the ideal of

the citizen, virtuous in his devotion to the public good and his engagement in relations of equality and ruling-and-being-ruled, but virtuous also in his independence of any relation which might render him corrupt. For this, the citizen required the autonomy of real property. . . . Property remained the assurance of virtue. It was hard to see how he could become involved in exchange relationships, or in relationships governed by the media of exchange (especially when these took the form of paper tokens of public credit) without becoming involved in dependence and corruption" (*Virtue, Commerce, and History,* 48).

See Michael McKeon, *The Origins of the English Novel, 1600–1740* (Baltimore: Johns Hopkins University Press, 1987), chap. 5, for a discussion of capitalist ideology that sought to supplant aristocratic values of service and obligation by naturalizing human appetite, validating "material self-interest," and creating value for the process of exchange (202–06). McKeon quotes Defoe, who, critical of the "'Power of Imagination' that rules the modern world of exchange value," refers to the activities of the money market as imaginary—"the Storms and Vapours of Human Fancy"—and Swift, who, attacking bankers and the cunning stock-jobbers for their "Knavery and Couzenge," is relieved by the passage of the Property Qualifications Act, which ensures that "our Properties lie no more at Mercy of those who have none themselves, or at least only what is transient or imaginary" (205, 207). See also R. D. Richards, *The Early History of Banking in England* (1929; reprint New York: Augustus M. Kelley, 1965), chap. 1, for early resistance to the money trade; for instance, "This dunghill trade of brokerie . . . newly sprung up and coined in the devil's minting house the shoppe of all mischiefe hath made many a theefe more than ever would have bin" (12).

18. The poor rate was a tax levied on property owners and distributed as charity on the parish level to the poor by a board made up of local gentry, clergy, and gentlemen-farmers.

19. William Clarkson, "Inquiry on Pauperism and Poor Rates," *Pamphleteer* 8 (1816): 390.

20. See, for instance, Patrick Colquhoun, *A Treatise on Indigence* (London, 1806), 5–7.

21. Some writers attributed the increase in the poor rates to the mismanagement and negligence of the Overseers of the Poor, the committee made up of local gentry appointed to care for the poor. Davies states that in the large parishes, "where the poor-rates amount to many hundred pounds a year, overseers of less scrupulous consciences have frequent opportunities of abusing their trust, and sometimes most iniquitously avail themselves of them, either by embezzling the public money, or by partial indulgence to favorites" (*The Case of Labourers in Husbandry,* 81). Eden reprinted in his treatise the text of the Act of Parliament "For the better Relief and Employment of the Poor" (1782), which states that more must be done for the poor "notwithstanding the great sums raised for those purposes" because "by the incapacity, negligence, or misconduct of overseers, the money raised for the relief of the Poor is frequently misapplied, and sometimes expended in defraying the charges of litigations about settlements indiscreetly and unadvisedly carried on" (reprinted in Sir Frederic Eden, *The State of the Poor,* 3 vols. [London, 1795], 3:clxxxii-iii).

22. Southey, *Colloquies,* 2:224–25.

23. Bandana, "Hints to the Country Gentlemen," *Blackwood's Magazine* 12 (1822): 96.

24. Whereas most social historians, E. P. Thompson and R. S. Neale among them, stress the disastrous consequences of enclosure on the laboring poor, most economic and agricultural historians tend to see enclosure and farm engrossment as important features of the agricultural revolution, arguing that contemporaries exaggerated the suffering of the displaced farmers and laborers. They argue that the increased productivity of the farmland made possible by enclosure and engrossment enabled England to feed its population and thus strengthened England's economic position in the world market. See Mingay, "Enclosure and the Small Farmer."

25. Kent, *Hints to Gentlemen of Landed Property,* 218–19.

26. Davies, "The Case of Labourers in Husbandry," 72–73.

27. Bandana, "Hints to the Country Gentlemen," *Blackwood's Magazine* 12 (1822): 90. This depiction of the landlord as someone who engrosses farmland and encloses common land because he is either greedy or lazy is an image that is repeated over and over in literature on landed estates, on population and poverty, and on the moral duties of the upper classes. For instance, a good landlord, Gisborne argues, is one who "regulates his life by principles of duty" ("Duties of Men," 393) and acts not in a "sordid and ungenerous manner" by consulting his "private advantage" (ibid., 398) only, and who does not depopulate the country by "turning multitudes of industrious poor adrift, by converting half a parish into an immense sheepwalk, which no longer affords occupation to a twentieth part of the former inhabitants; nor by combining many small farms into a few of great size, that he may save himself and his agent the trouble of attending petty accounts" (ibid., 393). Coleridge in his second lay sermon blames the landlords for their "unfaithful stewardship" (416), for their lack of "time or inclination" to oversee the management of their estates and the supervision of the people dependent on them. Passive landlords allow estate agents and farmers eager for profits to institute a policy of farm engrossment. The farmer "takes every particle of the land to himself, and re-lets the house to the labourers, who by these means is rendered miserable." This is, according to Coleridge, the "manner that the labourers have been dispossessed of their cow pastures" (427). See Samuel Taylor Coleridge, "A Lay Sermon addressed to the Higher and Middle Classes on the Existing Distresses and Discontents" (1817), in *On the Constitution of Church and State,* ed. Henry Nelson Coleridge (London, 1839).

28. Patrick Colquhoun, *A Treatise on the Wealth, Power, and Resources of the British Empire* (London, 1814), 106–09.

29. Nassau William Senior, *Two Lectures on Population* (London, 1829), 89.

30. Nassau William Senior, *Political Economy* (London, 1854), 89.

31. David Ricardo, *Principles of Political Economy and Taxation,* in *The Works and Correspondence of David Ricardo,* 11 vols., ed. Piero Sraffa and M. H. Dobbs (Cambridge: Cambridge University Press, 1951), 1:336.

32. Ricardo, *Essay on the External Corn Trade,* in *Works,* 4:21. Ricardo's position on landlords is quite different from Adam Smith's, at least according to

David McNally, who argues that, unlike Ricardo, Smith thought that the landlords' interests were "consistent with the general interest" of the nation (263). McNally demonstrates convincingly that Smith shared the physiocratic faith in landowners' "fixed and permanent interest in their country of residence" and their "permanent interest . . . in seeing that society is prosperous and well-governed" (263). For these reasons, Smith thought that "political power should be based upon the landed gentry" (264). See David McNally, *Political Economy and the Rise of Capitalism: A Reinterpretation* (Berkeley: University of California Press, 1988).

33. Thomas Evans, *Christian Policy* (1815), quoted in "Parliamentary Reform," *Quarterly Review* 16 (1816): 270. See William Cobbett, *Legacy to Labourers* (London, 1835).

34. See John Bohstedt, *Riots and Community Politics in England and Wales, 1790–1810* (Cambridge: Harvard University Press, 1983), chaps. 1, 8. The Corn Laws, passed in 1815, placed a tariff on imported grain and thus maintained the high wartime price of grain. Regarded as an act that promoted the welfare of the landed classes at the expense of every other rank, the Corn Laws infuriated the manufacturing interests and the laboring poor because they kept the price of bread and thus wages high.

35. Harold Perkin, *Origins of Modern English Society* (London: Routledge and Kegan Paul, 1969), 239.

36. W. Johnstone, "Our Domestic Policy," *Blackwood's* 26 (1829): 768.

37. Both David Hume and Adam Smith register their concern over the alienating and unstable nature of money derived from commerce and stock trading. Smith writes, "The capital . . . that is acquired to any country by commerce and manufacturers, is all a very precarious and uncertain possession till some part of it has been secured and realized in the cultivation and improvement of its lands" (*The Wealth of Nations,* bk. 3 [New York: Penguin, 1986], 519). Hume is also deeply suspicious of stockholders because of the unattached nature of their money: "These are men, who have no connexions with the state, who can enjoy their revenue in any part of the globe in which they chuse to reside, who will naturally bury themselves in the capital or in great cities, and who will sink into lethargy of a stupid and pampered luxury, without spirit, ambition, or enjoyment. Adieu to all ideas of nobility, gentry, and family" ("Of Public Credit," in *David Hume, Writings on Economics,* ed. Eugene Rotwein [Madison: University of Wisconsin Press, 1955], 98). Mr. Woodhouse seems to fit Hume's description of a stockholder who has declined into a state of pampered and stupid lethargy.

38. Arthur Young, *A Six Months Tour through the North of England,* 4 vols. (London, 1770), 1:307, 316–17.

39. For a discussion of the confiscation of church lands, see Karl Marx, *Capital,* 1:880–83.

40. Gisborne, "Duties of Men," 393, 398.

41. See James Thompson's discussion of marriage in his chapter on finance and romance in *Sense and Sensibility* in *Between Self and World,* 130–57.

42. Briggs, "Middle-Class Consciousness in English Politics, 1780–1846," *Past and Present* 9 (1956): 70.

43. Antonio Gramsci, *Selections from the Prison Notebooks of Antonio*

Gramsci, ed. and trans. Quintin Hoare and Geoffrey Nowell Smith (New York: International Publishers, 1971), 18.

CHAPTER FOUR. *MANSFIELD PARK* AND HANNAH MORE

1. In attempting to evaluate the degree to which Austen embraced Evangelicalism, I am reopening a topic that many might think has already been dealt with quite thoroughly by very able critics, among them Marilyn Butler, Alistair Duckworth, Avrom Fleishman, and David Monaghan. I offer an interpretation of *Mansfield Park* and of Evangelicalism that differs from previous interpretations, as it is informed by Leonore Davidoff and Catherine Hall's social history *Family Fortunes: Men and Women of the English Middle Class, 1780–1850,* by Nancy Armstrong's *Desire and Domestic Fiction: A Political History of the Novel,* and ultimately by Michel Foucault's *Discipline and Punish: The Birth of the Prison.*

2. For a discussion of the Evangelical "campaigns against worldliness, triviality, and irresponsibility in high life" (Butler, 284), see Butler's *War of Ideas,* esp. 162–67, 242–47, 284–87; Davidoff and Hall, *Family Fortunes,* chaps. 1–3; Perkin, *Origins of Modern English Society,* 280–88; F. K. Brown, *Fathers of the Victorians* (Cambridge: Cambridge University Press, 1961), chap. 1; Nancy F. Cott, "Passionlessness: An Interpretation of Victorian Sexual Ideology, 1790–1850," in *A Heritage of Her Own,* ed. Nancy F. Cott and Elizabeth H. Peck (New York: Simon and Schuster, 1979), 162–81; and Mitzi Myers, "Reform or Ruin: 'A Revolution in Female Manners,'" *Studies in Eighteenth-Century Culture* 11 (1982): 199–216.

3. Hannah More, *Coelebs in Search of a Wife: Comprehending Observations on Domestic Habits and Manners, Religion and Morals,* in *The Works of Hannah More* (1830; New York: Garland, 1982), 59. Subsequent references to this text appear in parentheses following the quotation.

4. Mary Wollstonecraft shares with More, despite their extreme political and philosophical differences, an abhorrence of the kind of education that renders a woman a fool, a bauble, "created to be the toy of man, his rattle, and it must jingle in his ears whenever, dismissing reason, he chooses to be amused" (118). See her *Vindication of the Rights of Woman* (1792; reprint New York: Penguin, 1983). See also Mitzi Myers's discussion of their similar positions on women's education in "Reform or Ruin: 'A Revolution in Female Manners.'"

5. Jane Austen, *Mansfield Park* (1814), in *The Novels of Jane Austen,* ed. R. W. Chapman (London: Oxford University Press, 1973), 3:463. Subsequent references to this text appear in parentheses following the quotation.

6. For a discussion of Fanny's Evangelical qualities, see Marian E. Fowler, "The Courtesy-Book Heroine of *Mansfield Park,*" *University of Toronto Quarterly* 44 (1974): 31–46. For an analysis of the concept of modesty and how it is played out in *Mansfield Park,* see Ruth Bernard Yeazell, *Fictions of Modesty: Women and Courtship in the English Novel* (Chicago: University of Chicago Press, 1991), chaps. 1–5, 9.

7. William Cowper, "Book III: The Garden," *The Task,* in *Cowper's Poems* (London: Dent, 1966), ll. 389–91. Cowper was a favorite with both Austen and More. More had in common with Cowper a friendship with John Newton, a leading Evangelical preacher. See Davidoff and Hall, *Family Fortunes,* 162–67.

8. Cowper, "Book IV: The Winter Evening," *The Task*, ll. 36–41.

9. R. W. Dale, *The Life and Letters of John Angell James,* quoted in Davidoff and Hall, *Family Fortunes,* 129.

10. As Kenneth L. Moler suggests ("The Two Voices of Fanny Price," in *Jane Austen: Bicentenary Essays,* ed. John Halperin [Cambridge: Cambridge University Press, 1975], 176), there is a childishness and a bookishness about Fanny's raptures over the stars. Fanny's rhapsody on stars is reminiscent of Jane Taylor's "Twinkle, twinkle little star," published in *Rhymes for the Nursery, by the Authors of 'Original Poems'* (1806). An Evangelical, Taylor also wrote a story about a girl who, looking out of a window, lets her mind revel "mid the stars" and her imagination to range "through the sky . . . with untold delight" to "watch the changing splendors of the night. . . . While thought is free, how'er enslaved the wretch, he has a circuit where no arm can reach" (*Memoirs* [1831], 295). See Davidoff and Hall for a fuller discussion of star imagery in Taylor's work (*Family Fortunes,* 450–54).

11. Davidoff and Hall, *Family Fortunes,* 87. For an insightful study of Hannah More, her relationship with the laboring poor she worked with, and her need to control their impulses and desires, see Beth Kowaleski-Wallace, *Their Fathers' Daughters: Hannah More, Maria Edgeworth, and Patriarchal Complicity* (New York: Oxford University Press, 1991), chaps. 2, 3.

12. Mrs. Helen Knight, *Hannah More or Life in Hall and Cottage* (New York: M. W. Dodd, 1851), 309. Knight quotes from More's writings profusely (and accurately as far as I can determine); however, she rarely cites the text, only occasionally mentioning the title of the piece she is quoting from. I have tracked down many but not all of the sources she cites. I cite from Knight when I cannot locate the original More quote. Subsequent references to this text appear in parentheses following the quotation.

13. Hannah More, *Thoughts on the Importance of the Manners of the Great to General Society,* in *The Works of Hannah More* (Philadelphia: J. D. Maxwell, 1818), 3:187.

14. Hannah More, *Christian Morals,* in *The Works of Hannah More* (1818), 3:99.

15. Ann Martin Taylor, *Practical Hints to Young Females on the Duties of a Wife, a Mother and a Mistress of a Family* (1815), 27.

16. More's concern that the gentry were giving alms to the wrong people—"the undeserving poor"—echoes William Cowper's description of the plight of the "deserving poor" at the hands of parish officials:

> . . . lib'ral of their aid
> To clam'rous importunity in rags,
> But oft-times deaf to suppliants, who would blush
> To wear a tatter'd garb however coarse,
> Whom famine cannot reconcile to filth:
> These ask with painful shyness, and, refus'd
> Because deserving, silently retire!
> ("Book IV: The Winter Evening," *The Task*, ll. 413–19)

Similar opinions are expressed by Joseph Townsend in his very influential tract on the poor laws. Townsend argues that the poor laws encourage "idleness and vice" by misapplying funds collected for "industry in distress." Men who wish to be charitable are "harassed by the clamours and distracted by the incessant demands of the most improvident and lazy of the surrounding poor; and he will have little inclination to seek for objects of distress, or to visit the sequestered cottage of the silent sufferer. It is generally found, that modest worth stands at a distance, or draws nigh with faltering tongue and broken accents to tell an artless tale; whilst the most worthless are the most unreasonable in their expectations, and the most importunate in their solicitation for relief" (*A Dissertation on the Poor Laws* [1786; reprint Berkeley: University of California Press, 1971], 17–19).

17. More, *Cheap Repository Tracts*, in *Works* (1818), 2:179–80.

18. More, *Estimate of the Religion of the Fashionable World*, in *Works* (1818), 3:221–22.

19. Ellis, *The Contested Castle*, 11. In "The Notion of Expenditure" Georges Bataille writes, "A fundamental grievance of the bourgeois was the prodigality of feudal society and, after coming to power, they believed that, because of their habits of accumulation, they were capable of acceptably dominating the poorer classes" (*Visions of Excess: Selected Writings, 1927–39*, trans. Alan Stoekl [Minneapolis: University of Minnesota Press, 1985], 125).

20. Davidoff and Hall, *Family Fortunes*, 76.

21. Andrew Ure, *Philosophy of Manufactures* (1835), quoted in E. P. Thompson, *The Making of the English Working Class* (New York: Random House, 1966), 360.

22. Armstrong, *Desire and Domestic Fiction*, 93.

23. Ellis, *The Contested Castle*, 49.

24. J. G. A. Pocock, *Virtue, Commerce, and History* (Cambridge: Cambridge University Press, 1985), 48.

25. Bataille, "The Notion of Expenditure," 121–23.

26. An example of Sir Thomas's consideration is his asking that a fire be lit in Fanny's room: "A fire! it seemed too much; just at that time to be giving her such an indulgence, was exciting even painful gratitude. . . . 'I must be a brute indeed, if I can be really ungrateful!' said she in soliloquy; 'Heaven defend me from being ungrateful!'" (322–23).

27. See Harold Perkin for a discussion of the hierarchy based on patronage and gratitude (*Origins of Modern English Society*, 40–49).

28. Crawford rarely visits his estate in Norfolk, choosing to spend his time in London and other places of pleasure. As a result the estate is run by a less-than-honest agent who has "imposed" (411) on Crawford and is engaged in "some underhand dealing" (404). Crawford knows that "the mischief such a man does on an estate, both as to the credit of his employer, and the welfare of the poor, is inconceivable" (412), and yet he does nothing to protect his estate community from his agent and his agent's crony, "a hard-hearted, griping fellow" (412). Crawford knows that he should return to his estate to set things right: "I must make him know that I will not be tricked . . . , that I will be master of my own property" (411). But Crawford does not go home to his estate to do his "duty" (404) and instead returns to London and his flirtation with Maria.

29. Bataille, "The Notion of Expenditure," 123.

30. This, of course, is Alistair Duckworth's point in *The Improvement of the Estate*. Fanny becomes the daughter Sir Thomas has always wanted because she has the "courage to maintain faith in 'principles' and 'rules of right' even when these are everywhere ignored and debased" (80).

31. See Mary Poovey's discussion of the rise of the middle classes in *Persuasion* in *The Proper Lady and the Woman Writer.* See Robert Hopkins's critique of Poovey's assertion that the gentry were on the decline in the beginning of the nineteenth century ("Moral Luck and Judgment in Jane Austen's *Persuasion,*" *Nineteenth-Century Literature* 42 (1987–88): 143–58. For an interesting discussion of the contradictions in Austen's treatment of the gentry in *Persuasion,* see David M. Monaghan, "The Decline of the Gentry: A Study of Jane Austen's Attitude to Formality in *Persuasion,*" *Studies in the Novel* 7 (1975): 73–87.

32. Austen, *Persuasion* (1818; reprint New York: Oxford University Press, 1989), 91, 96.

33. Mary Musgrove, always jealous of and competitive with her sisters, worries that when Anne marries Wentworth she will be "restored to the rights of seniority" but consoles herself by saying, "Anne had no Uppercross-hall before her, no landed estate, no headship of a family; and if they could but keep Captain Wentworth from being made a baronet, she would not change situations with Anne" (235). The implication here is that Anne, in marrying Wentworth, has not left the ranks of the landed gentry permanently; Captain Wentworth might have enough prize money to purchase an estate.

CHAPTER FIVE. WOMEN AND THE CLERGY

1. See Halevy's discussion of the Church of England in *A History of the English People in 1815* (1924; reprint London: Routledge, 1987), 341–52.

2. George Crabbe's portrait of a squarson:

> A jovial youth, who thinks his Sunday's task
> As much as God or man can fairly ask;
> The rest he gives to loves and labors light,
> To fields the morning, and to feasts the night;
> None better skilled the noisy pack to guide,
> To urge their chase, to cheer them or to chide;
> A sportsman keen, he shoots through half the day,
> And, skilled at whist, devotes the night to play.
> Then, while such honors bloom around his head,
> Shall he sit sadly by the sick man's bed,
> To raise the hope he feels not, or with zeal
> To combat fears that e'en the pious feel? (ll. 306–17)

George Crabbe, "The Village: Book I" (1783), in *The Complete Poetical Works of George Crabbe,* 3 vols., ed. Norma Dalrymple-Champneys and Arthur Pollard (Oxford: Clarendon Press, 1988), 1:165–66.

3. George Eliot, *Scenes of Clerical Life* (1858; reprint Oxford: Clarendon Press, 1985), 7.

4. Elizabeth Gaskell, *My Lady Ludlow and Other Stories* (1859, 1861; reprint New York: Oxford University Press, 1989), 14. Subsequent references to this text appear in parentheses following the quotation.

5. The Rump refers to the Long Parliament of 1640–60, which defied Charles I and was responsible for his beheading and the civil war between the Roundheads (Puritans) and the Cavaliers (royalists).

6. Anne Brontë, *Agnes Grey* (1847; reprint New York: Penguin, 1988),

140. Subsequent references to this text appear in parentheses following the quotation.

7. Cited in T. J. Wise and J. S. Symington, *The Brontës: Their Lives, Friendships and Correspondence,* 4 vols. (Oxford, 1932), 1:115.

8. See Ellis, *The Contested Castle,* chaps. 1, 2, for discussions of *Pamela* and the construction of domestic femininity. See Armstrong, *Desire and Domestic Fiction,* chaps. 2, esp. 3, on the middle-class construction of the self-contained domestic woman as a way to attack the hedonistic aristocracy.

9. For a study of the didactic fiction produced by Hannah More, see Mitzi Myers, "Hannah More's Tracts for the Times: Social Fiction and Female Ideology," in *Fetter'd or Free? British Women Novelists, 1670–1815,* ed. Mary Anne Schofield and Cecilia Macheski (Athens: Ohio University Press, 1986), 264–84. For More's position in the Blagdon controversy, see Mitzi Myers, "'A Peculiar Protection': Hannah More and the Cultural Politics of the Blagdon Controversy," forthcoming.

10. Hannah More assumed the paternal role of patron to the milkmaid poetess Ann Yearsley. She behaved as any male paternalist would have, exerting her power and authority and expecting in return for her patronage Yearsley's obedience and deference. For a discussion of Hannah More's patronage of Ann Yearsley, see Donna Landry, *The Muses of Resistance: Laboring-class Women's Poetry in Britain, 1739–1796* (Cambridge: Cambridge University Press, 1990), chap. 4.

11. *Memoirs of the Life and Correspondence of Mrs. Hannah More,* 2 vols., ed. William Roberts (New York: Harper and Brothers, 1837), 2:72. Subsequent references to this text appear in parentheses following the quotation.

12. Knight, *Hannah More,* 133.

13. Knight, *Hannah More,* 132. For a critical discussion of More's Sunday school work as a form of social control, see Beth Kowaleski-Wallace, chap. 3, "Hannah and Her Sister: Women and Evangelism," in *Their Fathers' Daughters,* 56–93, and Roger Sales, *English Literature in History, 1780–1830: Pastoral and Politics* (New York: St. Martin's Press, 1983), chap. 1.

14. More, *Cheap Repository Tracts,* in *Works,* 2:176. Subsequent references to this text appear in parentheses following the quotation.

15. M. G. Jones, *Hannah More* (Cambridge: Cambridge University Press, 1952), 179.

16. William Cobbett, *Weekly Political Register* 20 (April 1822); quoted in F. K. Brown, *Fathers of Victorians,* 216.

17. Martha More, *Mendip Annals: or, a Narrative of the Charitable Labours of Hannah and Martha More in their Neighbourhood. Being the Journal of Martha More,* ed. Arthur Roberts (New York: Carter and Brothers, 1859), 44.

18. See Martha More's *Mendip Annals* for a more lively account of Bere's accusations: "At Blagdon, likewise, Satan was busy, through the instrumentality of him who called himself a preacher of the gospel, and had the immediate care of these people's souls" (ibid., 220–21).

19. See Myers, "'A Peculiar Power,'" for an analysis of Brown's gender bias.

20. Hannah More, *Practical Piety; Or, the Influence of the Religion of the Heart on the Conduct of the Life,* 2 vols. (London, 1812), 1:11. Subsequent references to this volume appear in parentheses following the quotation.

21. Quoted in W. J. Sparrow Simpson, *The History of the Anglo-Catholic Revival from 1845* (London: Allen and Unwin, 1932), 70.

22. Davidoff and Hall argue that the Anglo-Catholic movement "can be interpreted as a search for a male-bonded culture which recovered the richness, colour and music increasingly denied to men while placing women firmly in separate sisterhoods as men recreated the religious world of ritual without female interference" (*Family Fortunes,* 451).

23. Patty writes, "A visit to Cheddar now surpassed, without exaggeration, everything we had hitherto met with. . . . We found the school crowded indeed, though the day was short and wet, and all appeared full of knowledge and zeal. We stayed and read to the evening congregation, crowded also. It was truly comfortable and consoling—the people cheerful upon the best principles, pious, humble, grateful. Mr Hyde—the once lofty, insolent, proud Mr Hyde—accosted us with all the humility of a Christian of the lowest rank. He is now well informed upon the great subject. This one man is full payment for all the toil of Cheddar" (*Mendip Annals,* 95–96). Religion, "the great subject," as Patty terms it, acts as a powerful source of social control, subduing not only the poor, ignorant rabble but also the insolent gentry.

24. Foucault, *Discipline and Punish,* 187. Subsequent references to this text appear in parentheses following the quotation.

25. Foucault's interest in tracing the evolution of the "disciplinary power" is limited to its transforming of public institutions, and so, he ignores the work of women and their more private incursions into the field of converting "residual forms of feudal power" and "local mechanisms of supervision" (Foucault, *Discipline and Punish,* 217) of that power into disciplinary power. More, along with her charitable women, was at least as significant a leader in this movement as was Bentham, and her legacy is one that has not left us untouched. As Nancy Armstrong remarks, "I will insist that those cultural functions which we automatically attribute to and embody as women—those, for example, of mother, nurse, teacher, social worker, and general overseer of service institutions—have been just as instrumental in bringing the new middle classes into power and maintaining their dominance as all the economic take-offs and political breakthroughs we automatically attribute to men" (*Desire and Domestic Fiction,* 26).

26. Maria Louisa Charlesworth, *The Cottage and Its Visitor* (New York: Carter and Bros., 1860), contains a description of the function of the Sunday school fête: "The good effects of Sunday-school instruction are not always perceptible in childhood, or if perceptible, the parent may not trace the connection or appreciate the result, but the happiness of their children they can and do sympathize in, and they are disposed to look with interest on that which promotes it; and one thankfully learns to call in every aid in winning the hearts of the poor, in order to the leading them onward and upward to the truth, which is LOVE" (187).

27. See, for instance, chap. 9, "Domestic Rebellion," in Elizabeth Hamilton, *The Cottagers of Glenburnie:* "'Bless me!' cried Mrs Mason, in amazement; 'how does your butter come to be so full of hairs? Where do they come from?' 'Oh they are a' frae the cows,' returned Mrs MacClarty. 'There has been lang a hole in the milk sythe, and I have never been at the fash to get it mended. But as I tak ay care to sythe the milk through my fingers, I wonder how sae

mony hairs win in.' 'Ye need na wonder at that,' observed Grizzel, 'for the house canna be soopit but the dirt flees into the kirn.' 'But do you not clean the churn before you put in the cream?' asked Mrs Mason, more and more astonished" (199).

28. Mary Leadbeater, *Cottage Dialogues among the Irish Peasantry* (1811; reprint Dublin, 1841), iii. Subsequent references to this text appear in parentheses following the quotation.

29. Elizabeth Hamilton, *The Cottagers of Glenburnie; A Tale for the Farmer's Ingle-nook* (Edinburgh: James Ballantyne, 1808), 274. Subsequent references to this text appear in parentheses following the quotation.

30. Myers, "Hannah More's Tracts," 277.

31. The 1840s were years of widespread and devastating unemployment of industrial labor owing to the instability of newly formed, high-risk manufacturing companies. This downturn in the economy was considered the unfortunate side effect of venture capitalism and its boom/bust cycle of prosperity and failure.

32. Harriet Ritvo, *The Animal Estate: The English and Other Creatures in the Victorian Age* (Cambridge: Harvard University Press, 1987), 131–35.

33. Anne Brontë, *Agnes Grey* (1847; reprint New York: Penguin, 1988), 69. Subsequent references to this text appear in parentheses following the quotation.

34. Charlotte Brontë, *Shirley* (1849, reprint New York: Oxford University Press, 1986), 6–7.

35. See Rosemarie Bodenheimer's study of Victorian fiction *The Politics of Story in Victorian Social Fiction* (Ithaca: Cornell University Press, 1988), particularly the chapter on the female paternalist. Bodenheimer argues that Brontë's version of female charity is rendered "socially impotent" (68). Cary "rejects the idea that charity work is a solution in the lives of single women," middle-class women who live idle, empty, purposeless lives. For Cary, "such a life looks like the death of the soul" (50).

36. This may be true in general, but I must note that Elizabeth Gaskell's *North and South* is perhaps an exception, for its heroine acts benevolently and successfully in the public realm. Discussing the female paternalist, Bodenheimer argues that "Gaskell creates a heroine whose life is responsibly and directly entangled with the male world of industrial politics" (ibid., 52–53). Bodenheimer points out, however, that Margaret does not behave like the typical female paternalist, like More's Lucilla. Gaskell's heroine recognizes "that her traditional charitable role is obsolete" (ibid., 56) and has to rethink her position in the complicated class relations of an industrial town. Contrasting *North and South* with *Shirley*, Bodenheimer contends that of the two, Gaskell's novel "is more progressive, more challenging to traditional conceptions of social order, and more self-conscious about those conceptions" (ibid., 53).

37. This epithet of Carlyle refers to Joe Manton, the famous gunmaker. His point is that the gentry and aristocracy have abdicated their roles of leadership and have failed the nation in this time of crisis because they are too busy enjoying themselves on their estates shooting partridges. See Carlyle, *Past and Present* (1843), in *Works* 10:214.

38. See Bodenheimer, *The Politics of Story,* 36–53, for an insightful discussion of Brontë's book. Shirley's marriage "suggests that her immense energies find their appropriate role in relation to a powerfully benevolent husband who can nourish and regulate her psychological life" (49).

CHAPTER SIX. SELF-REGULATION IN *BLEAK HOUSE*

1. Charles Dickens, *Bleak House* (1852–53, 1868; reprint New York: Bantam, 1985), 95. Subsequent references to this text appear in parentheses following the quotation.

2. *The Lady's Companion for Visiting the Poor* (London, 1813) provides its readers with set speeches "adapted to particular occasions" with "the idea that they may possibly be of assistance to those who are unprovided with better helps, and who complain of not readily finding verbal expressions suited to the occasion" (ix). There are addresses for "Lying-In Women," "to be used shortly after a Woman's Confinement"; there are prayers for a woman "who has lost her husband"; and there are many addresses for those in sickness, even a speech for "one who has led a careless Life, but who is now awakened to a Sense of his danger" (title page).

3. "The Ladies' Royal Benevolent Society for Visiting, Relieving, and Investigating the Conditions of the Poor at their own Habitations" (pamphlet) (London, 1818), 8.

4. Quoted in Norris Pope, *Dickens and Charity* (New York: Columbia University Press, 1978), 129. For a detailed description of Dickens's antipathy toward the Clapham sect, see Pope's book on Dickens and philanthropy.

5. For a study of women's charity, see F. K. Prochaska, *Women and Philanthropy in Nineteenth-Century England* (New York: Oxford University Press, 1980). See chapter 4 on cottage visiting and the very useful and quite extensive lists of charitable organizations in the appendixes. Prochaska focuses on charitable organizations, most of which are urban and middle-class; for a study of rural, upper-class charity performed by the wives and daughters of the landowners, see Jessica Gerard, "'Lady Bountiful': Women of the Landed Class and Rural Philanthropy," *Victorian Studies* 30 (1987): 183–210. For general histories of charity, see David Owen, *English Philanthropy, 1660–1960* (Cambridge: Harvard University Press, 1964), and Betsy Rodgers, *Cloak of Charity: Studies in Eighteenth-Century Philanthropy* (London: Methuen, 1949).

6. For instance, a pamphlet titled "The Nature, Design, and Rules of the Benevolent or Stranger's Friend Society; Instituted for the Purposes of Visiting and Relieving Sick and Distressed Strangers, and other Poor, at their Respective Habitations" (London, 1804) contains a compilation of statistics on the society's charitable activities for the year. The society made 10,632 visits in 1804; 2,683 families were visited (each 4 times approximately) in one year, averaging about 338 families a month; and £162 were distributed each month (3). Subsequent references to this text appear in parentheses following the quotation. An extract reporting on the work of a "London soup shop" describes how the committee that ran the shop had wanted to "visit the dwelling of every individual, who received the benefit of the institution; to inquire into circumstances and situation, and to record each particular case." Unfortunately, this plan proved "impractical"; the committee did not have the staff to gather what

might have been "a valuable body of information relative to the situation of the poor" (*Extracts from the Reports of the English Society for Bettering the Condition of the Poor* [Dublin, 1799], extract 4, by William Hillyer, 29).

7. See Hannah More's depiction of Sir John's largesse in "A Cure for Melancholy," in *Stories for Persons in the Middle Ranks*: "He had that sort of constitutional good nature which, if he had lived much within sight of misery, would have led him to be liberal: but he had that selfish love of ease, which prompted him to give to undeserving objects, rather than be at the pains to search out the deserving" (*Works*, 2:179).

8. David E. Musselwhite remarks that the brickmaker's speech is the only prose in *Bleak House* that rings with real feeling. See *Partings Welded Together: Politics and Desire in the Late Nineteenth-Century English Novel* (London: Methuen, 1987), 226.

9. "The Influence of Pious Women in Promoting a Revival of Religion," tract no. 800, published by the Religious Tract Society (the British Library's copy has "1830?" written on the title page), 2–3; "The Nature, Design, and Rules of the Benevolent or Stranger's Friend Society" (London, 1804), 9–10, 20.

10. Sarah Stickney Ellis wrote *Daughters of England, Wives of England, Mothers of England, Women of England.*

11. Maria Edgeworth, *True Charity* (1800; reprint 1827), 136–38; Anon., *The Young Ladies' Remembrancer of Obligations, Responsibilities, and Duties* (York, 1848), 70–71.

12. Harley's tears are plentiful in Mackenzie's *The Man of Feeling.*

13. Sarah Trimmer, *The Oeconomy of Charity; or, an Address to Ladies* (London, 1787), 3–4.

14. J. S. Mill, *Principles of Political Economy,* 119.

15. Jessica Gerard, "'Lady Bountiful': Women of the Landed Class and Rural Philanthropy," 185.

16. Newby, "The Deferential Dialectic," 155, and id., *The Deferential Worker,* 44. See chapter 1 above for a discussion of Newby's definition of *paternalism.*

17. *The Young Ladies' Faithful Remembrancer of Obligations, Responsibilities, and Duties* (author of "Marriage Offering" and "Holidays at Home") encourages young ladies to visit the homes of the poor and sympathize with them, offering them "the balm of soothing tenderness" (70).

18. See Mrs. Sarah Ellis on "disinterested" kindness as a woman's most admired attribute. In *The Women of England* she urges middle-class women to develop "habits of consideration" and repeatedly uses the word *disinterested* to describe women's selfless concern for "what is best to be done for the good and the happiness of those around them." When a woman is kind, considerate, and disinterested, the "self is annihilated," which, for Ellis, should be every woman's goal. See Ellis, *The Family Monitor and Domestic Guide: Comprising The Women of England, The Daughters of England, The Wives of England, The Mothers of England* (New York: Henry G. Langley, 1844), 62–72.

19. For a discussion of Esther as housekeeper and of her role as agent of the social police, see Martin A. Danahay, "Housekeeping and Hegemony in *Bleak House,*" *Studies in the Novel* 23 (1991): 416–31.

20. See Judith Newton, "Historicisms New and Old: 'Charles Dickens'

Meets Marxism, Feminism, and West Coast Foucault," *Feminist Studies* 16 (1990): 449–70, for a discussion of Esther's "economy of self-sacrifice" (460) and the containment of female desire.

21. Mitzi Myers, "Hannah More's Tracts," 277.

22. For a discussion of Dickens's representation of women's "limited sphere of action" (636), see Newton, "Historicisms New and Old"; Merryn Williams's chapter on Dickens in *Women in the English Novel, 1800–1900* (New York: St. Martin's Press, 1984), 73–87; Virginia Blain, "Double Vision and Double Standard in *Bleak House,* A Feminist Perspective," *Literature and History* 11 (Spring 1985): 31–46; and Carol Senf, "*Bleak House*: Dickens, Esther, and the Androgynous Mind," *Victorian Newsletter* 64 (1973): 21–27. For a historical perspective on the ideology of separate spheres, see ; Nancy F. Cott, *The Bonds of Womanhood: "Women's Sphere" in New England, 1780–1835* (New Haven: Yale University Press, 1977); Davidoff and Hall, *Family Fortunes*; Barbara Leslie Epstein, *The Politics of Domesticity: Women, Evangelism, and Temperance in Nineteenth-Century America* (Middletown, Conn.: Wesleyan University Press, 1981); Mary Poovey, *Uneven Developments: The Ideological Work of Gender in Mid-Victorian England* (Chicago: University of Chicago Press, 1988); Judith Rowbotham, *Good Girls Make Good Wives: Guidance for Girls in Victorian Fiction* (New York: Basil Blackwell, 1989); Martha Vicinus, ed., *Suffer and Be Still: Women in the Victorian Age* (Bloomington: Indiana University Press, 1972); and Eli Zaretsky, *Capitalism, the Family, and Personal Life* (New York: Harper and Row, 1976).

23. For a discussion of the function of the police and incarcerating institutions in *Bleak House,* see D. A. Miller, *The Novel and the Police* (Berkeley: University of California Press, 1988). For a history of the police, see Robert Reiner, *The Politics of the Police* (Brighton: Wheatsheaf Books, 1985), chap. 1, "Birth of the Blues," and Stanley H. Palmer, *Police and Protest in England and Ireland, 1780–1850* (Cambridge: Cambridge University Press, 1988), chaps. 1, 5, 10.

24. Sir Edwin Chadwick, "Preventive Police," pamphlet (London, 1829), 253. See also *The Beadle's, Headborough's, and Constable's Guide, as to their duty in respect to Coroner's Inquest,* comp. Thomas Bell (1837); "Orders and Instructions to be Observed by the Officers of the Manchester-Police" (Manchester, 1836); "Regulations for the Day-Patrol and Watchmen of the Edinburgh Police Establishment" (Edinburgh, 1838); and Joseph Ritson, *The Office of Constable: Being an entirely new Compendium of the Law concerning that ancient minister for the conservation of the Peace* (London, 1791), reprinted in 1815 and excerpted as *The Constable's Guide* (London, 1843).

25. Chadwick, "Preventive Police," 253.

26. *The Constable's Guide,* 11.

27. George B. Mainwaring, "Observations on the present State of the Police of the Metropolis," *Pamphleteer* 38 (1822): 217, 219.

28. Patrick Colquhoun, *Treatise on the Functions and Duties of a Constable* (London, 1803), 1.

29. Patrick Colquhoun, *A Treatise on Indigence,* 83, 82, 90.

30. "A Treatise on the Police of the Metropolis . . . by a Magistrate" (London, 1796), 5.

31. Chadwick, "Preventive Police," 281–82.

Works Cited

Addison, Joseph. *The Spectator,* no. 69 (Saturday, May 9, 1711). In *Addison and Steele: Selections from The Tatler and The Spectator,* 210–14, ed. Robert J. Allen. New York: Holt, Rinehart and Winston, 1970.

Armstrong, Nancy. *Desire and Domestic Fiction: A Political History of the Novel.* New York: Oxford University Press, 1987.

Austen, Jane. *Emma.* 1816; New York: Oxford University Press, 1989.

———. *Mansfield Park.* 1814. *The Novels of Jane Austen,* vol. 3, ed. R. W. Chapman. London: Oxford University Press, 1971, 1988.

———. *Persuasion.* 1817; New York: Oxford University Press, 1989.

———. *Price and Prejudice.* 1813; New York: Oxford University Press, 1989.

Bage, Robert. *Mount Henneth,* 2 vols. 1782; New York: Garland Publishing Co., 1979.

Bandana, "Hints to the Country Gentleman," *Blackwood's Magazine* 12 (1822): 90–96.

Barrell, John. *The Idea of Landscape and the Sense of Place, 1730–1840.* Cambridge: Cambridge University Press, 1972.

Bataille, George. "The Notion of Expenditure." In *Visions of Excess: Selected Writings, 1927–39,* trans. Alan Stoekl. Minneapolis: University of Minnesota Press, 1985.

Bell, Thomas. *The Beadle's, Headborough's, and Constable's Guide, as to their duty in respect to Coroner's Inquest.* 1837.

Blain, Virginia. "Double Vision and Double Standard in *Bleak House,* A Feminist Perspective." *Literature and History* 11 (Spring 1985): 31–46.

Bodenheimer, Rosemarie. *The Politics of Story in Victorian Social Fiction.* Knight: Cornell University Press, 1988.

Bohstedt, John. *Riots and Community Politics in England and Wales, 1790–1810.* Cambridge: Harvard University Press, 1983.

Briggs, Asa. *The Age of Improvement.* London: Longmans, 1959.

———. "The Language of 'Class' in Early Nineteenth-Century England." In *Essays in Labour History*, ed. Asa Briggs and John Saville. London: Macmillan, 1960.

———. "Middle-Class Consciousness in English Politics, 1780–1846." *Past and Present* 9 (1956): 65–74.

Brissenden, R. F. *Virtue in Distress: Studies in the Novel of Sentiment from Richardson to Sade*. New York: Barnes and Noble, 1974.

Brontë, Anne. *Agnes Grey*. 1847; New York: Penguin, 1988.

Brontë, Charlotte. *Shirley*. 1849; New York: Oxford University Press, 1979, 1986.

Brown, F. K. *Fathers of the Victorians*. Cambridge: Cambridge University Press, 1961.

Burke, Edmund. "Thoughts on Scarcity." 6 vols. *The Works of the Rt. Hon. Edmund Burke*. London: Oxford University Press, 1927.

Butler, Marilyn. *Jane Austen and the War of Ideas*. Oxford: Clarendon Press, 1975.

———. *Romantics, Rebels and Reactionaries*. New York: Oxford University Press, 1982.

Caird, Sir James. *The Landed Interest and the Supply of Food*. 1878; London: Cass, 1967.

Carlyle, Thomas. "Chartism." 1839. *The Works of Thomas Carlyle*. 30 vols. 1897; New York: AMS Press, 1974.

———. *Past and Present*. 1843. *The Works of Thomas Carlyle*. 30 vols. 1897; New York: AMS Press, 1974.

Chadwick, Sir Edwin. "Preventive Police." London, 1829.

Chambers, J. D., and G. E. Mingay. *The Agricultural Revolution 1750–1880*. New York: Schocken Books, 1966.

Chapman, R. W., ed. *Jane Austen's Letters to her Sister Cassandra and Others*. Oxford: Oxford University Press, 1952.

Charlesworth, Maria Louisa. *The Cottage and Its Visitor*. New York: Carter and Bros., 1860.

Clarkson, William. "Inquiry on Pauperism and Poor Rates." *Pamphleteer* 8 (1816): 385–420.

Cobbett, William. *Legacy to Labourers: What Is the Right which Lords, Baronets, and Squires, have to the Lands of England*. London, 1835.

———. *Cobbett's Weekly Political Register* (April 7 1821): 1–22.

Coleridge, Samuel Taylor. "A Lay Sermon addressed to the Higher and Middle Classes on the Existing Distresses and Discontents" (1817). In *On the Constitution of Church and State*, ed. Henry Nelson Coleridge. London, 1839.

Colquhoun, Patrick. *A Treatise on Indigence*. London, 1806.

———. *Treatise on the Functions and Duties of a Constable*. London, 1803.

———. *A Treatise on the Wealth, Power, and Resources of the British Empire*. London, 1814.

The Complete Family Piece: and, Country Gentleman and Farmer's Best Guide. London, 1741.

Corrigan, Philip, and Derek Sayer. *The Great Arch: English State Formation as Cultural Revolution*. New York: Basil Blackwell, 1985.

Cott, Nancy F. *The Bonds of Womanhood: "Woman's Sphere" in New England, 1780–1835*. New Haven: Yale University Press, 1977.

———. "Passionlessness: An Interpretation of Victorian Sexual Conduct." In *A Heritage of Her Own*, ed. Nancy F. Cott and Elizabeth H. Peck. New York: Simon and Schuster, 1979.

Cowper, William. *The Task. Cowper's Poems*. London: Dent, 1966.

Crabbe, George. "The Village: Book I." *The Complete Poetical Works of George Crabbe*. 3 vols. Ed. Norma Darrymple-Champneys and Arthur Pollard. Oxford: Clarendon Press, 1988.

Danaway, Martin A. "Housekeeping and Hegemony in *Bleak House*." *Studies in the Novel* 23 (1991): 416–31.

Davidoff, Leonore, and Catherine Hall. *Family Fortunes: Men and Women of the English Middle Class, 1780–1850*. Chicago: University of Chicago Press, 1987.

Davies, David. *The Case of Labourers in Husbandry*. London, 1795.

Defoe, Daniel. *Roxana, the Fortunate Mistress* (1724). Ed. David Blewett. New York: Penguin, 1982.

Dickens, Charles. *Bleak House*. 1852–53, 1868; New York: Bantam, 1985.

Dickinson, H. T. *British Radicalism and the French Revolution 1789–1815*. Oxford: Blackwell, 1985.

———. *Liberty and Property: Political Ideology in Eighteenth-Century Britain*. New York: Holmes and Meier, 1977.

Duckworth, Alistair. *The Improvement of the Estate*. Baltimore: Johns Hopkins University Press, 1971.

Eden, Sir Frederic. *The State of the Poor*. 3 vols. London, 1795.

Eliot, George. *Scenes of Clerical Life*. 1858; Oxford: Clarendon Press, 1985.

Ellis, Kate Ferguson. *The Contested Castle: Gothic Novels and the Subversion of Domestic Ideology*. Urbana: University of Illinois Press, 1989.

Ellis, Sarah. *The Family Monitor and Domestic Guide*. New York: Henry G. Langley, 1844.

Epstein, Barbara Leslie. *The Politics of Domesticity: Women, Evangelism, and Temperance in Nineteenth-Century America*. Middletown, Conn.: Wesleyan University Press, 1981.

Evans, Mary. *Jane Austen and the State*. London: Tavistock, 1987.

Evans, Thomas. *Christian Policy* (1815). Quoted in "Parliamentary Reform," *Quarterly Review* 16 (1816): 225–71.

Faulkner, Peter. *Robert Bage*. Boston: Twayne Publishers, 1979.

Folkenflik, Robert, ed. *The English Hero, 1660–1800*. Newark: University of Delaware Press, 1982.

Foucault, Michel. *Discipline and Punish: The Birth of the Prison*. Trans. Alan Sheridan. New York: Random House, 1979.

The Friendly Female Society for Relieving Poor, Infirm, and Aged Women of Good Character. London, 1803.

Fowler, Marian E. "The Courtesy-Book Heroine of *Mansfield Park*." *University of Toronto Quarterly* 44 (1974): 31–46.

Fox-Genovese, Elizabeth, and Eugene Genovese. *Fruits of Merchant Capital: Slavery and Bourgeois Property in the Rise and Expansion of Capitalism*. New York: Oxford University Press, 1983.

Gerard, Jessica. "'Lady Bountiful': Women of the Landed Class and Rural Philanthropy." *Victorian Studies* 30 (1987): 183–210.

Gisborne, Thomas. *An Enquiry into the Duties of Men in the Higher and Middle Classes of Society*. London, 1795.

Gaskell, Elizabeth. *My Lady Ludlow and Other Stories*. 1859; New York: Oxford University Press, 1989.

Godwin, William. *Things as They are, or the Adventures of Caleb Williams*. 1794; New York: Penguin, 1988.

Goldsmith, Oliver. "The Deserted Village." *Collected Works of Oliver Goldsmith*. 5 vols. Ed. Arthur Friedman. London: Oxford University Press, 1966.

Gramsci, Antonio. *Selections from the Prison Notebooks of Antonio Gramsci*. Trans. Quintin Hoare and Geoffrey Nowell Smith. New York: International Publishers, 1971.

Halevy, Elie. *A History of the English People in 1815*. 1924; London: Routledge, 1987.

Hamilton, Elizabeth. *The Cottagers of Glenburnie; a Tale for the Farmer's Ingle-nook*. Edinburgh: James Ballantyne, 1808.

Hammond, J. L., and Barbara Hammond. *The Village Labourer*. London: Longmans, Green, and Co., 1927.

Hillyer, William. *Extracts from the Reports of the English Society for Bettering the Condition of the Poor*. Dublin, 1799.

Hopkins, Robert. "Moral Luck and Judgement in Jane Austen's *Persuasion*." *Nineteenth-Century Literature* 42 (1987–88): 143–58.

Howlett, J. H. "Essay on Riches and Poverty." *Lady's Magazine* 20 (1790) 363–69.

Hume, David. "Of Public Credit." *David Hume: Writings on Economics*, ed. Eugene Rotwein. Madison: University of Wisconsin Press, 1970.

"The Influence of Pious Women in Promoting a Revival of Religion." Tract No. 800. Religious Tract Society, 1830.

Johnson, Claudia. *Jane Austen: Women, Politics, and the Novel*. Chicago: University of Chicago Press, 1988.

Johnstone, W. "Our Domestic Policy." *Blackwood's Magazine* 26 (1829): 768–74.

Jones, M. G. *Hannah More*. Cambridge: Cambridge University Press, 1952.

Kelly, Gary. *English Jacobin Novel*. Oxford: Clarendon Press, 1976.

———. "Jane Austen and the English Novel of the 1790s." In *Fetter'd or Free? British Women Novelists, 1670–1815*, ed. Mary Anne Schofield and Cecilia Macheski. Athens: Ohio University Press, 1986.

Kent, Nathaniel. *Hints to Gentlemen of Landed Property*. London, 1775.

———. "On the Size of Farms." *Georgical Essays* 5 (1803): 280–86.

———. "On the Poor." *Georgical Essays* 6 (1804): 468–71.

Knight, Helen. *Hannah More or Life in Hall and Cottage*. New York: M. W. Dodd, 1851.

Kowaleski-Wallace, Beth. *Their Fathers' Daughter: Hannah More, Maria Edgeworth, and Patriarchal Complicity*. New York: Oxford University Press, 1991.

———. "Milton's Daughters: The Education of Eighteenth-Century Women Writers." *Feminist Studies* 12 (1986): 275–93.

———. "Hannah and Her Sister: Women and Evangelism in Early Nineteenth-Century England." *Nineteenth-Century Contexts* 12 (1988): 29–51.

The Lady's Companion for Visiting the Poor. London, 1813.

"The Lady's Royal Benevolent Society for Visiting, Relieving, and Investigating the Conditions of the Poor at their own Habitations. Pamphlet published by organization." London, 1818.

Landry, Donna. *The Muses of Resistance: Laboring-class Women's Poetry in Britain, 1739–1796*. Cambridge: University of Cambridge Press, 1990.

Leadbeater, Mary. *Cottage Dialogues among the Irish Peasantry*. 1811; Dublin, 1841.

Lillo, George. *The London Merchant; or the History of George Barnwell*. In *British Dramatists From Dryden to Sheridan*, ed. George H. Nettleton et al. New York: Houghton Mifflin, 1969.

Lovell, Terry. "Jane Austen and Gentry Society." In *Literature, Society, and the Sociology of Literature*, ed. Francis Barker. University of Essex, 1976.

Mackenzie, Henry. *The Man of Feeling*. 1771; New York: Oxford University Press, 1987.

Mainwaring, George B. "Observations on the present State of the Police of the Metropolis." London, 1822.

Marshall, William. *On the Landed Property of England, an elementary and practical Treatise; containing the Purchase, the Improvement, and the Management of Landed Estates*. London, 1804.

———. *On the Management of Landed Estates*. London, 1806.

———. *The Rural Economy of Norfolk: Comprising the Management of Landed Estates and the Present Practice of Husbandry*. 2 vols. London, 1787.

————. *The Rural Economy of Yorkshire.* 2 vols. London, 1788.

Marx, Karl. *Capital: A Critique of Political Economy.* Vol. 1. 1867. Trans. Ben Fowkes. New York: Random House; Vintage Books, 1977.

McKeon, Michael. *The Origins of the English Novel, 1600–1740.* Baltimore: Johns Hopkins University Press, 1987.

McNally, David. *Political Economy and the Rise of Capitalism: A Reinterpretation.* Berkeley: University of California Press, 1988.

Mill, John Stuart. *Principles of Political Economy. Books IV and V.* 1848; New York: Penguin, 1985.

Miller, D. A. *The Novel and the Police.* Berkeley: University of California Press, 1988.

Mills, Dennis. *Lord and Peasant in Nineteenth-Century Britain.* London: Croom Helm, 1980.

Mingay, G. E. *English Landed Society in the Eighteenth Century.* London: Routledge and Kegan Paul, 1963.

————. "The Eighteenth-Century Land Steward." In *Land, Labour and Population in the Industrial Revolution,* ed. E. L. Jones and G. E. Mingay. London: Edward Arnold, 1967.

————. *The Gentry: The Rise and Fall of a Ruling Class.* London: Longman, 1976.

————, ed. *Victorian Countryside.* 2 vols. London: Routledge and Kegan Paul, 1981.

————. "Enclosure and the Small Farmer in the Age of the Industrial Revolution." Economic History Series. London: Macmillan, 1968.

Moler, Kenneth L. "The Two Voices of Fanny Price." In *Jane Austen: Bicentenary Essays,* ed. John Halperin. Cambridge: Cambridge University Press, 1975.

Monaghan, David. "The Decline of the Gentry: A Study of Jane Austen's Attitude to Formality in *Persuasion." Studies in the Novel* 7 (1975): 73–87.

————. "*Mansfield Park* and Evangelicalism: A Reassessment." *Nineteenth-Century Fiction* 33 (1978): 215–30.

Mordant, John. *The Complete Steward, or the Duty of a Steward to his Lord. Containing several new methods for the improvement of his Lord's estate.* 2 vols. London, 1761.

More, Hannah. *Cheap Repository Tracts. The Works of Hannah More.* Vol. I. Philadelphia: J. D. Maxwell, 1818.

————. *Coelebs in Search of a Wife: Comprehending Observations on Domestic Habits and Manners, Religion and Morals. The Works of Hannah More.* 1830; New York: Garland Publishing Co., 1982.

————. *Christian Morals. The Works of Hannah More.* Vol. VII. Philadelphia: J. D. Maxwell, 1818.

————. *Estimate of the Religion of the Fashionable World. The Works of Hannah More.* Vol. III. Philadelphia: J. D. Maxwell, 1818.

————. *Practical Piety.* 2 vols. London, 1812.

———. *Thoughts on the Importance of the Manners of the Great to General Society. The Works of Hannah More.* Vol. VII. Philadelphia: J. D. Maxwell, 1818.

More, Martha. *Mendip Annals: or, a Narrative of the Charitable Labours of Hannah and Martha More in their Neighbourhood. Being the Journal of Martha More,* ed. Arthur Roberts. New York: Carter and Brothers, 1859.

Mullan, John. *Sentiment and Sociability: The Language of Feeling in the Eighteenth Century.* Oxford: Clarendon Press, 1988.

Musselwhite, David E. *Partings Welded Together: Politics and Desire in the Nineteenth-Century English Novel.* London: Methuen, 1986.

Myers, Mitzi. "Hannah More's tracts for the Times: Social Fiction and Female Ideology." In *Fetter'd or Free? British Women Novelists, 1670–1815,* ed. Mary Anne Scofield and Cecilia Macheski. Athens: Ohio University Press, 1986.

———. "'A Peculiar Protection': Hannah More and the Cultural Politics of the Blagdon Controversy." In *History, Gender, and Eighteenth-Century British Literature,* ed. Beth Fowkes Tobin. Athens: University of Georgia Press, forthcoming.

———. "Reform or Ruin: 'A Revolution in Female Manners.'" *Studies in Eighteenth-Century Culture* 11 (1982): 199–216.

Nardin, Jane. "Charity in *Emma.*" *Studies in the Novel* 7 (1975): 61–72.

"The Nature, Design, and Rules of the Benevolent or Stranger's Friend Society; Instituted for the Purposes of Visiting and Relieving Sick and Distressed Strangers, and Other Poor, at their Respective Habitations." London, 1804.

Neale, R. S. "Zapp Zapped: Property and Alienation in *Mansfield Park.*" In *Writing Marxist History: British Society, Economy, and Culture since 1700.* Oxford: Basil Blackwell, 1985.

Newby, Howard. *Country Life: A Social History of Rural England.* London: Weidenfeld and Nicholson, 1987.

———. "Deferential Dialectic." *Comparative Studies in Society and History* 17 (1975): 139–64.

———. *The Deferential Worker: A Study of Farm Workers in East Anglia.* Madison: University of Wisconsin Press, 1979.

———. "Paternalism and Capitalism." In *Industrial Society: Class, Cleavage and Control,* ed. Richard Scase. New York: St. Martin's Press, 1977.

Newby, Howard, et al. *Property, Paternalism, and Power: Class and Control in Rural England.* Madison: University of Wisconsin Press, 1978.

Newton, Judith Lowder. *Women, Power, and Subversion: Social Strategies in British Fiction, 1770–1860.* New York: Methuen, 1985.

———. "Historicisms New and Old: 'Charles Dickens' meets Marxism, Feminism, and West Coast Foucault." *Feminist Studies* 16 (1990): 449–70.

"The Orders and Instructions to be Observed by the Officers of the Manchester-Police." Manchester, 1836.

Owen, David. *English Philanthropy, 1660–1960.* Cambridge: Harvard University Press, 1964.

Palmer, Stanley H. *Police and Protest in England and Ireland, 1750–1860.* Cambridge: Cambridge University Press, 1988.

Perkin, Harold. *Origins of Modern English Society.* 1969; London: Routledge and Kegan Paul, 1985.

Perry, Ruth. "Bluestockings in Utopia." In *History, Gender, and Eighteenth-Century British Literature,* ed. Beth Fowkes Tobin. Athens: University of Georgia Press, forthcoming.

Pocock, J. G. A. *Virtue, Commerce, and History.* New York: Cambridge University Press, 1988.

Poovey, Mary. *The Proper Lady and the Woman Writer: Ideology as Style in the Works of Mary Wollstonecraft, Mary Shelley, and Jane Austen.* Chicago: University of Chicago Press, 1984.

———. *Uneven Developments: The Ideological Work of Gender in Mid-Victorian England.* Chicago: University of Chicago Press, 1988.

Pope, Norris. *Dickens and Charity.* New York: Columbia University Press, 1978.

Prochaska, F. K. *Women and Philanthropy in Nineteenth-Century England.* Oxford: Clarendon, 1980.

Reiner, Robert. *The Politics of the Police.* Brighton: Wheatsheaf Books, 1985.

"Regulations for the Day-Patrol and Watchmen of the Edinburgh Police Establishment." Edinburgh, 1838.

Ricardo, David. *Essay on the External Corn Trade.* Vol. 4. *The Works and Correspondence of David Ricardo,* ed. Piero Sraffa and M. H. Dobbs. Cambridge: Cambridge University Press, 1951.

———. *On the Principles of Political Economy and Taxation.* Vol. 1. *The Works and Correspondence of David Ricardo,* 11 vols. ed. Piero Sraffa and M. H. Dobbs. Cambridge University Press, 1951.

Richards, R. D. *The Early History of Banking in England.* 1929; New York: Augustus M. Kelley, 1965.

Richardson, Samuel. *Pamela, or Virtue Rewarded.* 1740; New York: Penguin, 1980.

Riston, Joseph. *The Office of Constable: Being an entirely new Compendium of the Law concerning that ancient minister for the conservation of the Peace.* London, 1791.

Robbins, Bruce. "Telescopic Philanthropy: Professionalism and Responsibility in *Bleak House.*" in *Nation and Narration,* ed. Homi Bhabha. London: Routledge, 1990.

Roberts, David. *Paternalism in Early Victorian England.* New Brunswick, N.J.: Rutgers University Press, 1977.

Roberts, Warren. *Jane Austen and the French Revolution.* New York: St. Martin's Press, 1979.

Roberts, William, ed. *Memoirs of the Life and Correspondence of Mrs. Hannah More.* 2 vols. New York: Harper and Brothers, 1837.

Robinson, Lillian. "Why Marry Mr. Collins?" In *Sex, Class, and Culture.* New York: Methuen, 1986.

Rodgers, Betsy. *Cloak of Charity: Studies in Eighteenth-Century Philanthropy.* London: Metheun, 1949.

Rose, David, et al. "Ideologies of Property: A Case Study." *Sociological Review* n.s. (1976): 699–730.

Rowbottom, Judith. *Good Girls Make Good Wives: Guidance for Girls in Victorian Fiction.* New York: Basil Blackwell, 1989.

Sales, Roger. *Closer to Home: Writers and Places in England, 1780–1830.* Cambridge: Harvard University Press, 1986.

———. *English Literature in History, 1780–1830: Pastoral and Politics.* New York: St. Martin's Press, 1983.

Scheuermann, Mona. *Social Protest in the Eighteenth-Century Novel.* Columbus: Ohio State University Press, 1985.

Sekora, John. *The Concept of Luxury in Western Thought, Eden to Smollett.* Baltimore: Johns Hopkins University Press, 1977.

Senf, Carol. "*Bleak House:* Dickens, Esther, and the Androgynous Mind." *Victorian Newsletter* 64 (1973): 21–27.

Senior, Nassau William. *Political Economy.* London, 1854.

———. *Two Lectures on Population.* London, 1829.

Sheriff, John K. *The Good-Natured Man: The Evolution of a Moral Ideal, 1660–1800.* Tuscaloosa: University of Alabama Press, 1982.

Simpson, W. J. Sparrow. *The History of the Anglo-Catholic Revival from 1845.* London: Allen and Unwin, 1932.

Smith, Adam. *The Wealth of Nations: Books I–III.* 1776; New York: Penguin, 1986.

Southey, Robert. *Sir Thomas More; or, Colloquies on the Progress and Prospects of Society.* 2 vols. London, 1829.

Spring, David. *The English Landed Estate in the Nineteenth Century: Its Administration.* Baltimore: Johns Hopkins University Press, 1963.

———. "Interpreters of Jane Austen's Social World." In *Jane Austen: New Perspectives,* ed. Jane Todd. New York: Holmes and Meier, 1983.

Steele, Sir Richard. *The Conscious Lovers.* In *British Dramatists from Dryden to Sheridan,* ed. George H. Nettleton et al. New York: Houghton Mifflin, 1969.

Stone, Lawrence, and Jeanne C. Fawtier Stone. *An Open Elite? England 1540–1880.* Oxford: Oxford University Press, 1984.

Swift, Jonathan. *Gulliver's Travels.* 1726; New York: Oxford University Press, 1990.

Tave, Stuart. *The Amiable Humorist: A Study in the Comic Theory and*

Criticism of the Eighteenth and Early Nineteenth Centuries. Chicago: University of Chicago Press, 1960.

Taylor, Ann. *Practical Hints to Young Females on the Duties of a Wife, a Mother, and a Mistress of a Family.* London, 1815.

Taylor, Jane. *Rhymes for the Nursery, by the Authors of "Original Poems."* 1806.

Thompson, E. P. *The Making of the English Working Class.* New York: Random House, 1964.

———. "The Moral Economy of the English Crowd in the Eighteenth Century." *Past and Present* 50 (1971): 76–136.

———. "Patrician Society, Plebeian Culture." *Journal of Social History* 7 (1974): 384–405.

Thompson, F. M. L. *English Landed Society in the Nineteenth Century.* London: Routledge and Kegan Paul, 1963.

———. "Landowners and the Rural Community." In *The Victorian Countryside,* ed. G. E. Mingay, 2:457–74. London: Routledge and Kegan Paul, 1981.

Thompson, James. *Between Self and World.* University Park: Pennsylvania State University Press, 1988.

Throsby, John. *Select Views in Leicestershire.* 2 vols. Leicester and London, 1791.

Todd, Janet. *Sensibility, An Introduction.* New York: Methuen, 1986.

"A Treatise on the Police of the Metropolis." By a Magistrate. London, 1796.

Tompkins, J. M. S. *The Popular Novel in England 1770–1800.* 1932; Lincoln: University of Nebraska Press, 1961.

Townsend, Joseph. *A Dissertation on the Poor Laws.* 1786; Berkeley: University of California Press, 1971.

Tribe, Keith. *Land, Labour and Economic Discourse.* London: Routledge and Kegan Paul, 1978.

Trimmer, Sarah. *The Oeconomy of Charity; or, an Address to Ladies.* London, 1787.

Vicinus, Martha, ed. *Suffer and Be Still: Women in the Victorian Age.* Bloomington: Indiana University Press, 1972.

Wallerstein, Immanuel. *Historical Capitalism.* New York: Verso, 1983.

———. *The Modern World System III: The Second Era of Great Expansion of the Capitalist World-Economy, 1740s–1840s.* New York: Academic Press, 1989.

"The Warder, No. VII." *Blackwood's Magazine* 7 (1820): 90–102.

Weber, Max. *On Charisma and Institution Building.* Ed. S. N. Eisenstadt. Chicago: University of Chicago Press, 1968.

Williams, Merryn. *Women in the English Novel, 1800–1900.* New York: St. Martin's Press, 1984.

Williams, Raymond. *The Country and the City.* New York: Oxford University Press, 1973.

Wise, T. J., and J. S. Symington. *The Brontës: Their Lives, Friendships and Correspondence.* 4 vols. Oxford: Blackwell, 1932.

Wollstonecraft, Mary. *Vindication of the Rights of Woman.* 1792; New York: Penguin, 1983.

Wordie, J. R. *Estate Management in Eighteenth-Century England.* London: Royal Historical Society, 1982.

Young, Arthur. *The Farmer's Letters to the People of England.* London, 1767.

———. *The Farmer's Tour through the East of England.* 4 vols. London, 1771.

———. *A General View of the Agriculture of the County of Lincoln.* London, 1799.

———. *A Six Months Tour through the North of England.* 4 vols. London, 1770.

———. *A Six Weeks Tour, Through the Southern Counties of England and Wales.* London, 1768.

Yeazell, Ruth. *Fictions of Modesty: Women and Courtship in the English Novel.* Chicago: University of Chicago Press. 1991.

The Young Ladies' Faithful Remembrancer of Obligations, Responsibilities, and Duties. York, 1848.

Zaretsky, Eli. *Capitalism, the Family, and Personal Life.* New York: Harper and Row, 1976.

Index